7/2000

Imagining Paris

Imagining Paris

Exile, Writing, and American Identity

J. Gerald Kennedy

Yale University Press

New Haven & London

Designed by James J. Johnson.
Set in Trump type by Keystone
Typesetting, Inc., Orwigsburg,
Pennsylvania. Printed in the
United States of America by
Vail-Ballou Press, Binghamton,
New York.

A catalogue record for this book
is available from the British
Library.

The paper in this book meets
the guidelines for permanence
and durability of the
Committee on Production
Guidelines for Book Longevity
of the Council on Library
Resources.

10 9 8 7 6 5 4 3 2

*Library of Congress
Cataloging-in-Publication Data*

Kennedy, J. Gerald.
  Imagining Paris : exile,
writing, and American
identity / J. Gerald Kennedy.
    p. cm.
  Includes bibliographical
references and index.
ISBN 0-300-05747-4 (cloth)
    0-300-06102-1 (pbk.)
  1. Authors, American—20th
century—Homes and haunts—
France—Paris. 2. Authors,
American—20th century—
Biography. 3. American
literature—20th century—
History and criticism. 4. Paris
(France)—Intellectual life—
20th century.
PS144.P37K46   1993
810.9'324436—dc20   92–19535

Endpaper maps from *Baedeker's
Paris 1924* reproduced courtesy
of Jarrold Printing.

*Dedicated to
Ben and Molly
and to the memory
of Gérard Tondeur*

Contents

Illustrations

Preface

One December evening fourteen years ago, a Parisian acquaintance whom I chanced to meet on the Pont de l'Alma gestured toward the lights along the Seine. "Really," she said, "don't you think Paris is the center of the world?" The notion, so transparently ethnocentric, had never before occurred to me, but I agreed easily, dismissing the question as an instance of civic pride and visual delight. I, too, had noticed the gleaming spectacle, and if my critical instincts reminded me that this panorama did not epitomize Paris—that other, mundane scenes were more typical—I nevertheless felt then what I have often felt: the presence of place, so overwhelming in the capital of France. Whether or not this was the *axis mundi*, I wondered how to account for its palpable sense of place.

Returning to Paris year after year with the Louisiana State University summer program has enabled me during the past decade to gain a somewhat clearer sense of the topographical and architectural intricacies which compose the surface of the city. But the experience of place has remained an elusive and perplexing phenomenon. While guiding the students in my "lost generation" course through short stories, novels, and memoirs depicting expatriate life in Paris, I have been brought back repeatedly to a set of related questions: What is place? How do we conceptualize and assimilate our surroundings? How does place affect our sense of who we are? Why do we remember and dream about places? What does it mean to "represent" a place in narrative?

Although here I consider these issues largely in relation to the complex reality of Paris and to particular literary versions of the city by American writers earlier in this century, the problem of place obviously extends far beyond the responses of a given national group to a specific foreign city. Geographers have been actively theorizing about the nature of place for more than two decades, and, to judge from the appearance of several recent titles, literary critics now seem poised to undertake a concerted inquiry into the poetics of place. My hope is that this discussion of Paris will stimulate further thinking about the problem of place as it enters into the practice of writing.

That an interest in place should develop in the last decade of a century marked by massive shifts of population, by rootlessness and emigration, and by relentless, worldwide leisure travel seems hardly surprising. The epoch of global exploration which began with the Vikings and Columbus has perhaps, in the wake of the Apollo moon landings, reached an apocalyptic final phase, marked by the frantic search for that great good dwelling place not already depleted, poisoned, bombed out, or overpopulated. Yet even as throngs of travelers and immigrants surge across international borders—some to relocate, others merely to reconnoiter—the differences between one locale and another become increasingly indistinct. Technology has worked inexorably toward homogenization; television, that most insidious instrument of postmodern culture, has (according to Joshua Meyrowitz) deeply undermined our sense of place by enabling us to witness events occurring simultaneously all over the world. "When we are everywhere," he contends, "we are nowhere in particular." [1] As shopping malls and fast-food restaurants proliferate, the placelessness engendered by rampant capitalism poses an increasing threat to personal orientation and identity. In ways too numerous to specify, we have all depended on places—and the different opportunities which they represent—to nurture aspects of our human growth. Perhaps criticism and theory have now turned to the question of place in response to a growing suspicion that the inhuman landscape of postmodernism makes us all displaced persons by denying the grounding which would allow us to locate and define our lives.

My effort to work out a theory of place (confined mainly to the first chapter) provides what I believe is a fresh approach to

American expatriate writing. By focusing on the works of Gertrude Stein, Ernest Hemingway, Henry Miller, F. Scott Fitzgerald, and Djuna Barnes, I have tried to indicate how exile in France affected the career of each writer and how Paris became for each a complex image of the possibilities of metamorphosis. These writers represented the city in contrasting ways; they came from various parts of the United States and chose to live abroad for diverse reasons. In Paris, they inhabited different *quartiers*, had their own idiosyncratic haunts, and projected their relation to place in quite different terms. Yet these patterns of attachment reveal much about each writer's individual crises, particularly those dilemmas of identity rooted in personal origins, family ties, ingrained beliefs and values, literary ambitions and anxieties, sexual desires and compulsions, and unresolved psychic conflicts. Their patterns of geographical association, moreover, reveal much about the human tendency to regard places as focuses of activity and purpose; they reflect as well upon the curious situation of the exile who lives between two worlds yet belongs to neither and perhaps cannot say where "home" might be.

In a poem first composed in 1928 in a letter to the expatriate Gerald Murphy, Archibald MacLeish asked his friend: "How can a wise man have two countries?" Having just returned to the United States after five years in France, MacLeish wondered how he could feel homesick for "the red roofs and the olives, / And the foreign words and the smell of the sea fall." His poem "American Letter" probes the tensions felt by an exile torn between the "country-earth" from which he had sprung and that "land far off, alien" which has become the locus of his daydreams. It also clarifies the peculiar way in which the superficiality of place-identity in the United States complicates the American experience of exile and perhaps triggers that hunger for place implicit in so much expatriate writing. MacLeish says of this country:

> Neither a place it is nor a blood name.
> America is West and the wind blowing.
> America is a great word and the snow,
> A way, a white bird, and the wind falling,
> A shining thing in the mind and the gulls' call.
> America is neither a land nor a people,
> A word's shape it is, a wind's sweep.[2]

The poet's claim that America represents an idea rather than a distinctive place helps to account for the problem of national identity which surfaces recurrently in the texts examined here. Ironically, as these writers work to construct new identities abroad, most betray a preoccupation with those American surroundings from which they have emerged, framing tenuous recollections of native scenes against which these identities might be more clearly outlined. But their principal orientation is toward Paris, which supplies symbolic material for the construction of an expatriate self. Through features of place, each writer figures a relation to the city which clarifies the emergent identity made possible by the conditions of exile.

The American expatriate movement in France has of course already generated a plethora of memoirs, anecdotal histories, street guides, and coffee-table photographic studies. In the wake of Malcolm Cowley's *Exile's Return* (1934), much attention has been given to piquant tales of ambition, rivalry, betrayal, and excess—to the high jinks of the "lost generation." But there has been little cogent discussion of the writing which emerged from this collective adventure. Two exceptions, both indispensable books, must be hailed: George Wickes' *Americans in Paris* (1969) remains a significant, ground-breaking work, with major sections on Stein, Cummings, Hemingway, and Miller which combine biography with apt critical commentary. Shari Benstock's provocative *Women of the Left Bank* (1986) merges biography with critical analysis and feminist theory as she characterizes the experiences of literary women in Paris. Another study worth noting here, Noel Riley Fitch's *Sylvia Beach and the Lost Generation*, offers an informative history of Beach, her famous bookstore, and her involvement in the careers of Joyce, Hemingway, and others. More recently, Jean Méral's *Paris in American Literature* (1989) provides a thorough survey of works from Poe to Baldwin which portray the Paris scene.

Readers expecting to find in the present book a comprehensive account of the American expatriate movement in France should be forewarned. Of the dozens of important American authors who worked in Paris from 1900–1940, only a handful receive attention here; such key figures as Edith Wharton and Ezra Pound receive only brief mention, while the Parisian experiences of others—John Dos Passos, H. D., William Carlos Williams, Langston Hughes, Thomas Wolfe—go quietly unnoticed. This book presents not a comprehensive historical view but rather a revisionary account of certain exemplary writers from a specific critical and theoretical perspective. In a broad sense I treat these figures and their narratives of exile as instances of the profound effect of place on writing and self-identity.

Since I began working on this book in 1986, many people have contributed to its development by suggesting books to consult, archives to visit, and ideas to consider. From the outset, Ellen Graham at Yale University Press offered encouragement and later made valuable suggestions about the Hemingway chapter. My regret about not completing the manuscript prior to her retirement has been eased by the enthusiastic support of her successor, Jonathan Brent. Yet another member of the press staff, Noreen O'Connor, has improved the book by her fine copyediting.

A number of good folk have read portions of the manuscript and offered scholarly advice; these include Michael Reynolds, George Wickes, Shari Benstock, Paul Smith, Wallace Fowlie, and Jackson Bryer. Michael Reynolds deserves special thanks for sharing his unpublished manuscripts with me and saving me from many biographical blunders. James Olney and Lewis Simpson, my esteemed colleagues at Louisiana State University, also read parts of the manuscript, expressed support, and passed on useful materials. I am grateful to Mary Dearborn for sharing her knowledge of Henry Miller and to the children of Henry Miller—Barbara, Tony, and Valentine—for permission to quote from the Miller papers at UCLA. Novelist Maurice Denuzière provided retrospective articles from the *International Herald Tribune*, Robert E. Gajdusek made available his wonderful photographs of Paris, Richard Lehan sent his work-in-progress on Scott Fitzgerald, and the late Jim Hinkle shared his superb unpublished annotations of *The Sun Also Rises*. My father, John R. Kennedy, found many of the postcards of Paris used in this book. James Brasch and Timothy Dow Adams also brought helpful materials to my attention. I also appreciate the professional support of Daniel Hoffman, James M. Cox, John T. Irwin, John Carlos Rowe, William M. Chace, Louis J. Budd, Terence Martin, and Donald Pizer.

Staff members at several research centers also showed great kindness: the John F. Kennedy Library in Boston; the Beinecke Rare Book and Manuscript Library at Yale; the Firestone Library at Princeton; the Perkins Library at Duke; the Humanities Research Center at the University of Texas; the Research Library at UCLA; the McKeldin Library at the University of Maryland; the Cecil Green Library at Stanford University; the Bancroft Library at Berkeley; Les Archives de la Ville de Paris; and the Middleton Library at Louisiana State University. Special thanks should go to Megan Desnoyers, curator of the Hemingway Collection at the Kennedy Library, to Jean Preston and Ann Van Arsdale at Princeton, to David Zeidberg at UCLA, and to Judy Choe at the University of Maryland. Thanks also to Floris St. Amant at LSU for the library carrel in which most of this book has been written. Other friends at LSU have provided helpful suggestions, pertinent information, or relevant materials: Daniel Mark Fogel, Miles Richardson, Kent Mathewson, Adelaide Russo, and Richard Cox. My sister, Kathleen Kennedy, shared her own suggestive research on place. Three graduate students also deserve thanks: William Watson did preliminary research, Kirk Curnutt read several chapters, and Rob Hale helped with proofreading and checked quotations.

I am especially grateful to the Council on Research at Louisiana State University for the 1990 summer research grant which supported work on this project. The National Endowment for the Humanities also provided a 1988 Travel-to-Collections grant which facilitated my work at Princeton and the University of Maryland.

I wish to thank the editors of the *Southern Review* and *American Literature* for permission to reprint material incorporated in the first and third chapters.

Finally, I wish to express my gratitude to my wife, Sarah, who capably directs the freshman English program at Louisiana State University. Despite her many other labors—including the memorable one which brought our daughter Molly into the world—she has read and critiqued every chapter, checked my revisions, helped with research, and encouraged me when the end of this book seemed very far away. I cannot adequately thank her for all that she has done; I can only cherish her and promise a *framboise* at the Select.

Imagining Paris

CHAPTER ONE

Place, Self, and Writing:
Toward a Poetics of Exile

SHORTLY after returning from a prison camp in France, E. E. Cummings composed *The Enormous Room* (1922), an experimental novel recounting his ordeal as a Norton Harjes ambulance driver arrested (with his friend Slater Brown) on suspicion of German sympathy and incarcerated by French authorities. From his confinement with a motley assortment of men, Cummings created an exuberant, heterogeneous narrative mixing French with English, traditional allegory with naturalistic detail, and verbal portraiture with stream-of-consciousness impressionism. As implied by the title, the broad subject of this autobiographical account is the experience of place; the camp at La Ferté Macé and the "enormous room"—a dark, oblong enclosure "unmistakably ecclesiastical in feeling"—comprise Cummings' minimal world.[1] In this dismal compound, as he vents his scorn for French officialdom, the writer forms memorable friendships with fellow prisoners and thus recovers a faith in human goodness. His experience transforms the enormous room from a chamber of horror echoing with "weird cries, oaths, laughter" (42) into a scene of community filled with "a new and beautiful darkness" (233).

Oddly enough, however, the place which most clearly reflects the inner change in Cummings is Paris. He passes through the city twice: once on his way to the prison, when the idea of his arrest still seems preposterous, and then again after his discharge, en route to America. The earlier scene indeed depicts an ecstatic return to the city where Cummings and Brown had enjoyed a five-week revel before going to the Western Front. As the crowded night train approaches a station, the idea of Paris explodes into consciousness; the city's very name becomes a magical incantation: "Some permissionaires cried 'Paris.' The woman across from me said 'Paris, Paris.' A great shout came up from every insane drowsy brain that had travelled with us—a fierce and beautiful cry, which went the length of the train . . . . Paris where one forgets, Paris which is Pleasure, Paris in whom our souls live, Paris the beautiful, Paris enfin" (30). In a chapter significantly titled "A Pilgrim's Progress," Cummings enters a Celestial City which promises to satisfy all human longings. Richard S. Kennedy observes that "when the train reaches Paris, it is a holy place: the people on the streets are 'divine,' a motherly woman sells [Cummings] coffee, a 'sacredly delicious' brew."[2] Yet we know that Cummings is merely in transit; unlike Bunyan's pilgrim, his ultimate destination is "La Misere," the place of misery.

When the dazed Cummings finally obtains his release from prison, he can barely comprehend an order to report to the American Embassy in Paris. After four months in a dark pen, he feels disoriented: "Where in Hell am I? What is Paris—a place, a somewhere, a city, life, to live: infinitive. . . . Paris. Life. Liberté. La Liberté. 'La Liberté'—I almost shouted in agony" (237). From the mud and filth of La Ferté Macé, Paris is simply an idea of survival and freedom. By the time Cummings reaches the city, however, he finds quite a different place:

> The streets. Les rues de Paris. I walked past Notre Dame. I bought tobacco. Jews are peddling things with American trademarks on them, because in a day or two it's Christmas I suppose. Jesus it is cold. Dirty snow. Huddling people. La guerre. Always la guerre. And chill. Goes through these big mittens. Tomorrow I shall be on the ocean. . . . Les rues sont tristes. Perhaps there's no Christmas, perhaps the French government has forbidden Christmas. Clerk at Norton Harjes seemed astonished to see me. O God it is cold in Paris. Every-

one looks hard under lamplight, because it's winter I suppose.
Everyone hurried. Everyone hard. Everyone cold. Everyone
huddling. Everyone alive; alive: alive. (240–41)

After his stint in prison (where he has heard about the horrors of
war from other inmates), Cummings sees the city as a site not of
beauty or pleasure but of suffering. The air is cold, the snow dirty,
the streets sad, the faces hard; even Cummings' style seems aus-
tere. The city has been transformed by winter and "la guerre." The
authorities who threw him into prison may even cancel Christmas, but thanks to the brotherhood he has discovered at La Misère, Cummings now experiences place as a focus of community;
in winter Paris is bearable because everyone is "alive." That perspective, so different from his earlier, effusive vision of "Paris the
beautiful," marks a crucial change in Cummings himself, whose
experience of hardship now enables him to set aside his illusions
of Paris, to recognize its wartime sadness and to value its defiant
vitality.

Three decades later, in *I: Six Nonlectures* (1953), Cummings
looked back upon Paris (to which he had returned in the twenties
as a painter-poet) not as an aggregate of buildings and monuments
but as a place manifesting "the humanness of humanity": "Everywhere I sensed a miraculous presence, not of mere children and
women and men, but of living beings; and the fact that I could
scarcely understand their language seemed irrelevant, since the
truth of our momentarily mutual aliveness created an imperish-
able communion." From the perspective of his sixtieth year he
sees Paris as the meeting place of two realms, the sacred and the
secular. He recalls an image from his "Post Impressions" of the
twenties:

> Paris; this April sunset completely utters
> utters serenely silently a cathedral
> before whose upward lean magnificent face
> the streets turn young with rain.[3]

These lines, he asserts, demonstrate the happy coexistence of the
material and the ethereal; he claims to have celebrated in Paris
"an immediate reconciling of spirit and flesh, now and forever,
heaven and earth." In retrospect, Cummings translates the city of

exile into a symbol of his own contradictory desires: "Paris was
for me precisely and complexly this homogeneous duality: this
accepting transcendence; this living and dying more than death or
life."[4]

What do these separate representations of *la ville lumière*
suggest about the nature of place? What do they imply about the
way human beings conceptualize places and form attachments to
them? In the progression of responses sketched above—from the
novel to the poem to the late philosophical "nonlecture"—we see
that Paris changes: not the actual city (although the novel implies
a change of seasons) but the city of words constructed by Cummings. Through these brief passages, we witness the evolution of
an imaginary city while regarding its transformation as a sign of
the changes which Cummings (or his persona) has undergone. The
phrases which constitute this imaginary city are mimetic, but
what they "represent" are the psychic and emotional conditions
under which he has contemplated Paris or his own mental image
of Paris. These fugitive references, supposedly to a real city, thus
mirror certain changes in the writer's own consciousness and
sensibility. In this respect they suggest the potential function of
place in every textual representation of self; more broadly, they
imply that identity itself inheres in the relation which the self
assumes to its surroundings (material and human). We see in
Cummings' novel that he makes sense of his wartime ordeal
through a contemplation of two sites: the "enormous room" at La
Misère—which becomes a microcosm of Europe and an emblem
of the human community—and the city of Paris, which in its
contrasting aspects discloses his own growth. Recounting his
transformative experiences, Cummings reveals the orienting
function of place; he can tell his story only through the reconstruction of those sites. For him, as for other American writers,
Paris was a scene of metamorphosis; the city's image, inscribed in
the expatriate text, inescapably reflects the creation of an exilic
self.

To pose the question of place is to revive an issue which
criticism apparently disposed of decades ago with the concept of
"setting." Yet as Leonard Lutwack has recently remarked, we still
lack "a theory of the formal use of place in literature." Though all
narrative action unfolds in space and time, criticism has con-

cerned itself almost exclusively with temporality; we have barely begun to consider the textual implications of place. Lutwack proposes that all literary projections of locale express "symbolic purposes even though in their descriptiveness they may be rooted in fact."[5] This figurality derives from both archetypal associations (mountains connote vision, spirituality, and so on) and particular implications of place generated by a given work (the vulgarity of Yonville, for example, in *Madame Bovary*). Lutwack asserts that "the most elemental orientation of a reader to a narrative text is through its evocation of places" (37). Here he refers to "those aspects of the actual environment" forming the world inhabited by fictive characters; he claims that correlations between real and fictional topography determine the reader's preliminary assumptions about narrative form and mode.

If Lutwack establishes the importance of place in literature and the diversity of its treatment, however, his distinction between the "actual environment" and an imaginative landscape bears reexamination. A real environment becomes intelligible— and comparable—only after it enters into language as an instance of place; yet as geographical theorists have suggested, all conceptions of place are inherently and inescapably subjective. According to Yi-Fu Tuan, "place" is a "concretion of value," space endowed with value; Edward Relph speaks of places as "focuses of intention."[6] For both, the notion of place implies the projection of human sensibility upon the natural or built environment. Hence one cannot compare an "actual" place with its literary representation, since there is literally no "place" apart from an interpreting consciousness. The only possible comparison for the critic is thus between a personal, readerly concept of place (perhaps informed by knowledge of an existent site) and a textual, writerly image. This distinction forces a rethinking of the status of literary topography, for the salient difference lies not in the relation between real and fictive environments but between textual scenes and the symbolic experiences of place which they inscribe. In the case of Cummings' novel, Paris is first synonymous with beauty and pleasure, then with life and liberty, and finally with the persistence of humanity in the face of war. What matters is not the discrepancy between his version of the city and that of the Baedeker guide but rather the connection between his city of words and the internalized place to which it refers. Perhaps every textual construction of place implies just such a mapping or symbolic re-presentation of an interior terrain.

In everyday conversation, the word *place* designates a portion of the physical world, detaches it from its surroundings, and tacitly attributes a distinctiveness: "Vienna is a place I want to visit." The uniqueness or difference assumed by such a statement resides not in the material configuration of streets, buildings, trees, or rivers but in an *idea* of place already embedded in consciousness and shaped by cultural forces (art, literature, advertising, journalism), as well as personal fantasy. The same place may, as we know, hold radically different meanings for different persons: on a visit to London, the traveler who loses her passport and gets food poisoning will have a significantly different sense of the city than someone who falls in love in Hyde Park. Relph shows how the identity of a place derives from three intertwined yet irreducible elements—"physical features or appearance, observable activities and functions, and meanings or symbols." Some of these components seem fixed, objective, and independent of subjective judgment; yet even so empirical a criterion as the "appearance" of a place implies its contemplation from a certain vantage point or through a particular representation. We can distinguish between a popularly held image (Rome, the eternal city) and an individual perception of place, but both are ultimately human constructions; the supposed "identity" of a place may be little more than the dominant popular image. A person's sense of place emerges from a fusion of perceptions occurring on several levels—a process which inevitably remains conditional and arbitrary. Such an operation hinges, according to Relph, on one's existential relation to place, which may be characterized by some form of "insideness" or "outsideness."[7] The extent of one's psychic involvement in or identification with a given place affects—and is affected by—the symbolic meanings associated with that site. "Outsideness" connotes the persistent sense of exclusion from or disregard for one's material surroundings. From the converse perspective of "insideness," place becomes (as Tuan says) a "calm center of established values," a symbolic constant amid change and movement; he thus ascribes a groundedness, a sense of orientation and identity to the root concept of meaningful space. Here place connotes security and belonging, as in the expression "my place," a synonym for home.[8]

Feelings of "insideness" and "outsideness" occur as more or less conscious responses to milieu; but we can also experience place as space which has penetrated to the level of the unconscious. Pierre Sansot appositely remarks: "To the rather embarrassing question 'What is the essence of a place?' one must often substitute another question: 'What can one dream about it?'" To dream of place is to experience the intrusion of landscape into the deepest recesses of the psyche and to recognize the inevitably symbolic structure which our perceptions of the environment assume. But dreams typically manifest a topography quite different from conscious perceptions. Our residual, waking remembrance of dreamscapes may, for example, call to mind a place in childhood, a scene of trauma or pleasure, without providing any specific visual correlation; we recognize through pure intuition the site of an essential though repressed episode. This phenomenon of intuitive recognition suggests that one's sense of place is determined less by specific geographical features than by experiential associations. It also implies, however, that the assimilation of experience in the unconscious—the processing of everyday life—depends in some way upon these spatial and topical attachments. Beyond their conscious symbolic or functional importance, places thus invade the unconscious and acquire oneiric potency. According to Gaston Bachelard, the most powerful psychospatial image is the house in which we were raised, which is "physically inscribed in us" and "imbued with dream values which remain after the house is gone."[9] The house of childhood recurs in the unconscious as a phantasmic repository of early impressions and sensations, ordinarily as the embodiment of at-homeness.

Summing up the multiple implications of place for what Heidegger might call our being-in-the-world, Relph argues that

> the essence of place lies in the largely unselfconscious intentionality that defines places as profound centers of human existence. There is for virtually everyone a deep association with and consciousness of the places where we were born and

grew up, where we live now, or where we have had particularly moving experiences. This association seems to constitute a vital source of both individual and cultural identity and security, a point of departure from which we orient ourselves in the world.[10]

This process of orientation, of situating ourselves in space and coming to know the surrounding environment, seems indispensable to the recognition of the self as a self. The elements of place to which we are most responsive (consciously or unconsciously) comprise the physical signs of our deepest intentions and desires. Gabriel Marcel once observed that "an individual is not distinct from his place; he is that place." His contention is not that geography determines personality (otherwise all natives of a region would be indistinguishable) but that we find or know ourselves principally through the attachments we form to a place.

Similarly, we organize our experiences with other people through associations with place; to recall an acquaintance is to visualize scenes and contexts in which we have known that individual. This is precisely the psychic connection between identity and setting evoked when we try to "place" someone who looks vaguely familiar: we recollect a college lecture hall and instantly recognize an old classmate. The identification occurs not through a rational calculation of time or chronology but by recalling some physical scene which condenses past experience as a nexus of associations. Roger M. Downs and David Stea make the intriguing suggestion that we can have no awareness of past events in our lives "without a sense of the place in which they happened."[11] They contend that we reconstruct the past largely through the imagery of place and imply that memory is less the retrieval of bygone time than a recovery of symbolic space.

Despite its title (which underscores the passage of time), Proust's *A la recherche du temps perdu* demonstrates this point: in the first volume, *Du côté de chez Swann*, the narrator recovers an earlier self by evoking the village of Combray, a place associated with childhood visits to his aunt's house. Through the lapse of time, his image of the town had become dim and unreal: "These Combray streets exist in so remote a corner of my memory, painted in colors so different from those in which the world is decked for me today, that in fact one and all of them, and the church which towered above them on the Square, seem to me now more unsubstantial than the projections of my magic-lantern."[12] Conjured up by the taste of lime tea and *petites madeleines*, however, the memory of that lost world returns: the church of Sainte-Hilaire, Tante Léonie's house, the streets and lanes of the village, the "two ways" (the Méséglise and Guermantes), the ruined castle, and all of the other images of Combray which compose its particularity. For Proust the village is that network of associations within which he locates himself as a subject. Yet he also knows that the place of memory bears little relation to contemporary Combray, where even the landscape has changed; he recalls promenades along the rue des Perchamps, "a street for which one might search in vain through the Combray of today, for the public school [which in the actual village of Illiers has been renamed the Lycée Marcel Proust] now rises upon its site" (213).

The remembered sites which hold the key to our being thus have a shadowy, precarious existence:

> The places that we have known belong now only to the little world of space on which we map them for our own convenience. None of them was ever more than a thin slice, held between the contiguous impressions that composed our life at that time; remembrance of a particular form is but regret for a particular moment; and houses, roads, avenues are as fugitive, alas, as the years. (551)

Despite their evanescent nature, however, places known in the past remain with us like certain tastes and smells, ready to be summoned into consciousness and to unfold a profusion of meaning; according to Proust these places form part of the "vast structure of recollection" (58) through which we order and interpret our past lives. He uses the metaphor of Japanese cutouts that expand in a bowl of water from tiny crumbs to recognizable shapes of "flowers or houses or people" to suggest how a single image or impression may evoke a detailed recollection of place. Throughout his later experiences in Balbec and Paris, Proust's narrator draws upon memories of Combray as a point of reference and a source of coherence. The quintessential episode associated with Combray—his mother's refusal to bestow the goodnight

kiss—indeed holds the key to Marcel's subsequent preoccupation
with the paradoxes of desire.

A shorter modernist text, Hemingway's "Snows of Kilimanjaro," enables us to examine with perhaps greater efficiency this
complicated relation between place and memory. Here, a dying
writer on safari in Africa visualizes a series of mental scenes—the
rail station at Karagatch, the Alpine village of Schruns, a trout
stream in the Black Forest—each of which evokes certain moments or phases of consciousness. Set against the immediate
environment of the African plain, these flashbacks imply a process of re-collection, a psychic review *in extremis* of experiences
which have shaped a life. In effect, the narrative enacts the gesture
of autobiography, the effort to locate in past experience those
episodes in which the self has defined itself through its responses
to the world. As the writer, Harry, recalls these sites of being, he
acknowledges the function of place in remembrance; each separate locale, evoked by sensory images, epitomizes an entire episode. More poignantly, these scenes signify stories which will go
untold, for Harry recognizes that "he would never write the things
that he had saved to write until he knew enough to write them
well."[13] Hemingway here manifests more than self-pity: Harry's
remorse betrays a profound attachment to places where he has
glimpsed basic truths. These sites mark moments in which he has
been fully alive to the world, and in the chagrin of lost opportunity, the writer virtually equates place with writing. The "things
that he had saved to write" all reside within recollections of
physical scenes: the ranch out West, his grandfather's log house
on a hill above the lake, the streets of Constantinople, the working-class neighborhood in Paris.

In the italicized passages which comprise Harry's reveries,
Hemingway implies that in some fundamental way, we do not
inhabit places so much as they inhabit us. Each of the physical
scenes, linked (in Relph's phrase) with "particularly moving experiences," persists in memory and dream as a psychic landmark.
The writer's life is obviously more than the sum of those places in
which he has lived, but the difference between one place and
another makes possible the recollection of that life and in effect
determines the very structure of remembrance. Wyoming, Paris,

and Constantinople constitute more than settings in which meaningful events have unfolded; they designate separate spheres of
being, each marked by specific impressions, desires, and con-
tingencies. As Harry recalls these scenes, he implicitly takes the
measure of his existence, trying to discern in memory some
scheme or pattern which will account for the cruel irony of his
death in Africa by gangrenous infection. But in depicting this
"recherche du temps perdu," Hemingway reflects less on time
than on the primacy of place in the writer's conception of self. If
memory is the crux of identity, images of place determine the act
of remembrance. Late in his career Hemingway wrote: "We live by
accidents of terrain, you know. And terrain is what remains in the
dreaming part of your mind."[14] In "The Snows of Kilimanjaro," the
dying writer surveys that inner terrain, the symbolic landscape of
his life, to understand who he is and what he has been; like
Tolstoy's Ivan Ilych, Harry confronts the enigma of self in the
imminence of annihilation. Each of the places in which he has
lived holds a clue to the essential identity threatened by the
absolute displacement of death.

As if to preserve these memories of place (and hence the
remembering self) from oblivion, the writer at one point considers dictating his recollections to Helen, the wife at his bedside.
He recalls one site so integral to his self-conception, however,
that it cannot be thus transcribed:

> *You could dictate [the fishing trip to the Black Forest], but
> you could not dictate the Place Contrescarpe where the
> flower sellers dyed their flowers in the street and the dye ran
> over the paving where the autobus started and the old men
> and the women, always drunk on wine and bad marc; and
> the children with their noses running in the cold; the smell
> of dirty sweat and poverty and drunkenness at the Café des
> Amateurs and the whores at the Bal Musette they lived
> above.* (69)

The significance of the Left Bank setting is not immediately clear.
The flashback follows two previous allusions to Paris in dialogue
with Helen; Paris also figures in a recollection of the writer's
encounter with the Dadaists of Montparnasse, evoked by the
image of an *"American poet with . . . a stupid look on his potato*

face" (identified in manuscript as Malcolm Cowley) talking in a café *"with a Roumanian who said his name was Tristan Tzara"* (66). Through these references Hemingway draws an implicit contrast between the elegant Parisian haunts Harry has known with his wealthy second wife and the more modest environs associated with a previous marriage and the beginnings of his career.

But why is the author unable to dictate a description of the quarter around the place de la Contrescarpe? Why does that sketch seem possible only if he writes it himself? In two sentences Hemingway discloses the psychic importance of this place for Harry's conception of himself:

> *In that poverty, and in that quarter across the street from a Boucherie Chevaline and a wine co-operative he had written the start of all he was to do. There never was another part of Paris that he loved like that, the sprawling trees, the old white plastered houses painted brown below, the long green of the autobus in the round square, the purple flower dye upon the paving, the sudden drop down the hill of the rue Cardinal Lemoine to the River, and the other way the narrow crowded world of the rue Mouffetard.* (70)

This section of Paris—the very milieu where Hemingway served his apprenticeship in 1922–23—thus becomes associated with the life of writing and with a period of ambition and hard work prior to the dissipation of Harry's middle years. Throughout the passage, he recalls with disdain the drunken locals, contrasting their *ivresse* with his own industry and recollecting the room he rented in the hotel where Verlaine died: *"He had a room on the top floor of that hotel that cost him sixty francs a month where he did his writing, and from it he could see the roofs and chimney pots and all the hills of Paris."* While the view from his apartment is restricted (*"you could only see the wood and coal man's place"*), the writing room significantly affords a panorama; by this vertical ascent, a secular, urban mode of transcendence, the writer claims a position of symbolic dominion. Seen in its totality, the confusing maze of Paris reveals its ultimate form and organization. From this loft, in a hotel which once housed a famous poet, Harry knows where he is and who he is. The old neighborhood, recollected in vivid colors, becomes associated with the formation of this writing self; it is appropriately only through an act of writing that he can recover the immediacy of that place which, in its remembered details, yields his original identity as an author.

But that task remains uncompleted, and Harry's lingering regret is that *"he had never written about Paris. Not the Paris that he cared about"* (71). Hemingway here discloses a nostalgia for the lost world of his own youth. By the mid-1930s he had realized the importance to his development of those lucky years on the Left Bank; yet not until the late fifties, as he struggled against infirmity and despair, did he compose (in *A Moveable Feast*) his memoirs of "the Paris that he cared about." The dying protagonist of "Snows" receives no second chance to preserve the story of a life lived in and shaped by memorable places. Instead, like the doomed hero of Borges' "Secret Miracle," he must content himself with the cerebral projection of never-to-be-completed writing. In the end, his memories reveal the psychic fusion of topography and experience, as desire resolves into the forms and features of place. Hemingway's story culminates in a vision of Kilimanjaro, which in the spatial dynamic of the narrative marks an apotheosis of place, the geographical concretion of the longing for artistic transcendence figured in Harry's climb to the top-floor room. In this final fantasy, the dying writer reinscribes the dream of a younger self, confirming again the symbolic status of landscape in the conceptualizing of a life story.

Although Hemingway's story enables us to consider the role of place in the structure of remembrance, we must look elsewhere for insight into the daily process by which one internalizes surroundings and thus orients and defines the self. Downs and Stea call this phenomenon "cognitive mapping" and define it as "a series of psychological transformations by which an individual acquires, codes, stores, recalls, and decodes information about the relative locations and attributes of phenomena in his everyday spatial environment."[15] That is, cognitive mapping describes the assimilation of sensory information about the places we inhabit or traverse not as raw impressions but as a "code" of meaningful signs which collectively produce a mental map. This cartography enables us to function by providing a sense of distance and relation and by schematizing our experiential world in terms of val-

ued or significant sites. Social scientists have examined spatial
behavior dependent on cognitive mapping: giving directions, taking shortcuts, determining shopping routes, or even choosing
one's place of residence. They have acknowledged, moreover, that
beyond the conduct of daily business, this topographical orientation seems vital to personal survival in a complex environment;
without this internalized map we would literally be unable to find
our way home.[16]

But cognitive mapping surely affects more than spatial behavior. We have already seen in Proust and Hemingway how
encoded landscape figures in the operation of memory; other
literary texts suggest that place enters importantly into the day-
to-day construction of the self. Of particular relevance here is the
autobiographical form most attentive to everyday life: the journal
or diary. In her *Early Diary*, the French-born American writer
Anaïs Nin records her agonizing return to Paris in late 1924.
Before leaving the United States she had mused: "The New
Yorker dreams of Paris while the Parisian wonders about New
York. And we go through life without definitely realizing any
place. They all remain unreal for us."[17] Yet her experience proved
otherwise; after moving to Paris with her husband, Hugh Guiler,
Nin became obsessed with the reality of the city, which for nearly
three years seemed to determine the course of her existence. Her
profound ambivalence toward Paris forms a key to her diary during this period and mirrors an ongoing psychological conflict.

Perhaps because she recalled the Paris of her childhood, Nin
returned full of illusions. Her first weeks there established a
pattern of sharply vacillating emotion: one day the air was sweet,
and Nin felt "the pleasure of being in Paris" (81); a few days later
"Paris was gloomy," and she wished that she had never come back
(84). But she nevertheless began to reorient herself, walking with
Hugh through the Tuileries (fig. 1), beside the river, and along the
grand boulevards. Recurrent references in the diary indicate sites
of personal significance: the place des Vosges, the Louvre, Notre
Dame, the Luxembourg Gardens, and the bookstalls along the
Seine. For a few months in 1925 Nin lived on the Right Bank near
the Etoile and enjoyed promenades along the fashionable boulevard Haussmann; the couple subsequently took a Left Bank apartment on the rue Schoelcher in Montparnasse. Nin took a skeptical

Figure 1. The Tuileries, looking toward the Obelisk and the Arc de Triomphe.

view of this quarter (then teeming with expatriate artists) and preferred little side streets—like the rue Vavin—to the broad boulevard du Montparnasse. When urban crowds aroused her disgust, Nin alternately sought out quiet parks or remained ensconced in the apartment. But despite a reclusive tendency, she also loved walking and became familiar with the streets of the city's central arrondissements. Her perambulations reflect a seemingly deliberate effort to absorb the geography of the city—as if absolute spatial orientation might somehow reconcile her to the invisible Paris which oppressed her.

Much as she tried to understand the city, though, Nin felt a revulsion toward it and confided in her diary: "This Parisian life, I am convinced now, is a constant source of irritation to me" (142). We can identify three separate sources of dis-ease which undermined "the pleasure of being in Paris." The first was the "intolerable pain" inflicted upon the modest young wife by the spectacle of "impurities"—public displays of sensuality or vulgarity. Prior to the awakening which plunged her into sexual adventures as well as the composition of erotica, Nin discovered in Parisian culture a bawdiness which tainted her perception of the physical city:

Paris is like a giant park, riotous in coloring, festive in its fountains and flowers, glorious in its monuments. When I stand at the top of the Champs-Elysées, with its chestnut trees in flower, its undulations of shining cars, its white spaciousness, I feel as if I were biting into a utopian fruit, something velvety and lustrous and rich and vivid.

But the worms are gnawing it. A repugnant phrase in a book, a coarse breath of the theatre, a look from sacrilegious eyes, the smell of something foul and abysmal, . . . and the fruit turns bitter in my mouth. I stand in the same place, but shivering, nauseated.

My reaction to sensuality causes me infinite pain. (142–43)

Nin's reaction was complicated by her relationship to her philandering father—who personified "intelligent, insidious, cultured Paris"—and to her husband Hugh, the "humorous banker" whose character would be corrupted, she worried, by the "poisoned life" of the city. Reading between the lines, we see that Nin also feared the transformation of her own nature—specifically, the loss of those constraints which protected her from the seductive influence of Paris. Like Lambert Strether in James's *Ambassadors* (a novel she greatly admired), Nin felt strangely intrigued and repelled by the complicated amours of the French.

A second source of unhappiness was the climate of Paris. Weather seems to have determined both her mood and her perception of the city; with keen self-awareness she observed: "I react with the exactitude of a barometer to the atmosphere" (95). On 2 January 1925 she confessed: "Tonight I hate Paris. The wind is blowing heavy rain-drops about; the streets are wet and muddy; the automobile horns, more discordant and insistent than ever" (82). Nin's attentiveness to climate illustrates the influence of weather on the experience of place. Rain and gloomy skies triggered her most despairing characterizations of Paris:

Hateful gray days—short and dark and oppressing, wrapped in mists, with a pale, powerless sun appearing occasionally through them like a mockery. You see the copper circle, but its rays cannot reach you—the fog swallows them and cuts up the warmth halfway. And to me it is even sadder to see the sun and not to feel it, to be reminded that on other worlds it shines so deliciously. . . . I want to go *anywhere*, but away from loathsome Paris. (243)

Yet pleasant weather could transform the city: "Paris on a sunny day is such a different thing!" (84). Sometimes atmospheric conditions enabled her to recover a romantic perspective: "Today, in the dense fog, I saw Paris like a magic city. The shadowy people, the muffled sounds, the fantastic air that hung over the most common *voitures à bras,* over the vague and featureless heads of the vendors. The Seine has completely disappeared. I walked over a bridge that spanned two clouds" (89). But such moments came infrequently. Throughout the diary, Nin traced a curious relationship to Paris in which she had seemingly surrendered her will: the city in its various seasonal and meteorological aspects controlled her emotional life.

Finally, Nin felt oppressed by the weight of French literary tradition. Unlike most Americans in Paris, she enjoyed fluency in French; she read the literary journals, attended lectures at the Sorbonne, and retained from childhood a reverence for the *grands hommes* of French letters. Nin registered the ordeal of finding her literary identity in the shadow of such brilliance; she conceived herself as the victim of "a Monster, . . . the perpetual presence of Letters" in Paris which "swallows your individuality." Sensing that she had become paralyzed, she wrote in the dramatic entry of 11 April 1926: "Paris kills my writing. I have been oppressed and belittled and silenced in Paris. As soon as I leave it, I feel free again, vivid, enthusiastic, fervent, creative. . . . I have been spiritually crucified in Paris" (189). Nin here acknowledges the intimidating—and patently masculine—authority of French tradition as enshrined at the Sorbonne, the Panthéon, and the Académie Française. She felt that her survival depended upon relocating, finding a milieu in which writing would be possible: "All I need now," she wrote, "is a chance to develop in a place where I am allowed to breathe" (191).

For a time Nin imagined that a room above the rooftops might enable her to come to terms with the city she described as "hell on earth" (198). After seeing a movie with aerial views of the capital, she felt a need to "get a sweeping sight of the whole" for

she had seen "only parts of Paris at a time" (99–100). She thought
that a panoramic view would disclose "the beauty of the whole"
which—in her experience—was often "lost in the sourness of the
details." Nin couched in aesthetic terms her own desire for an
elevated perspective: to scan the horizon, note landmarks, and
absorb the spatial configuration is to conduct an essential remapping, to place oneself above a landscape thus rendered coherent,
picturesque, and benign. By surmounting Paris literally she hoped
to conquer the effects of the oppressive, internalized city. This
desire for "a sweeping sight of the whole" led to the discovery in
May 1926 of a top-floor servant's room on the rue Schoelcher,
which the couple rented as "a Secret Refuge, a workroom." Nin
called it "the High Place" and recognized its psychic importance:
"On this little terrace, seeing Paris from such a high plane, nothing can affect us" (205). Although not quite a room of her own, the
loft offered "peace and books and sunshine" (224) as well as superb views of Montmartre and Sacré Coeur. But Nin found the
loneliness "intolerable"; four months after renting the top-floor
room, she acknowledged a "fear of the High Place, where I am
alone with my ideas, alone with my hate of Paris" (233).

Unable to relieve her anguish by positioning herself above the
city, Nin tried yet another strategy of adjustment. In December
1926 she vowed: "I shall try to turn my hate of Paris into writing
and make it harmless" (248). Hugh had suggested that she consolidate her journal entries under the title "Two Years in Paris," and
she initially undertook an analysis of Montparnasse: "I am going
to study my quarter, my neighbors, and their life." She examined
the bohemianism of the Rotonde and the Dôme (fig. 2), concluding that the great cafés were "fake in spirit," crowded with "men
and women who make sport of art" (252). But Nin wanted to take
a wider view of Paris; in a passage framed as the opening of her
book, she offered a striking parallel:

> Night and day the gargoyles of Notre Dame look down
> upon Paris with a sinister expression, with derision, mockery,
> amusement, with hate, fear, disgust. For two years I looked
> down into Paris, and tried to understand why the gargoyles
> had such expressions.
>
> It seemed strange that they should be able to look in such

Figure 2. The Dôme, around 1930.

a manner at the lovely river, the graceful bridges, the ancient palaces, the gardens, the majestic avenues, the flowers, the quays and the old books, the bird market, the lovers, the students. What do they see beneath these attractive surfaces? Why do they frown perpetually and mock eternally? What monstrous secrets made their eyes bulge out, twisted their mouths, filled their heads with wrinkles and grimaces?

I know now. (253)

Observing a disparity between the city's "attractive surfaces" and its "monstrous secrets," Nin conducts a further remapping of the visible Paris in order to disclose an invisible world. The avenues, bridges, and palaces merely point toward an unspeakable abyss. But while this passage seems initially to reinscribe Nin's misery, we should note that by bringing Paris into her own discourse she has achieved a conceptual breakthrough implied by the final claim "I know now." Precisely *what* she knows remains unspecified, but the comparison of her vantage point with that of the gargoyles seems revealing. For Nin has found at the geographical and symbolic center of Paris, literally amid the stones of its most fabled monument, a figure for her own relation to the city. She has in effect metaphorized her alienation from Paris in the gargoyle's sardonic gaze; she has articulated her displacement through a recognizable sign of place (fig. 3).

Figure 3. Gargoyles of Notre Dame. Anaïs Nin imagined that their sinister
expressions were inspired by the city they looked down upon.

Nin's "Two Years in Paris" apparently never reached completion. But the project seems to have marked a turning point in her relation to the city. In early 1927, she listed an achievement of the preceding year: "I faced and accepted Paris as a test of my courage" (258). A visit to America that summer placed her life in France in a new perspective; recounting for a friend her experiences in Paris, Nin confessed: "I found myself drawing an intensely ·interesting picture, full of color, movement, rhythm, meaning and beauty. And unexpectedly, I was struck by the conviction that the life in New York could not hold me, that I longed to return to Paris" (283). Into the quarrel with Paris she had of course projected other struggles: with loneliness and depression, with the burden of household duties, with doubt about her talent, with worries about her "perfect" marriage, with suppressed desires and disturbing temptations. But her relentless contemplation of the city—"the lovely river, the graceful bridges, the ancient palaces, the gardens, the majestic avenues, the flowers, and the quays and the old books"— finally culminated in a reconciliation to place, renewed purpose in her writing, and a growing acceptance of her sensuality.

Nin's diary displays, to be sure, many other facets of her emotional and intellectual life. But her encounter with the city reflects with remarkable precision the course of that life and illuminates its essential unfolding. Because the diary provides only a selective condensation of daily thoughts and activities, however, we cannot reconstruct Nin's response to Paris in its full complexity; what remains is at best a partial, residual image of the city she had internalized, suggesting certain reference points in a private, symbolic cartography. But the diary nevertheless testifies to the function of such mapping in realizing a sense of self; if Nin's vision of the Champs-Elysées in 1925 exposes an initial uncertainty and vulnerability, her identification with the gargoyles of Notre Dame in late 1926 manifests a perspective that is at once more cynical and more secure. As she absorbed the topographical subtleties of Paris and demystified its monstrous presence, she gained a more confident sense of her literary identity. By August 1927 Nin had returned to the High Place to work, and at year's end she reported in her diary: "Every day I feel surer of myself, my desires soar higher, I feel power in myself, conviction."[18]

Beyond their autobiographical interest, Nin's many allusions to Paris raise the question of how cognitive mapping affects textual versions of place. Downs and Stea have noted that mapping consists of two basic stages, encoding and decoding. That is, the mind converts perceptions of place into images that are symbolic, schematic, and functional.[19] Theoretically this mental grid helps us resolve spatial questions—which route is most direct? which is most scenic?—and implicitly directs our movement toward centers of value or interest. But does *writing* about place entail the same encoding and decoding? Or does the textual representation of place reverse the process of mapping by depositing reformulated signs of spatial experience? Insofar as Nin's diary sheds light on this problem, allusions to her apartment, the Luxembourg Gardens, the Louvre, the Seine, and other locales may describe important nodes of an internal map; but her attention to these sites also forms part of a deliberate strategy of self-presentation. Despite its apparent status as a truthful, uncensored record, Nin's diary (like all diaries) betrays a self-conscious selection and manipulation of details to produce an ultimately fictive image.[20] It yields a portrait of the writing self constructed from the diverse signs by which personality inscribes itself—especially from those reencoded signs of place which encompass and epitomize the struggle for identity. In Nin's diary, the gargoyles of Notre Dame figure crucially in her fabulation and illustrate the textual encoding of the city by which the self discovers and defines itself.

Not all prose forms, of course, entail the representation of place. Nor does place invariably indicate a writer's effort to articulate an image of self. Certain genres, such as travel narratives or landscape sketches, emphasize topography to assert the charm or distinctiveness of particular sites. The writer's attachment to place may color the account but remains incidental to the task of delineation. Other types of prose (the reflective essay, for example) incorporate physical scenes chiefly when locus figures as an explicit object of contemplation. In short stories and novels, however, place often plays an integral role in narrative conception as the matrix of action. Indeed, we speak of plot as what "takes place," what assumes localized form, in fiction. The French expression *avoir lieu* captures this same sense of an action or incident which literally must "have a place" in order to happen at all.

Localization is, however, scarcely a uniform principle of fiction; some writers, curiously indifferent to geography, have seemed content to embed plot in obscure or generalized settings. Lutwack notes that after Fielding locates the story of *Tom Jones* in Somersetshire and depicts the house of Squire Allworthy in pastoral terms, "place ceases to function in the novel."[21] For the most part, Poe's tales of effect employ vague, unlocatable European settings to lend remoteness to events and underscore their ambiguity. In Kafka's fiction, the physical scene also remains ambiguous, a dreamscape which metaphorizes the protagonist's anxieties but which in its surreal figurality resists facile biographical association. Recently the more realistic stories of Raymond Carver have inscribed a postmodern placelessness—a flat, undifferentiated suburban scene marked by anomie and emptiness.

But fiction more often embodies a purposive image of place, as we see in evocations of locale by Hawthorne, Flaubert, and Hardy.[22] In this century, both Anderson's *Winesburg, Ohio* and Faulkner's *Absalom! Absalom!* have appeared with maps tracing the configuration of imaginary towns and thus called attention to spatial relations within these fictive worlds. Faulkner's representation of Yoknapatawpha County indeed remains an unparalleled instance of the literary concretion of place. Modern fiction presents other notable instances of what Bachelard has called "topophilia": Joyce's obsessive attention to the geography of his native city in *Dubliners, Portrait of the Artist as a Young Man,* and *Ulysses;* Virginia Woolf's material evocation of place (her parents' summer house in Cornwall) in the brilliant "Time Passes" section of *To the Lighthouse;* Thomas Wolfe's meticulous rendering of his mother's boarding house and the streets of Asheville in *Look Homeward, Angel.*

These last three examples suggest a possible correlation in fiction between an elaboration of place and an autobiographical project. I do not mean to suggest that all novels which emphasize locale should be read as autobiography; it seems more plausible to assume that a writer's fixation with place may signal the *desire* of autobiography: the longing to reconstruct—albeit in fictive terms—the relation between an authorial self and a world of located experience. As we have seen, this is precisely the gap bridged in Hemingway's "Snows of Kilimanjaro." Autobiographies like Nabokov's *Speak, Memory* and Soyinka's *Aké: The*

Years of Childhood reinforce the impression that place may be crucial to autobiography; both writers reconstruct their early years through evocations of specific, almost magical sites associated with indelible, formative experiences. Indeed, in theoretical terms it is difficult to imagine the recounting of a life story apart from the tangible, physical scenes where important episodes have occurred. As Plato observed in the *Timaeus*, place is a veritable matrix of energies, the "nurturing container" of experience. Summing up Plato's ideas on *chora* (place), E. V. Walter writes: "People and things in a place participate in one another's natures. Place is a location of mutual immanence, a unity of effective presences abiding together." Chora is more than mere position, more than a constellation of material forms or structures: it is "the active receptacle of shapes, powers, feelings, and meanings, organizing the qualities within it, energizing experience."[23] It would thus seem imperative for a writer constructing a narrative of lived experience to acknowledge the receptacle which gives that experience definition and sustenance.

Yet autobiography as a form exhibits as much variety in treatment of place as fiction; although numerous critical discussions examine time in autobiography, place remains an apparently incidental issue.[24] Whether the autobiographer acknowledges the influence of certain locations or, conversely, ignores locale seems finally to hinge upon the life itself, upon the degree of the writer's attachment to indigenous or customary scenes. Milton's Satan insisted that "the mind is its own place," and for writers ensconced in their own mental worlds, the physical environment may indeed remain an irrelevant background. But for writers attentive to lived, sensory experience, place proves (as Plato insisted) a nurturing medium, a source of both thought and identity.

Insofar as all writers of fiction and autobiography display differing attachments to place and different patterns of habitation and movement, one might conceive a range of possible spatial attachments. There are, at one end of the scale, writers whose work is rooted in the life and landscape of a specific region and whose projections of place imply a groundedness, a sense of belonging. Eudora Welty serves here as the representative figure; her *Place in Fiction* acknowledges the determinative role of locale in narrative:

Place in fiction is the named, identifiable, concrete, exact and exacting, and therefore credible, gathering-spot of all that has been felt, is about to be experienced, in the novel's progress. Location pertains to feeling; feeling profoundly pertains to place; place in history partakes of feeling, as feeling about history partakes of place. Every story would be another story, and unrecognizable as art, if it took up its characters and plot and happened somewhere else.[25]

Then there are those diverse writers for whom place is a matter of happenstance or preference, simply the present locus of activity. Their fiction tends to register the commonalities of contemporary culture rather than regional peculiarities. Some attachment to roots may remain, but these writers inhabit a changing, megalopolitan scene which has little meaning *as place* in their writing, however realistic its portrayal. Among current American writers, John Updike and Anne Tyler may perhaps be said to possess such an orientation. Perceptibly more dislocated are those writers of internal exile whose attachments to place have been complicated by feelings of alienation, marginalization, or exclusion. Their identification with a given locale may be as intense as that of the regionalist but is accompanied by a complex, ironic detachment. In quite different ways, Flannery O'Connor and Ralph Ellison may be seen as figures of domestic exile, projecting into their fiction a contradictory, often hostile relation to place. Finally, at the other end of the spectrum, we locate those writers whose careers have been marked by prolonged absence or even permanent exile from homeland. Their passage from familiar, native grounds to an alien scene poses in the sharpest terms the difference between one place and another and produces the perspective of displacement. Conrad, Joyce, and Mann all drew upon that perspective to reconstruct the geography of their own experience.[26]

Reductive as this scheme may be, it helps to explain the singular importance of expatriate writings for a study of place. It might be argued that, among all forms of prose discourse, narratives of exile (including novels, short stories, autobiographies, and diaries) seem most likely to incorporate reflections on the problem of place and the relation of place to writing. Near the end of a career marked by his own relentless search for what his protagonist Nick Adams called "the good place," Hemingway speculated in *A Moveable Feast* that "transplanting" might be as necessary for the writer as for other growing things, insofar as relocation produced a new perspective from which a previous haunt might be written about. His theory is revealing: like many a modernist, Hemingway regarded displacement as an elective strategy of re-plenishment, a way of shifting one's angle of vision. Unlike such precursors as Ovid or Dante, who were banished for political reasons, the modern literary expatriate has (with certain excep-tions) often experienced exile as a quest for a more productive milieu. In his determination to "fly the nets" of language, religion, and country, Joyce's Stephen Dedalus may be seen as the exem-plary exiled modernist, though of course Joyce himself made a career of self-exile in Trieste, Zurich, and Paris. Gertrude Stein observed pointedly that in the twentieth century writers needed two countries because the creative life depended upon that de-tachment or ungrounding only available in a foreign place.[27] Stein's claim resonates with Henry Miller's declaration in *Tropic of Cancer:* "I'm not an American any more, nor a New Yorker, and even less a European, or a Parisian. . . . I'm a neutral."[28] What Stein and Miller identify is the expatriate's oddly indeterminate status of being imaginatively neither *here* nor *there*. Moving from the place where one "belongs" to an unreal second country implies a deliberate renunciation of origins and the assumption of an am-biguous position between "outsideness" and "insideness."

Yet as Hemingway realized, this deliberate dislocation can become a mode of vision. Lloyd S. Kramer has observed that the situation of exile produces a heightened consciousness of the physical and social environment; more significantly, Kramer adds, "the experience of living among alien people, languages, and in-stitutions can alter the individual's sense of self . . . [provoking] important changes in self-perception and consciousness."[29] The writing which emerges from this experience tends to reflect both an intensified awareness of place and an instinctive preoccupation with the identity of the alienated self. In an essay on the expatriate "avant-garde autobiography," William Boelhower claims that this type of narrative embodies "the larger crisis of *habitare* that char-acterizes the modernist condition." In this form of discourse, "the avant-garde autobiographer, in his attempt to create a coherent grammar of the self out of the spatial vocabulary of the metropolis, ends up with a loosely bound inventory of fragmented forms."[30] That is, the city of exile offers a source of signs from which the author constructs a provisional expatriate identity.

In this sense the modern expatriate writer also reenacts an ancient human predicament, the dilemma of the ungrounded self. Reconsidering Freud's reading of Sophocles' Oedipus cycle, E. V. Walter shows how the psychoanalyst abstracted the mythic hero from his environment to underscore the "universal drives of infantile mental life." But Freud thus overlooked (and quite literally displaced) an important dimension of the tragic myth, the relation of sacred or portentous sites to the mystery of identity: "Taken together, *Oedipus the King* and *Oedipus at Colonus* go beyond psychological insight to grounded insight. They present the drama of place and the crisis of the placeless self. Together, they probe the riddle of alienation and explore the relation between the self and its place."[31] This dilemma continues to inscribe itself in Western cultural attitudes. Whatever differences may be seen in the experiences of the aforementioned expatriates, each to some extent participated in and wrote about the crisis of the displaced self—a crisis which, to be sure, has certain modernist aspects but which in the search for identity and grounding traces an archetypal struggle.

Although expatriation remains a problematic concept, often loosely invoked to claim dubious commonalities, we can nevertheless recognize that a lengthy stay in an alien place must produce certain changes in the way one feels, thinks, sees, and writes. In the difference between the immediate scene of exile, the "unreal" site of expatriation (as Stein would have it), and those real, remembered scenes of homeland, one confronts the anxiety of the ungrounded self. No mere homesickness, this condition exposes a radical uncertainty about one's relation to "home" and to the self one has been. In *Invisible Cities*, Italo Calvino depicts the situation of the wandering expatriate in paradoxical terms: "Arriving at each new city, the traveler finds again a past of his that he did not know he had: the foreignness of what you no longer are or no longer possess lies in wait for you in foreign, unpossessed places."[32] The experience of exile reveals a different, foreign self while disclosing the stranger whom one no longer resembles. As it calls identity into question, expatriation forces a rethinking of the relation between place and self.

To dwell in another country also opens the expatriate to awareness of another kind of exile, the homelessness that may be traced in Western, Judeo-Christian culture to the loss of Eden. Perhaps our longing for and attachment to earthly places derives from an ineradicable collective memory of that forfeited paradise. Heidegger suggests that a consciousness of this plight may ironically provide the basis for dwelling: "As soon as man *gives thought* to his homelessness, it is a misery no longer. Rightly considered and kept well in mind, it is the sole summons that *calls* mortals into their dwelling."[33] If a sense of homelessness indeed leads to dwelling, then exile must be seen as an enabling exercise, an ironic means of inserting the self into the world so as to "bring dwelling to the fullness of its nature." In effect, expatriation creates a space for being, thinking, and writing by rupturing those relations to place which obscure the nature of our homelessness. In exile, the longing of the self for place reveals itself as pure nostalgia—as a futile yearning for *nostos* (home), for a ground of being. This is the desire identified by Plato and later expressed by Hemingway and Nin, the desire to discover the "good place" or the "high place" wherein the ungrounded self might at last escape homelessness and find bliss. But exile also makes literal one's existential displacement, and it is this consciousness which impels the writer's effort to construct a city of words which may be inhabited by a textual self.

Just as exile foregrounds the problem of place by posing an implicit contrast between new surroundings and old, it also produces a fresh perspective on cultural differences. Kramer points out that "extended contact with a foreign *mentalité* helps [exiles] to recognize the unconscious social or ideological hierarchies that create order and meaning in their native culture but pass unnoticed by people who never leave home. The 'normal' (or normative) values of the home country become more relative: simply *one* way of explaining reality or social experience rather than *the* way."[34] This vantage point "on the margin of two cultures" also works the other way, enabling the emigré to see revealing features of daily life in a foreign country which might escape the notice of the native. For the writer, exile thus provides an immediate spectacle that yields material for reflection and composition as it supplies a new perspective from which to contemplate the distant homeland.

While the tradition of literary exile extends back to the classical period, the condition of expatriation has become so pervasive in the twentieth century that, according to Andrew Gurr, we should regard exile itself as "the essential characteristic of the modern writer."[35] By definition a separation from a familiar and significant native landscape, exile presupposes no particular destination. Yet displaced writers of the modern age have in fact converged mainly upon a half-dozen great cities, presumably finding in them the cosmopolitan density of experience and urban energy conducive to the production of modern literature.[36] Among these centers of emigré activity, Paris has since the mid-nineteenth century claimed preeminence as a city of exile. We may summarize those key cultural factors which made it a haven for expatriates, taking note of a few earlier writers who sojourned in Paris and began to explore the vantage point of modern literary exile.

As Kramer and others have demonstrated, the conditions of Parisian life during the nineteenth century made the city powerfully attractive to a large population of exiled artists, writers, and intellectuals. Under the relaxed regime of Louis-Philippe (1830–48), France enjoyed "more freedom for publishing and political activity" than any country in "southern or central Europe"; Paris consequently became a "refuge for displaced radicals" escaping repressive conditions in Italy, Germany, Poland, and Russia.[37] The so-called "bourgeois monarchy" of Louis-Philippe also produced material prosperity and cultural dynamism; the rise of bourgeois capitalism inspired a lively counter-culture known as Bohemia, an underworld populated by students, artists, and intellectuals linked mainly by their desire to scandalize the bourgeoisie and to repudiate its materialism.[38] Though caricatured in Murger's *Scènes de la Vie Bohème* (1851), Bohemia developed a romantic allure as a site of rebellious creativity; it defined a climate hospitable to the marginalized artist-exile by rejecting social distinctions and setting itself in opposition to elitist (and xenophobic) high culture. Paris also attracted exiles as the "capital of the nineteenth century," placing on display the most advanced forms and styles of what Walter Benjamin has called "commodity fetishism." Through such projects as the construction of the arcades in the 1830s, the staging of world exhibitions, and the modernization of Parisian streets under Baron Haussmann, "Paris was confirmed in its position as the capital of luxury and fashion" and presented a "dreamworld" of progress which fascinated even the politically disaffected.[39]

The figure whose career most fully embodies the tensions of nineteenth-century French culture and who serves ironically as a prototype of the exiled writer is the Parisian Charles Baudelaire. His brooding sense of isolation, his cultivation of the contradictory roles of dandy and bohemian, his identification with the *poète maudit* Edgar Allan Poe, his obsession with the crowd and the city streets, his diabolism, and his participation in "the cult of multiplied sensation" all defined aspects of Baudelaire's estrangement from middle-class life. In the poems grouped as *Tableaux parisiens* and in the prose-poems titled *Le Spleen de Paris* (now available in English as *The Parisian Prowler*), he uncovered the grim, fantastic world of the streets, using his sense of self-exile from the Paris of bourgeois splendor as a lens through which to observe the grotesque low-life types—beggars, degenerates, freaks—whose misery appalled and fascinated him. An inveterate *flâneur* (stroller), Baudelaire metaphorized Paris now as an "ant-like city, full of dreams," now as a "terrifying landscape," now as a "gloomy old man doomed to toil." Benjamin contends that "the Paris of his poems is a sunken city, and more submarine than subterranean," a city upon which Baudelaire cast "the allegorist's gaze" while accentuating "the modern" in his poetry.[40] Contemplating a Parisian underclass of victims, misfits, and outcasts, he constructed a model of metropolitan exploration which would influence not only later French *symbolistes* (especially Jules LaForgue) but also such international exiles as Rilke and Eliot, who came to Paris and briefly adopted what Benjamin calls "the gaze of the *flâneur*."

So many notable exiles lived and worked in Paris during the century preceding the expatriate invasion of the 1920s that a separate book would be necessary to do justice to the topic. Kramer's fine study treats three exemplary figures—Heine, Marx, and Mickiewicz—who experienced self-discovery and developed new perspectives on modernity while living in France under the "bourgeois monarchy." Yet he does not mention another important literary expatriate, Turgenev, who during the revolutionary epoch of 1847–50 composed in Paris the majority of the pieces included in *A Sportsman's Sketches* (1852), the collection of stories about Russian peasant life which helped to bring about the abolition of serfdom in 1861.[41] Exile apparently enabled Turgenev to see more clearly the distinctive features of the rural subculture he sought to represent. After returning to Russia and suffering internal exile—banishment to a remote provincial town—Turgenev resumed a pattern of periodic visits to France in the late 1850s, primarily to be close to his love, Pauline Viardot. From 1871–83 he lived more or less continuously in Paris, establishing literary connections with Flaubert, Zola, Sand, Daudet, and the brothers Goncourt; during this prolonged exile he wrote *The Torrents of Spring*, a novel which a half century later provided an American expatriate, Ernest Hemingway, with the title for a parody.

Through his participation in Flaubert's salon, Turgenev made the acquaintance of another international exile, Henry James, who spent a crucial year in Paris (1875–76) before establishing residence in England. As a correspondent for the *New York Tribune*, James reported on developments in Parisian culture, with emphasis on literary and theatrical fashions. In his first dispatch, he reflected on the American obsession with Paris, the inevitability of recurrent visits, and the effect of leaving and returning upon the perception of place: "No American, certainly, since Americans were, has come to Paris but once, and it is when he returns, hungrily, inevitably, fatally, that his sense of Parisian things becomes supremely acute."[42] James found his own "sense of Parisian things" so intense that he shortly began to write a novel dramatizing an American encounter with the city and its vast social complexity. In *The American* (1876) he analyzed the dazzling effect of culture, tradition, and manners upon a crass but good-hearted entrepreneur from the West who falls in love with a French noblewoman in the waning years of the Second Empire. The famous opening scene, set in the Salon Carré of the Louvre, epitomizes that craving for cultural refinement which in the case of Christopher Newman nearly becomes a destructive obsession. Perhaps fearing his own susceptibility to the charms of Paris,

James retreated to England but retained throughout his career (as Edwin Sill Fussell has shown) a veritable preoccupation with France and its capital, as well as with French language and literature.[43]

With the suppression of the Commune of 1871 and the rise of the Third Republic, the buoyant Parisian cultural scene produced, as Roger Shattuck has shown, a lively avant-garde movement which, like the earlier Bohemian movement, flaunted the sort of creative freedom enticing to international exiles of art.[44] During the "banquet years" celebrated by Shattuck, August Strindberg returned to France, determined to win fame. The Swedish playwright had visited Paris twice before, but in August 1894 he returned for a longer stay. Already celebrated as the author of such naturalistic dramas as *The Father* and *Miss Julie*, Strindberg considered Paris as his "intellectual Mecca" and hoped to promote the French translation and production of his works. But he also feared a loss of identity in the great, indifferent city; and the sudden departure of his wife Frida in October 1894 effectively signalled the failure of his second marriage. Beyond these anxieties he also suffered increasingly from bizarre hallucinations and delusions, including recurrent paranoia. As if to insulate himself from neglect as an expatriate dramatist, he pursued a fugitive career as a scientist, conducting experiments to determine the chemical composition of iodine and to extract gold from sulphur.

The record of Strindberg's strange two years in Paris appears in *Inferno*, the somewhat exaggerated memoir he composed in Sweden in 1897. The account traces the development of his mania partly through adventures in the streets of Paris; his chance discoveries, clairvoyant experiences, and occult intuitions curiously anticipate the narratives of French surrealists like Breton, Aragon, and Soupault three decades later. One evening, for example, Strindberg takes a walk in a gloomy *quartier* on the Right Bank:

> I crossed the Canal St. Martin, black as a grave, a most suitable place for drowning oneself in. I stopped at the corner of the rue Alibert. Why Alibert? Who was he? Wasn't the graphite that the analytical chemist had found in my sample of sulphur called Alibert graphite? What did that imply? It was

odd, but I could not rid my mind of the impression that there was something inexplicable about this.[45]

His stroll becomes progressively nightmarish: "Suspicious-looking persons brushed past me," he reports, "shouting out coarse words as they did so." He stumbles into a blind alley "that seemed to be the abode of human trash, vice, and crime" before finding his way to the Porte Saint-Martin. On another occasion, he notices in the Montparnasse cemetery a monument to "Orfila, Chemist and Toxicologist"; a week later on the rue d'Assas, he comes upon the Hôtel Orfila. Assuming this to be a mystical sign, Strindberg takes a room there in February 1896, but the place becomes his "purgatory" as weird, unnerving experiences recur. In the hotel vestibule he notices a letter addressed to a person with the surname of his estranged wife; the letter has come, coincidentally, from the very Austrian village where his wife and child are living. Later he hears someone playing a familiar song on the piano and suspects that a former disciple has followed him from Berlin to Paris to kill him. Finally, in July, he interprets odd noises in adjacent rooms as evidence of a plot by one or more strangers to pass an electric current through him. Horrified, Strindberg flees the Orfila and shortly thereafter leaves France to seek treatment for his delusions.

Unlike Turgenev, who during his first long stay in Paris wrote about the Russian countryside, Strindberg exploited the estrangement of exile to describe uncanny aspects of Parisian life. Both perspectives, however, figure in Rainer Maria Rilke's *The Notebooks of Malte Laurids Brigge,* a work which begins (like Strindberg's *Inferno*) with a slightly fictionalized memoir of the writer's first sojourn in Paris but ends with haunting childhood memories of family and homeland. As Naomi Segal points out, the *Notebooks* thus involve a subtle fusion of past and present, remembrance and perception: "We must ask ourselves whether this strange, often grim childhood produced an adult destined to receive Paris in precisely this way, or whether the stimuli of Paris induced him to remember certain things in a certain way."[46] Rilke arrived in Paris in late August 1902 and stayed for six months, principally to write a book about his hero, the sculptor Auguste Rodin. But the young poet from Prague also felt the influence of

Baudelaire and composed a number of poems about the city generally reminiscent of the *Tableaux parisiens.*

His most complex response to the city came in the *Notebooks,* however, where he registered what Segal calls "the ubiquity and anonymity of urban death." His persona and alter-ego
Brigge defines his principal task as "learning to see" and quickly
begins to notice the horrors of the metropolis. In a key paragraph
he reflects on his progress as a writer and considers the effects of
his exile:

> I am in Paris; those who learn this are glad, most of them
> envy me. They are right. It is a great city; great and full of
> strange temptations. As concerns myself, I must admit that I
> have in certain respects succumbed to them. I believe there is
> no other way of saying it. I have succumbed to these tempta-
> tions, and this has brought about certain changes, if not in my
> character, at least in my outlook on the world, and, in any
> case, in my life. An entirely different conception of all things
> has developed in me under these influences; certain differ-
> ences have appeared that separate me from other men, more
> than anything heretofore. A world transformed. A new life
> filled with new meanings. For the moment I find it a little
> hard because everything is too new. I am a beginner in my
> own circumstances.[47]

Brigge realizes that his experiences in the city have produced a
"new life" and a different understanding of the world; his stay has
also clarified what it is that separates him from others. This sense
of alienation appears to motivate the reflections on his childhood
which fill the last half of the *Notebooks.* Though he visited Paris
many times, Rilke discovered during his first sojourn there the
peculiarly stimulating effect of solitude in the city of exile.

These few figures—Turgenev, James, Strindberg, and Rilke—
represent a much larger contingent of expatriate writers who
established at least temporary residence in Paris during the period stretching from about 1850 until the outbreak of the Great
War. Discussions of such diverse figures as Knut Hamson, Oscar
Wilde, and Edith Wharton might enlarge or modify the emerging
model of exilic experience. But the cases briefly outlined above at
least indicate certain potential consequences of displacement and

identify a basic tension between the new, different, and perhaps disorienting conditions of an unfamiliar foreign scene and the remembered features of an abandoned native scene, now made strange by the perspective of exile. Kramer writes of the three subjects of his study: "All felt themselves to be alienated from the French culture in which they lived, alienated from their native countries, and also alienated from the general development of nineteenth-century European capitalist society."[48] Although later exiles seem to have been generally less troubled by capitalism, the experience of living in an alien culture did (as I will suggest later) complicate some responses to the changes associated with modernity.

Reduced to elemental terms, the situation of exile produces a revealing contrast between one place and another, a contrast which implicitly poses the question of which qualities or features determine the distinctive identity of a place. But this question leads us back to an earlier, more basic question: what is a place? Does place exist "out there" in a purely objective form susceptible to empirical analysis, or does it lie within the human mind, as a set of internalized images always already contained and determined by language? In a recent discussion of this problem, J. Nicholas Entrikin describes the "betweenness of place," arguing for a concept of liminality which sees place as a shifting function of reciprocal but contradictory realities.[49] He thus sees place as a construct caught between the subjective and the objective. This formulation recalls an idea advanced by Henri Bergson, who in *Time and Free Will* commented on the interpenetration of subject and object while analyzing the relation between time and memory:

> Every day I perceive the same houses, and as I know that they are the same objects, I always call them by the same name and I fancy that they always look the same to me. But if I recur, at the end of a sufficiently long period, to the impression which I experienced during the first few years, I am surprised at the remarkable, inexplicable, and indeed inexpressible change which has taken place. It seems that these objects, continually perceived by me and constantly impressing themselves on my mind, have ended by borrowing from

me something of my own conscious existence; like myself
they have lived, and like myself they have grown old.[50]

Bergson's sense that these houses have been "impressing themselves" on his consciousness and "borrowing" from it at the same
time provides a revealing gloss on many of the representations of
Paris to be examined in subsequent chapters. It also suggests that
the problem of place is caught up in the phenomenology of sub-
ject-object relations and perhaps belongs to that intermediate
reality which Bergson calls the "image"—that construction halfway between an idea and a thing, determined by objective reality
but registered only through perception—or additionally through
inscription. For the writing of place, the textual construction of a
perceived environment, gives at least a tentative account of the
interplay between the inner and outer realities which merge to
produce our sense of where we are.

This notion of place remains crucial, for as Entrikin reminds
us, "place serves as an important component of our sense of
identity as subjects."[51] No experience intensifies our consciousness of this fact more than immersion in a foreign environment,
which exposes not only our complex dependence upon knowledge of topography, climate, language, and culture (among the
most obvious determinants of place) but also reveals the considerable extent to which we are creatures of place, deriving our most
basic sense of self from the relation which we have formed with
the place or chora in which we have our being. The experience of
expatriation often discloses an alternate self, responsive to the
differences which constitute the foreignness of another place.

Precisely this dilemma of identity accounts for the dramatic
power of James's late novel *The Ambassadors*. His American
protagonist, Lambert Strether, comes to Paris with the delicate
mission of retrieving the errant son of wealthy Mrs. Newsome.
But Strether recognizes first in the prodigal behavior of Chad
Newsome and then in his own fascination with Chad's lover,
Madame de Vionnet, the potential transformation of perspective
and sensibility which the expatriate may undergo in Paris. To his
astonishment, Strether finds his notions of New England pro-
priety undermined by what Chad calls "the charm of life over
here"; the struggle between Strether's sense of duty to Mrs. New-

some and his attraction to the European sophistication of Madame de Vionnet persists to the final page in his quandary about remaining abroad and marrying Maria Gostrey.[52] James's novel also poses the special problem of American expatriation in Europe, a return to the Old World from which the New has obtained much of its cultural identity. Strether's conflict of values is inherently a crisis of self-conception, and in the following chapters we shall explore other versions of this predicament. Exile affords the opportunity for change, growth, and insight as well as the possibility of alienation, confusion, and corruption. The terms of this crisis are different for Stein, Hemingway, Miller, Fitzgerald, and Barnes, but their representations of Paris enable us to trace the implications of each writer's attachment to the city of exile.

CHAPTER TWO

The Outside and the
Inside of Stein's Paris

ALTHOUGH scores of expatriate writers and literary hopefuls surged through Paris during the era of high modernism, Gertrude Stein was one of the few to become a permanent Parisian, spending her last forty-three years in France before her burial in Père Lachaise cemetery in 1946. Stein's relationship to the city began in 1878–79 when, as a little girl, she lived with her mother in Passy and attended a French kindergarten. She later declared that "this visit to Paris made a very great impression," and throughout her California childhood the city's image persisted, its memory evoked by editions of Balzac and Verne, by Millet's painting *The Man with the Hoe*, by the smell of hats and gloves direct from Paris, and by the appearance in San Francisco of the French actress Sarah Bernhardt. Early in her life, Stein came to associate Paris with writing, painting, fashion, and fame. Thoughts of France recurred at Radcliffe, where she read Zola, Maupassant, and others; one day in Cambridge she shared a railway car with a Frenchman who spoke passionately of the poet Alfred de Musset. Not until 1900, however, on the final stage of a European tour with her brother Leo, did Stein revisit Paris; there she saw Eiffel's controversial tower (fig. 4), ambled through the world exposition, and bought prints at Hessel's gallery. Three years later, at the age of twenty-nine, she made a decisive return

Figure 4. A postcard showing the Eiffel Tower at the turn of the century when Gertrude Stein first saw it.

to the city, partly to rejoin Leo (who had taken up residence there)
and partly to escape the chagrin of an abandoned medical career at
Johns Hopkins and an awkward romance with a young woman
named May Bookstaver.[1]

Headstrong and unconventional, Stein moved to France to
refashion her life and to free herself from prudish attitudes about
the role and behavior of young women. Even as she made a bid for
independence, however, she signaled both a residual dependence
upon her older brother and a need to define herself through the
intellectual rivalry which marked their relationship. Leon Katz
contends that after installing herself on the rue de Fleurus, Stein
suffered prolonged disorientation and lethargy; but the competi-
tiveness between Gertrude and Leo—which contributed to the
rupture between them ten years later—eventually quickened her
literary ambition.[2] Through audacity and self-proclaimed genius,
she became the avant-garde author she had imagined herself to be,
producing texts which defied belletristic and grammatical convention. Amid the creative commotion of Paris, Stein (anticipat-
ing the portrait Picasso would paint of her) invented a new image
of herself which she steadily came to resemble. Leaving behind
the environs of Oakland, Cambridge, and Baltimore, she discovered in the French capital a new identity and *métier*.

Not until much later, however, did Stein begin to analyze her
relation to Paris. In a 1936 lecture delivered to the French club at
Oxford, she spoke of the city as the "hometown" where she had
lived half of her life: "not the half that made me but the half in
which I made what I made." Acknowledging the effect of geography upon personality ("anybody is as their land and air is"), she
made a crucial distinction between the civilization which forms
one's sensibility and that second civilization which has nothing to
do with "those who create things" and which thus remains "a
romantic other." Living amid this otherness, the writer enjoys an
unconstrained subjectivity, for the second civilization imposes
no claims upon the creative consciousness. Stein maintained
that the outside, the external scene, remained separate from the
writer's inner life. Moreover, the foreign milieu granted her "a
special language to write," because there, English differed from
"the language that was spoken" around her. Art itself, she insisted,
derives from this differential, fecundating relation between cul-

tures: "Creation is the opposition of one of them to the other." Before the Oxford crowd, Stein thus ruled out the possibility of an American achieving such freedom in England, where history, culture, and language seemed all too familiar. "And so Americans go to Paris," she explained, because "they are free not to be connected with anything happening." The American could work in prewar Paris because France "let you alone," its indifference guaranteeing the solitude indispensable to writing. In a formulation she liked to quote, Stein remarked: "It is not what France gave you but what it did not take away from you that was important."[3]

Stein's lecture implies a paradoxical relationship to Paris, one rooted not in the particularity and concreteness of place but in a theory of literary creativity. Indeed, reduced to its essential argument, her address (originally titled "An American and Paris") contends that the city affords the ideal situation for an American writer because its "romantic" ambience exerts no influence and holds no meaning. In some basic sense, Paris does not exist for Stein except as a locus of production; it remains an imaginary construct, conceptually distant and extrinsic to her work. The Oxford lecture suggests that the city, the site of much of her composition, is a scene destined to be forever effaced in her texts. Yet this programmatic exclusion poses a problem, for Stein assumes that she can somehow express what is inside herself without reference to what is outside—as if the writing self might arbitrarily dissociate itself from the world in which writing occurs. This denial of contingency complements her self-reflexive attention to that which is "inside." But despite this rationale, traces of externality inhere in Stein's discourse, for consciousness itself entails a constant internalizing of circumstance, just as it implies a relentless projection of subjectivity upon space and place. To borrow her terminology (if not her conclusion), we might say that in the mental exercise of writing, outside and inside invariably converge and redefine each other.

Stein's insistence that Paris has nothing to do with her—or she with it—must finally be regarded as an operative fiction consonant with her self-image as the independent founder of modern writing. If she "made what [she] made" in Paris, the city just as surely formed and made her. Shari Benstock observes that "a definite change of personality occurred after her arrival in

Paris," and over the decades Stein became profoundly attached to the city.[4] From the cryptic allusiveness of such portraits as "Rue de Rennes" and "Bon Marché Weather" to the more explicit disclosures of *The Autobiography of Alice B. Toklas* and *Everybody's Autobiography,* she wove the long narrative of her relationship to Paris. Yet that narrative resists easy reconstruction: her earlier, experimental writings offer only sporadic glimpses of the city in a play of phrases poised on the verge of intelligibility; her later, autobiographical texts confirm an attachment to Paris but seem to provide mainly interior scenes and anecdotal allusions. Although her biography reveals that she did a prodigious amount of walking, knew the streets of the city, frequented art galleries, exhibitions, and studios, enjoyed shopping, and spent many afternoons in the Luxembourg Gardens (fig. 5), nowhere did she undertake a detailed representation of the physical scene. Instead she constructed an oblique collage of Parisian images, leaving to the reader the task of composing from scattered hints the story of her metamorphosis in the city of writing.

No text by Stein reveals more about her attachment to the *ville lumière*—and her curious tendency to suppress or exclude its physical aspect—than the late narrative, *Paris, France.* This quasi-autobiographical account of her adopted hometown, which grew out of the 1936 lecture, arrests the reader precisely because the city figures not as a literal place but as a multifaceted impression of the French mind and temperament. Apart from fleeting references to Notre Dame, the boulevard Raspail, and her quartier, geographical reality scarcely obtrudes. This gathering of recollections, anecdotes, digressions, and pronouncements forms a notion of "Paris" as a space of theoretical oppositions. From the first sentence Stein insists that "Paris, France is exciting and peaceful," and—as Judith P. Saunders remarks—"all her important perceptions continue to fall into pairs of linked opposites."[5] Stein's fundamental claim is that aesthetic change, literary and artistic modernism, can occur only in the context of an unchanging, traditional way of life—and not as a revolution against that tradition (she chides "the sur-realist crowd" for its defiant posturing) but as a private revolt, an autonomous activity made possible by the stability of *la vie française.* Stein declared: "I cannot write too much upon how necessary it is to be completely conservative that is particularly traditional in order to be free" (38). Paris epitomizes the paradoxical fusion of change and changelessness, while Parisians (and the French generally) exhibit an analogous devotion to changing fashion and timeless logic.

Because France had absorbed the technological revolution of modernity ("scientific methods, machines and electricity") without losing its faith in human nature, daily living, and the sacredness of French soil, its capital provided the obvious base for those seeking "a new way" in arts and letters. "Paris was where the twentieth century was," Stein observed, because the city could assimilate the unconventional without jeopardizing its traditional character (11). Indeed, as we know from studies by Joanna Richardson and Jerrold Seigel, an active bohemian movement had flourished there since the 1830s, and the French veneration for writers and artists assured a certain respect for even the most unorthodox creative projects.[6] The logical, unsentimental mind of the French permitted them to take an interest in the new wave without being scandalized: "Their tradition kept them from changing and yet naturally they saw things as they were, and accepted life as it is" (17). Imperturbable Paris formed "the inevitable background" for modern art and literature; its secure cultural heritage guaranteed the freedom to create what Robert Hughes has called "the shock of the new."

But according to Stein, Paris also provoked "the emotion of unreality," reinforcing her view that the modern writer works from a sense of displacement. In a key theoretical observation she remarked:

> After all everybody, that is, everybody who writes is interested in living inside themselves in order to tell what is inside themselves. That is why writers have to have two countries, the one where they belong and the one in which they live really. The second one is romantic, it is separate from themselves, it is not real but it is really there. (2)

Indulging in apparent paradox to express the complex relation between the writer and the scene of writing, Stein claims that the second country of literary exile is simultaneously "not real" and "really there." The writer's actual, everyday life unfolds in a setting which seems "separate" and fantastic, a place which *has* no place in the expatriate text. This second country is manifestly "there," but the writing self remains apart from it, displaced (presumably) by the very act of writing. Committing herself to an absolute interiority, Stein grounds her project in a double rejection: a geographical flight from the country where she "belongs" and an imaginative detachment from the "romantic" country in which she lives. Her repudiation of place, a kind of auto-displacement, becomes an index of integrity, a sign of commitment to what is inside herself.

In effect, Stein announces at the outset the impossibility of writing a book about Paris. Or rather, she warns that her title designates an unreal place—not the actual, physical milieu but an imagined space of writing, a city of words. She sets herself the task of describing a zone of activity, a situation conducive to the production of modernist texts. Stein composes her city through a strategy of indirection and abstraction: instead of sketching streets and landmarks, she isolates essential qualities reflected by gestures, habits, or attitudes. Discrete impressions of things seen or heard produce generalizations about France which illustrate its attractions for the modern writer. She notes, for example, that it takes about seven men in Paris to accomplish a job: "several to talk several to look on and one or two to work." This absurdity (actually, an ethnic joke) exemplifies the "background of unreality" said to be "very necessary for anybody having to create the twentieth century" (13). She further remarks of Parisians crossing streets: "Nothing startles them nothing frightens them nothing makes them go faster or slower not the most violent or unexpected noise makes them jump, or change their pace or direction" (2). This pedestrian style, which mixes boldness and indifference, typifies the "peaceful and exciting" atmosphere which sustains the artistic imagination. Even food expresses this paradoxical doubleness; Stein observes of the cuisine at the Café Anglais that "their pride in French cooking expressed itself in the perfection of simple dishes, a saddle of mutton so perfectly and so delicately roasted that in itself it became peaceful and exciting" (51).

Another aspect of Paris—the formality of human relationships—insures the privacy of the writer's personal life. It would be unthinkable for someone to intrude upon a recognized author because, as she explains, "nobody knows anybody whom they do not know" (11). In Paris the writer has an important cultural status; Stein gleefully recounts how the attendant of an overcrowded garage finds a place for her car because she is "a woman of letters." She fancies that "the police treat artists and writers respectfully too" (21). Stein also acknowledges the stimulus of Parisian fashions: "When we came to Paris the men wearing their silk hats on the side of their head and leaning heavily on their cane toward the other side making a balance, the heavy head the heavy hand on the cane were the elegance of Paris" (111). To encounter such elegance on a daily basis is exciting, because "fashion is the real thing in abstraction," embodying fundamental transformations of sensibility: "It was in Paris that the fashions were made, and it is always in the great moments when everything changes that fashions are important" (11).

By such hints Stein constructs a fragmentary, notional view of the city. Her allusions to the physical, literal scene seem almost incidental, as when she opens part two of *Paris, France* with a rumor: "Alice Toklas said, my grandmother's cousin's wife told me that her daughter had married the son of the engineer who had built the Eiffel Tower and his name was not Eiffel" (8). Here the tower functions not as an icon or landmark but as a detail which lends interest to gossip. What matters to Stein is the human connection, not the visual spectacle; Paris is simply a place where one hears stories about the son of Gustav Eiffel. Stein later mentions dramatic changes between 1900 and 1930 in "the Paris that one can see":

> We lived in the rue de Fleurus just a hundred year old quarter, a great many of us lived around there and on the boulevard Raspail which was not even cut through then and when it was cut through all the rats and animals came underneath our house and we had to have one of the vermin catchers of Paris come and clean us out, I wonder if they exist any more now, they have disappeared along with the horses and enormous wagons that used to clean out the sewers under the houses that were not in the new sewerage system, now even the oldest houses are in the new sewerage system. It is nice in France they adapt themselves to everything slowly they change completely but all the time they know that they are as they were. (15–16)

Figure 5. Gertrude Stein in the Luxembourg Gardens, around 1905.

This reflection on changes in the visible city might have generated a broad sketch of the urban scene, but Stein's focus remains
resolutely personal. Passing references to the boulevard Raspail,
the rats, the horse-drawn wagons, and the sewerage system lead to
an observation not about "the Paris that one can see" but about
the invisible city constituted by people who adapt slowly and
change completely while remaining as they were.

In the same passage, Stein comments on the intense attachment of the Parisian to his quartier: "Take the quarter in which
one lives, it is lovely, it is a place rare and beautiful and to leave it
is awful." She adds that "we all had our quarters" but notes ironically that "when later we left them and went back to them they
did look dreary" (14). This comment leads to a revealing observation on the quarters preferred by artists:

> So from 1900 to 1930 those of us who lived in Paris did
> not live in picturesque quarters even those who lived in
> Montmartre like Picasso and Bracque did not live in old
> houses, they lived in fifty year old houses at most and now we
> all live in the ancient quarter by the river, now that the
> twentieth century is decided and has its character we all tend
> to want to live in seventeenth century houses, not barracks of
> ateliers as we did then. (17)

Here in a complex gesture Stein associates herself with modern art, implies the existence of an artistic community, and explains how "those of us who lived in Paris" worked first in nineteenth-century ateliers in "dreary" quarters before moving to older, more spacious places "in the ancient quarter by the river."[7] Her remark draws a symbolic connection between place and productivity. While Picasso, Braque, and Stein were (in her view) shaping the art and literature of the twentieth century, they lived in dull, modern neighborhoods; but once they had determined the aesthetics of modernity, they preferred the "picturesque" environs of the ancien régime.

Stein's most sustained glimpse of the city comes near the end of the volume in an anecdote about a schoolboy weeping "down by the quays in Paris." The youth has failed his examinations, but the woman who accompanies him sits by "quite impersonally," assuring him that "sorrow passes." This riverside tableau epitomizes the continuity of traditional French life: "The quays of Paris have never changed, that is to say they look different but the life that goes on there is always the same" (102). Stein has discovered this part of the city while walking to her parking garage near Notre Dame; along the quays she finds a pleasant world that has "nothing whatever to do with the life of a city" (102). Sketching the same milieu Hemingway would limn in the "People of the Seine" chapter of *A Moveable Feast*, she writes:

> It is a queer life down there by the river. One day I was coming along and there were two men, one of them had found a high hat and also some orange flowers which he had pinned on the hat, and as they came along, the one presented the other to everyone, he is my brother, he said of the other.
>
> The barges always grow flowers and the men always come down with mimosa in their hand and disappear somewhere with it, and there are cardboard beds under the bridges, cardboard apparently is good against the cold anyway they use it, and the women wash their clothes and the men fish there and artists paint there and everybody minds their own business. They talk and grumble mostly to themselves but nobody fights with anybody else. (105–06)

Beside the Seine, Stein finds a place where one may escape convention to express sorrow or whimsy; its denizens respect each other's eccentricities. Amid the metropolis lies a space of leisure and creativity ("artists paint there") defined by the absence of "city life." The banks of the river thereby disclose a paradox: at its geographical center, the city disappears; axis becomes periphery. In effect, the quays epitomize the narrative itself, which marginalizes the essential, salient Paris and essentializes the marginal.

Stein's sketch of the river also implies a reciprocity between the rural and the urban: "That is one of the characteristic things of the French, the city and country the country and city are not separated" (102). This contiguity reveals itself not only in the pastoral world along the Seine but also in elements of provincial life (such as regional cooking) which infuse Parisian experience. Although this view has descriptive validity, Stein's claim that "the country and the city are not separated" must also be understood as a compensatory fantasy, for she composed her book "quite far away" from Paris, ensconced in her summer home at Bilignin in the months preceding the Nazi invasion. From the Rhône valley, the city seems to her unreal:

> I really have never known Paris in the midst of a declaration of war. Wars always take place in vacation time and in vacation weather, so one is not in Paris. Paris is always there, at least we in the country suppose so although at such a time we are not very conscious of its existence, the beginning of war is so occupying where you are, that even Paris is not there. (109)

She inscribes her narrative in "the concentration of isolation" and reflects upon the capital from a distance that is both geographical and conceptual, juxtaposing general impressions of Parisian life with details of her rustication. Her refusal to concretize the city mirrors the predicament of displacement; Paris is simply "not there" as the ground of being. It has become a forbidden city, bracing for war and German occupation.

Judith Saunders rightly argues that the city projected by Stein should be regarded as "an imaginative construct, . . . a spiritual rather than a literal place, where apparent contradictions are a source of wholeness."[8] Yet we must bear in mind that the narrative registers Stein's dislocation, her enforced departure (all the more necessary as a Jew) from her apartment and her quartier. Her

Figure 6. The cover illustration for Gertrude
Stein's *Paris, France* by Francis Rose.

Paris emerges as a *ville manquée,* an absent city; through the
feints, shifts, and asides which comprise the narrative, Stein
seems perpetually to defer a portrait of the capital. Instead she
offers two prints (among others in the 1940 edition) which "represent" the Parisian scene: Lascaux's "Le Sacré Coeur" and Picasso's
"Café Intérieur." But these illustrations disclose just what the
author and the reader both miss: a view of Paris. In his cover
illustration (fig. 6) Stein's friend Francis Rose presents the volume
as an unpacking (from a trunk labeled "Gertrude Stein") of five
paintings, each depicting a familiar landmark—the Opéra, the
Eiffel Tower, the Arc de Triomphe, the place Vendôme, and the
place de la Concorde. As enormous tears fall upon the French flag
serving as a backdrop, workmen ready the paintings for exhibition. But as George Wickes remarks, "Stein pays no attention to
the official glories in *Paris, France.*"[9] Indeed, Rose's cover com-

ments ironically on the absence of cityscapes in the narrative to follow: aside from her reference to the Eiffel Tower, the author ignores monumental Paris, concentrating instead on its quotidian, human aspect. This appears to be the point of her frontispiece, Juan Gris' "Roses," an elegant, domestic collage of cups, saucers, napkins, and roses in bud vases, with a copy of *Le Monde* tucked discreetly in the background to signify the Parisian scene. From her place in exile, Stein misses the city of intimate, daily life.

For many years Stein had conceived of the capital primarily in relation to painting; in a 1936 letter to W. G. Rogers, she observed, "Paris is never quite itself unless painting is its subject."[10] She felt that the city's distinctiveness lay in its respect for painters and in its serious regard for fine art. Perhaps as a concomitant sign of this regard, Paris had been the subject of many paintings (as in the prints by Lascaux and Picasso), and Stein's inclusion of such illustrations suggests that the visible city interested her mainly insofar as it generated what T. J. Clark has called "the painting of modern life." Her writing—over four decades—suggests that in fact Stein felt a curious indifference to the topography of Paris. With a few exceptions, she left the task of representing cafés, streets, statues, bridges, cathedrals, and parks to her male literary contemporaries, preferring instead to insinuate through anecdotal detail and esoteric allusion the deep attachment she felt for her adopted "hometown." For Stein, Paris could be understood and represented only as a series of complex interior scenes; the grand, external spectacle remained unreal to her and unrelated to the project of writing.

To speak of Stein's literary relation to Paris is to confront the perplexing fact that, until she turned to autobiographical writing in the thirties, she rarely particularized place or time in her compositions. Her early narratives—*Q.E.D.*, *Fernhurst*, and *Three Lives*—possess minimal "settings" implied by vague allusions to New York, Baltimore, or such ostensibly American towns as "Bridgepoint" and "Farnham." But place has no real function in the elaboration of these stories. *The Making of Americans* (in progress from 1906 to 1911) stands as an interesting exception, as Stein reconstructs from memory a number of identifiable sites including her childhood home in Oakland, figured as the Hersland residence in "Gossols": "a not very large wooden house standing on the rising ground . . . with a winding avenue of eucalyptus, blue gum, leading from it to the gateway."[11] But in the experimental work which she produced from about 1911 onward—poems, sketches, portraits, plays, and texts eluding classification—place references seem at best incidental to the play of sound and sense. Only a handful of her experimental texts seem related in any discernible way to the city in which she pursued much of her work. This fact seems curious, for in *The Autobiography of Alice B. Toklas* Stein acknowledges a deep emotional attachment to Paris. Yet with the exception of "Bon Marché Weather," "Flirting at the Bon Marché," "Rue de Rennes," "Galeries Lafayette," and perhaps one or two other pieces, it is difficult to draw any definite connections between her writing and the Parisian scene.

Stein's department store portraits apparently date from 1911–12. Of this group, "Galeries Lafayette" is the most opaquely repetitive: the phrase "each one is one" recurs more than seventy times in the four-page composition, and this count does not include variant forms ("each one is that one" or "each one is being one").[12] With the opening declaration—"one, one, one, one, there are many of them"—Stein seems to allude to the hordes of shoppers in the department store. Each is "one," an individual being, and at the same time part of the crowd, the "many." Each person presumably possesses qualities which form a pattern of identity, and each shopper is "accustomed to being that one." But amid this mass of human forms individual differences blur, and Stein sees only sameness. Hence her monotonous repetition—"each one is one"—acknowledges the gulf between subjects, between the observing writer and those individuals striving to be "the especial one that one is being." Again and again they pass her by; she knows that each is settled into a separate identity and is "quite used to being that one," but she can observe only impassive external aspects.

The other department store sketches register more specific insights. Richard Bridgman points out the possible link between the two Bon Marché compositions and Picasso's 1913 collage "Au Bon Marché," which Stein later reproduced in her 1938 book,

Picasso.[13] It seems plausible that the writer and the painter had discussed the aesthetic problem of rendering in analytical terms the mammoth department store located on the rue de Sèvres not far from Stein's pavilion and Picasso's new studio. "Bon Marché Weather" plays with both the pleasantries of sales clerks ("Very nice weather everybody is having") and the repetitious absurdity of conjugation exercises: "Very comfortable travelling they are having. Very comfortable travelling you are having. Very comfortable travelling I am having. Very comfortable travelling everybody is having."[14] Perhaps Stein means to parody the hesitant, rehearsed French spoken by foreigners at Au Bon Marché. Using the paradigm of the language exercise, she turns from phrases about "pleasant weather," "nice eating," and "comfortable travelling" to speak of the "very bad season everybody is having." Stein does not exempt herself: "A very bad season I am having." This allusion to a period of turmoil or despair may account for the shopping habits characterized in subsequent paragraphs: everybody is buying "many things" but there are also many things "not any one is buying." She sees the behavior of shoppers as symptomatic of psychic need ("Some are ones needing to go very often to buy something they are not then buying") and shrewdly implies a relation between shopping and the process of aging. Many shoppers, she writes, "are not going to be any taller and their proportions will later be like those of their mother." Working variations on the premise that shoppers will or will not be taller and will or will not resemble a parent's proportions, Stein sees the shopping activity at the department store as a moment fixed in time and yet impelled by the consciousness of time. By implication, the acquisition of goods figures as a symbolic defiance of mortality; Stein perhaps means to suggest that in buying an object, we also hope to purchase the time to use or enjoy it.

The companion piece, "Flirting at the Bon Marché," contains a complementary analysis of the motives for shopping. This sketch exposes the quiet desperation of certain shoppers: "Some know very well that their way of living is a sad one." For others, their lives are "dreary," "tedious," or "dull." What draws these unhappy types to the department store, Stein suggests, is the secret adventure of shopping—the possibility of change: "Everything is changing because the place where they shop is a place where every one is needing to be finding that there are ways of living that are not dreary ones, ways of living that are not sad ones, ways of living that are not dull ones, ways of living that are not tedious ones" (354). The Bon Marché is thus a scene of fantasy in which the "quite interesting" experience of shopping may become "completely exciting." This excitement derives from the implicitly sexual transactions between those who are selling and those who are buying: "very many men and very many women, very many women, very many men, very many women." Stein finally traces the impulse for change to the play of seduction and resistance between seller and buyer. The transformation of the unhappy shopper occurs not by capitulating to desire but ironically by resisting the enticements of the seller: "Changing is not in being one buying, changing is in being one having some one be one selling something and not selling that thing" (358). In Stein's analysis, the "flirting" of the sales personnel generates exciting fantasies for the shopper, but only by refusing to buy does the shopper validate his or her life and initiate the changing of "a very sad way of living."

"Rue de Rennes" extends this line of speculation, evoking by its title a busy street scene to disclose the private fears of a certain pedestrian. Stein distinguishes between an unidentified "some one" who is "frightened" by "a thing" and the rest of the crowd ("every one") which is conversely certain that this unnamed thing is not frightening. Bridgman suggests that, as in "Ada," Stein's use of "some one" alludes to the author herself.[15] The more problematic referent in this composition, however, is the "thing" respectively regarded by some as "dreary," by others as "dirty," "solid," "noble," "steady," "common," "simple," "important," "pleasant," "ugly," "charming," "serene," "troubled," "sturdy," or "the only complete thing." Yet it remains "frightening" to that someone who tells about it "again and again." Stein's only hint concerning the nature of this controversial entity occurs in a single sentence: "This thing that is such a thing, this thing that is existing, that is a frightening thing to one, is a way of living of very many being living" (349). Perhaps, as Marianne DeKoven suggests, Stein alludes to a fear of poverty and lower-class drudgery.[16] But one might also infer that the text intimates an attitude toward heterosexual relations, a pervasive "way of living" which could evoke among different persons the adjectives attributed above. Stein may thus mean to imply that heterosexuality is for some a source of anxiety or disgust. But her ambiguous, repeated phrases resist precise interpretation; with greater certainty one may conclude that the sketch conveys a general sense of alienation and panic within the impersonal modern city.

To extract even provisional readings from these "Paris" sketches is to force difficult texts into the tradition of referential prose. In each case, the reading of a supposed urban scene depends upon the title, which designates a specific locus and thereby seems to signal a topographical description. As in the case of nonrepresentational visual art, the title performs not only its customary function of identification (distinguishing one work from others); it also provides a necessary clue to the idea of the composition itself. It does so by what Gérard Genette would call "antiphrasis" or irony, insofar as the place designation displays "a provocative absence of thematic relevance."[17] Without the aid of the title, no one could identify the specified site from internal detail; none of the repeated phrases "refer" to a recognizable physical scene. What Stein seems to produce instead is a melange of thoughts and impressions evoked by certain Parisian locations, a record (it may be) of her intuitions about the human beings circulating in these places. Because she builds up these compositions—like her other experimental works—through what DeKoven concisely terms "fecund incoherence," Paris has only an oblique relationship to the manifest content.[18]

Indeed, throughout the challenging texts Stein composed over two decades (1911–32), one must read closely to find any allusions to the city in which the author "made what she made." One such reference occurs at the end of *Geography and Plays* (1922), in a piece titled "The Psychology of Nations or What Are You Looking At":

> We make a little dance.
> Willie Jewetts dance in the tenth century chateau.
> Soultz Alsace dance on the Boulevard Raspail
> Spanish French dance on the rue de la Boetie
> Russian Flemish dance on the docks.[19]

Incredibly, this brief passage on multi-ethnic street dances is perhaps Stein's most capacious comment—during her experimental phase—on "the Paris that one can see." While making brief mention elsewhere of such places as the Louvre, the Seine, St. Cloud, and the Porte Maillot, Stein nowhere concentrates detail into a cityscape. She refers to the capital by name in a score of compositions, sometimes in connection with departing or returning ("When we left Paris we had rain") and other times in gnomic phrases, such as her characterization in "Making Sense" of a concierge's wife who was "ahead of the game because Paris is so kind." Similarly, in "A New Happiness" Stein blandly affirms: "Paris is nice. Our curtains are up and we are very happy."[20] The banality of "nice" conveys her minimal interest in the metropolitan scene; she immediately reduces Paris to intimate, domestic details. The city is simply *there*, an indefinite setting for the comfortable routine of daily life.

Curious as Stein's indifference to Paris may be, this phenomenon relates to the larger problem of place in her experimental work. Even in compositions which ostensibly concern "geography" or "landscape," she avoids localizing detail. One finds references to cities and countries; to roads and streets; to mountains, hills, rivers, and fields; to rooms, furniture, walls, and windows. In "France" she even suggests how one might analyze internal space: "Notice a room, in noticing a room what is there to notice, the first thing to notice is the room and the windows and the door and the table and the place where there are divisions and the center of the room and the rest of the people."[21] But Stein typically refuses to arrange spatial or scenic elements into a concrete representation of place; instead she challenges the concept of referentiality and descriptive coherence, producing phrases that approximate the language of conventional discourse only to slide into seeming nonsense. By situating her compositions on the margin of intelligibility and by toying with the phrases and formulas of visual description, she places in question the process by which words may be said to produce an image of place.

Her composition "To Call It A Day" appears, for example, to meditate on the relation between landscape and its reconstitution in language. This work explicitly offers "a description of the scarecrows and monuments of the war in and near Belly [Belley] which is in Bugey, which makes part of the department of the Ain, a department in the East of France and equidistant from Chambery Lyon Grenoble and Bourg in Bresse." Stein's precision, however, seems to mock the notion that topographical location has any-thing to do with the experience of place. More pointedly, her later allusion to scarecrows raises the question of whether language can indeed make place present and visible:

> And this is a scare a scarecrow. A scarecrow can be made in various ways usually it consists of hanging and stuffing and if a failure comes then can leaning be earlier. As this a scare and as this and seen so. Seen so the three in leaning and sitting and standing and renouncing soldiering. Is this a scene and seen and seen and seen.[22]

While the scarecrow is a makeshift contrivance to produce a visual effect, Stein asks whether her verbal play—which refers obliquely to three monuments—likewise creates a "scene" that is "seen." Throughout the piece Stein juggles the images of moun-tains, monuments, and scarecrows. But by defying the rhetoric and logic of place description ("Monuments erected small figures and often smaller than that when they are larger and there"), she treats landscape as an arbitrary deployment of verbal signs.[23]

A similar practice informs Stein's "landscape" novel, *Lucy Church Amiably* (1930), which begins: "To bring them back to an appreciation of natural beauty or the beauty of nature hills valleys fields and birds. They will say it is beautiful but will they sit in it." Marshaling the formal elements of the scene, Stein tries to evoke a landscape in which her readers will want to sit: "Trees fields hills valleys birds pinks butterflies clouds and oxen and walls of a part of a building which is up."[24] Her narrative—if it may be so regarded—is set in the village of Lucey; but despite the regional place names (Chambéry, Bourg, Nantua, Grenoble) and continual references to mountains, meadows, rivers, trees, and flowers, there is only an obscure sense of place. The elements of the natural scene remain, in effect, indefinite and abstract markers, having none of the specificity of landscape description. The fol-lowing passage, which ostensibly compares the village of Lucey ("here") with an unidentified "there," offers another inventory of natural components:

> Was Lucy Church pleased she was very pleased with the difference between here and there. There there is a lake here there is a lake. There there is a garden and woods and trees and here here there is a garden and woods and trees. Here there are

meadows and a moon. There there are not meadows and there
is a moon. Here there are lights and trees there there are lights
and trees. Here there are sounds due to marshes there there are
sometimes sounds due to marshes. There is this there. There
there is this there and so there is. (113)

The difference between "here" and "there" reduces to the presence or absence of meadows and to the frequency of marsh
sounds. But this discourse never moves beyond generic terminology. For Stein, place is a function of abstract, constituent features,
and landscape writing is thus the playful arrangement of those
signs by which "nature" is conventionally inscribed.[25]

Stein's treatment of landscape repeatedly calls attention to
the words and phrases by which we represent place. She obviously
understood that just as landscape painting resorts to visual
sleight-of-hand to produce the illusion of a panorama, so the
writer "composes" a natural scene by manipulating the tokens of
verbal representation. Like the rest of her experimental work,
Stein's writings on landscape thus comment on the possibilities
of language, for as Ulla Dydo aptly observes: "What holds them
together is words, not ideas. . . . Her word constructions cohere
through the tension between words as things and words as signs,
between their centripetal and their centrifugal energy."[26] In her
avant-garde compositions, Stein defies semantics and syntax, repeats key words over and over, plays with puns and homonyms,
works endless variations on familiar phrases, and vacillates between coherence and incoherence—all to call attention (it would
seem) to the constrictive system of English grammar. She exhibits
the same disdain for the generic conventions of drama, poetry, and
narrative, devising experimental forms which flaunt their lack of
continuity and development. Within such a program, place literally has no place or function, except as a concept to be dismantled
through parody, as in "Geography": "I stands for Iowa and Italy. M
stands for Mexico and Monte Carlo. G stands for geographic and
geographically."[27] In Stein's experimental texts, which are concerned from first to last with the arbitrariness of language, she has
no need to ground her writing in the external reality of Paris.

In 1932, however, events pushed her work in a new direction.
That spring Stein made the acquaintance of an English baronet, Sir

Robert "Bertie" Abdy, who asked Stein "to tell of Paris as it had been"; his prodding induced her to spin a story which made those early years "come alive again." A few months later, when a stretch of "unusually dry and beautiful" fall weather kept Stein in Bilignin through mid-November, she began to write the Paris narrative and in six productive weeks composed an autobiography that would, she believed, secure her rightful place at the head of the modernist movement. James Mellow speculates that the author had "come to some natural break in the routine of her life; she had severed connections with the young writers and artists who had surrounded her, her older acquaintances were dying—it was a time for taking stock of herself."[28] Approaching her sixtieth year, Stein felt increasing anxiety about the judgment of posterity, and as if to compensate for lack of critical acclaim, she filled her autobiography with blatant self-tribute (declaring, at one juncture, that in modern literature she was "the only one"). By the early thirties, her friends Picasso and Matisse had become luminaries in the world of modern art, and even Hemingway—the youngster she had obligingly tutored—enjoyed international fame. But to portray herself as a modern genius (on a par with Picasso and Alfred North Whitehead) and thus to win the admiration that she craved, Stein had to modify or abandon the hermetic style she had been developing over two decades. She could only project an autobiographical identity by telling a story—by placing herself in a specific, material scene at a particular historical moment. That is, Stein could only say who she was by grounding the narrative of her life in the details of the Parisian milieu she had inhabited for nearly thirty years.

Because such a representational strategy would seriously compromise her theories of writing (and perhaps risk disclosures that she was not prepared to make), Stein adopted the expedient of telling her story from the vantage point of her companion, Alice B. Toklas. Through this persona she could tell a more or less straightforward story without seeming to betray her own experimental poetics. Shirley Neuman contends that imagining a narrative "written as though by someone else" also liberated Stein from the autobiographer's implicit duty to account for one's formation, to explain the chronological shaping of identity. Assuming the voice and perspective of Toklas allowed the author to merge "historical time" and "writing time" into a "continuous present" and thus to escape the linear scheme of the conventional life story.[29] Neuman's theory explains Stein's tactic of circling back upon specific moments and scenes; and it accounts for the curiously static personality of "Gertrude Stein." But it does not explain the powerful fiction of self-begetting which forms the book's subject.

To be sure, this identity does not emerge from a story of apprenticeship; Stein downplays tutelary influences, and even William James, her mentor at Radcliffe, figures more precisely as a discoverer of her genius: "He gave her work the highest mark in his course." While autobiography typically recounts the education of the self, Stein emerges as a character in some ways already herself, an autogenous and original personality. Yet the book just as surely traces the process by which the author makes herself into a modernist presence. Through the narratorial persona of her friend (hereafter "Toklas"), the author projects this self-becoming through three main strategies of representation. The first is her attention to recurrent thoughts and impressions: she registers aesthetic values, literary theories, character judgments, ethnic and national biases, and sundry other opinions. She thus explains at one point why commas are unnecessary, at another argues that Americans and Spaniards are "abstract and cruel," and describes elsewhere her passion for "exactitude in the description of inner and outer reality."[30] Through the observations of "Toklas," Stein offers a compendium of characteristic ideas and thereby represents her mental life.

She also displays identity through social actions—conversations, gestures, encounters—which dramatize essential qualities. By recalling the luncheon at rue de Fleurus when she seated each painter opposite one of his own works, Stein exemplifies both her clever control of social situations and her insight into artistic narcissism. Just as he was leaving the luncheon, Matisse is said to have recognized the ploy and remarked, "Mademoiselle Gertrude, the world is a theatre for you" (15). Indeed, Stein tended to treat social gatherings as theatrical events, opportunities to manifest her genius or exercise her wit. But the luncheon scene also illustrates the function of place in autobiographical narrative, projecting a sense of the Stein residence as a mythic space, a site of

legendary encounters. The famous paintings which partly compose Stein's domestic space simultaneously enable her to carry off
the game of subliminal flattery and to signify (to visitors and
readers) important personal and aesthetic preferences.

This distinction clarifies Stein's third stratagem of self-
presentation, the delineation of her experiential world. The center of that world is of course the apartment on the rue de Fleurus;
but the *Autobiography* also constructs a surprisingly detailed
image of Paris as a broader stage for Stein's modernist performance. As she projects the complex relation of self and place, the
city emerges as both a symbolic landscape mirroring her preoccupations and as a creative ambience, or chora infusing her work.
Above all, Stein's Paris emerges as a scene of discovery: she defines her identity by recounting her delving into the galleries,
studios, and exhibition halls of Paris in search of modern art.
When Stein writes about the pupil of Matisse who declared, "je
cherche le neuf" (I seek the new), she announces the implicit
theme of her own self-portrait in the *Autobiography*. Through the
representation of scenes in which Stein discovers the work of an
original artist or articulates the principle of an unconventional
painting, she inscribes herself within the modernist avant-garde.
Unlike the word portraits of her experimental period, however,
she conveys this likeness not through verbal play but through the
narrative of her contacts with people and her explorations of
place.

Stein's expeditions around Paris include several exemplary
episodes which establish her identity and status as a modernist.
The earliest chronologically is the account of her 1904 foray with
Leo (figured anonymously as "her brother") to the gallery of Am-
broise Vollard on the rue Laffitte. Stein recalls: "It was an incredible place. It did not look like a picture gallery. Inside there were a
couple of canvases turned to the wall, in one corner was a small
pile of big and little canvases thrown pell mell on top of one
another, in the centre of the room stood a huge dark man gloom-
ing" (30). Stein and her brother have come to the cluttered gallery
in quest of a landscape by Cézanne. Three times Vollard slips
behind a partition to fetch works from an upstairs room where he
keeps the Cézannes. As "the early winter evening of Paris was
closing in" two old charwomen come down the back stairs, and

Stein jokes that Vollard employs the charwomen to paint his Cézannes. Finally Vollard brings down "a wonderful small green landscape" which the Steins purchase; they become regular clients, gain the right to sort through Vollard's canvases, and later buy works by Manet, Renoir, and Gauguin. Toward the end of the winter, the brother and sister decide to buy a Cézanne portrait and are "introduced into the room above the steps behind the partition." This is a symbolic breakthrough: the Steins have gained privileged access to a cache of important modern paintings (thus signifying their status as connoisseurs), and the Cézanne which they purchase—the portrait of a woman—gives a fillip to Stein's literary career. She later insisted that "in looking and looking at this picture Gertrude Stein wrote Three Lives," repeating the gerund to convey her fixation with Cézanne's female subject as she composed the stories of the Good Anna, Melanctha, and Lena.

Another emblematic site which influenced *Three Lives* was the studio of Pablo Picasso on the rue Ravignan in Montmartre. Leo Stein had discovered the Spaniard's work at the gallery of Sagot (also on the rue Laffitte), and through H. P. Roché, the "general introducer," the Steins soon made Picasso's acquaintance. During the winter of 1905–06, Gertrude began a series of some eighty sittings in Picasso's studio for the portrait which figures so importantly in the *Autobiography*. Stein (as "Toklas") recalls the "disorder" of the studio: "There was a large broken armchair where Gertrude Stein posed. There was a couch where everybody sat and slept. There was a little kitchen chair upon which Picasso sat to paint, there was a large easel and there were very many large canvases" (46). This is a scene of enormous productivity; the chaos of the studio reflects the painter's explosive energy. Stein makes the ambitious but doubtful claim that these sittings (and the resulting portrait) somehow changed the painter's career: "In the long struggle with the portrait of Gertrude Stein, Picasso passed from the Harlequin, the charming early italian period to the intensive struggle which was to end in cubism" (54). In effect Stein implies that her sessions with Picasso and the problem of portraying her complex nature produced the Cubist movement. She also explains, more plausibly, how these sessions affected her own work: "Practically every afternoon Gertrude Stein went to Montmartre, posed and then later wandered down the hill usually walking across Paris to the rue de Fleurus. . . . During these long poses and these long walks Gertrude Stein meditated and made sentences. She was then in the middle of her negro story Melanctha Herbert, the second story of Three Lives and the poignant incidents that she wove into the life of Melanctha were often these she noticed in walking down the hill from the rue Ravignan" (49). In this passage, Stein comments revealingly on place, writing, and influence. As Picasso fashions her portrait, she meditates on the portrait of Melanctha. In the crowded studio two kinds of modern art take shape simultaneously; Stein composes sentences as Picasso works from the "brown grey" palette, adding dabs and streaks to the canvas. The long walk from Montmartre to the rue de Fleurus also enters into Stein's composition, suggesting street scenes and tableaux; that is, she transposes the immediate Parisian scene into the American background of *Three Lives*.

In yet another place of art, Stein displays her developing role as an interpreter of modern painting. In 1907, the Salon des Indépendents featured several controversial, even scandalous works. Stein recalls the temporary structure housing the exhibition as "beautifully alight with Paris light" (17) and describes the puzzlement of Alice Toklas (who had then just arrived in France) upon viewing the strange paintings. Out of the crowd—which resembles "the vie de Bohème just as one had seen it in the opera"—appears Gertrude Stein to explain that Toklas has seated herself "admirably" on a bench facing works by Braque and Derain: "They were strange pictures of strangely formed rather wooden blocked figures." Magisterially Stein declares: "Right here in front of you is the whole story" (18). In an art-historical context, the scene coincides with the beginnings of Cubism, but within the *Autobiography* it more importantly epitomizes Stein's avant-garde sensibility. Her presence at the *vernissage,* her friendship with Picasso, and her impressive grasp of major developments in modern art (all figured in this anecdote) identify her as an insider; six years before the Armory Show that would introduce Fauvism and Cubism to the American public, Stein had successfully situated herself "in the heart of an art movement of which the outside world at that time knew nothing" (28).

These three scenes—at Vollard's gallery, at Picasso's studio, and at the Salon des Indépendents—describe Stein's transition from the periphery to the center of a brilliant circle. They signify a transformation involving her successful penetration of the world of male modernism, her discovery of the principles of avant-garde art, and her ostensible acceptance (by Matisse, Picasso, and others) as an intellectual equal. Her reception in the sanctuaries of male modernism culminates, of course, in Stein's account of the famous 1908 banquet for Henri Rousseau, organized by Picasso as a playful tribute to the older painter. Roger Shattuck has characterized the event, staged in Picasso's *bateau lavoir* studio, as a "serious-farcical hoax," a prototypical expression of the comic irreverence of the avant-garde. Stein describes the decorations for the event, which consisted of flags, wreaths, and statues arranged around the makeshift banquet table: "It was very magnificent and very festive" (105). If she did not join in the carousing, her very presence there (as the only woman not invited as a wife or mistress) marks a tacit recognition of her creative status.[31]

Her attendance may be further seen as the definitive instance of a recurrent pattern in the *Autobiography:* Stein's journey from the rue de Fleurus (from home, domesticity, female space) through the terrain of urban Paris to another interior site made significant by modern art and its male artificers. Stein thus portrays a rite de passage through a series of symbolic tests or proofs which unfold in privileged spaces associated with the creation and diffusion of the new art. Lying behind this pattern—which mirrors the spatial poetics of the masculine quest motif—is Stein's anxiety about her female nature and her capacity as a woman to enter into the channels of modernist production. Shari Benstock has provided an illuminating analysis of this crisis of gender in relation to differing male and female versions of modernism. Stein's habit of "seeing only male Modernists as her colleagues and competitors" compelled her to prove herself in masculine terms, to gain the acceptance of Matisse, Picasso, Braque, Apollinaire, and others. Such a project could not be completed, it seemed, on the rue de Fleurus; she could only satisfy this compulsion by an outward movement, by thrusting herself into the exclusive sites of modernist production—the studios of her painter friends and the galleries featuring their work—and there evincing her mastery (in its gendered connotation) of the difficulties of modernism.[32]

Other episodes in the *Autobiography* trace comparably revealing adventures in Paris. In 1913 Stein and Toklas witnessed
the second performance (at the Théâtre des Champs Elysées) of
Stravinsky's controversial *Sacré du printemps*, choreographed for
the Ballets Russes by Nijinsky. The debut had provoked a "terrible
uproar" which was repeated on the night Stein attended: "No
sooner had it commenced when the excitement began. The scene
now so well known with its brilliantly coloured background now
not at all extraordinary, outraged the Paris audience. No sooner
did the music begin and the dancing than they began to hiss"
(137). Far from being outraged or scandalized, however, Stein enjoyed the spectacle; clearly aligned with the avant-garde (she noticed Apollinaire sitting nearby), she judged the dancing to be
"very fine" and claimed critical expertise: "Dancing excites me
tremendously and it is a thing I know a great deal about" (136).
Though her opinion of Stravinsky's score is unclear, the bizarre
mechanical movements of the dancers—which shocked ballet
purists—gratified Stein's craving for the New and enabled her to
contrast her own progressive response with the recoil of "the Paris
audience."

Whatever its historical interest, this anecdote reenacts on a
symbolic level another incident in the *Autobiography*, Stein's
attendance at the Autumn Salon of 1905 in the Petit Palais. There,
at the first exhibition of the Fauves ("savages"), Matisse's *Femme
au Chapeau* had "infuriated the public, [and] they tried to scratch
off the paint" (34). Stein, however, had a completely different
response:

> This picture by Matisse seemed perfectly natural and she
> could not understand why it infuriated everybody. Her brother
> was less attracted but all the same he agreed and they bought
> it. She then went back to look at it and it upset her to see them
> all mocking at it. It bothered her and angered her because she
> did not understand why because to her it was so alright, just as
> later she did not understand why since the writing was all so
> clear and natural they mocked at and were enraged by her
> work. (35)

Stein's defense of *La Femme au Chapeau*, like her later praise of
Le Sacré du Printemps, expresses more than a chic affiliation

with the avant-garde; it manifests an identification with the suffering of modernists whose work was initially misunderstood and despised. But it is important to note the extent to which these paradigmatic episodes superimpose the emotions of the 1930s upon the experiences of the prewar years. Stein depicts herself in 1905 (before she had published anything avant-garde) in a place of controversy, angered by a public unable to recognize genius or accept the New. She thus retroactively anticipates the anguish of her later career; in the early thirties Stein was still widely ridiculed as a writer, a situation that gives added force to the stories of *La Femme au Chapeau* and *Le Sacré du Printemps*.

In yet another glimpse of Stein's "wanderings" in Paris, the problem of recognition and acceptance comes into sharper focus. Toward the end of the *Autobiography* she describes her pleasure at finally seeing her own work on display in Parisian bookstores. In 1930 Alice Toklas had become Stein's publisher under the name Plain Edition and in this capacity arranged for local distribution of the first volume, *Lucy Church Amiably:*

> It was easy to get the book put in the window of all the booksellers in Paris that sold english books. This event gave Gertrude Stein a childish delight amounting almost to ecstasy. She had never seen a book of hers in a bookstore window before, except a french translation of The Ten Portraits, and she spent all her time in her wanderings about Paris looking at the copies of Lucy Church Amiably in the windows and coming back and telling me about it. (243)

There are few other anecdotes in the *Autobiography* so genuinely touching: by revealing her "childish delight," Stein simultaneously discloses the depth of her anxiety about authorship. We can readily imagine her setting out from the rue to Fleurus to check the window at Shakespeare and Company on the rue de l'Odéon or tramping the Right Bank to Galignani's and Brentano's. For years Stein had been frequenting these bookstores and seeing there mainly the works of male rivals. Now the showcasing of her novel provided a kind of certification; Paris itself had begun to take notice of her.

Even as these excursions in the great city served to authenticate her status as a modernist writer, Stein also pursued an alternate strategy, developing an ultimately feminist identity on the rue de Fleurus. The construction of this identity coincides closely with Alice's taking up residence with the Steins in 1909. Explaining the effect of this friendship, Benstock has observed: "The relationship with Toklas allowed Stein to assert her individual contribution to literature because it established a boundary of significant experience, a separate, interior space within the larger world of Paris." On the rue de Fleurus, Stein isolated herself from "the world of patriarchal power outside the walls of her apartment."[33] She established an inner domain which, especially after the departure of Leo in 1914, seemed to mirror the contradictions of her personality, with the heavy Renaissance furniture and bold, contemporary paintings reflecting that tension between the traditional and modern which marked her sensibility. In the *Autobiography*, this "separate, interior space" forms the essential scene of Stein's genius; here she held court, staging the theatrical Saturday evening salons which became legendary, and here too she did her writing in the quiet hours of the night as Alice slept.

The most detailed sketch of Stein's dwelling informs the book's second chapter, in which "Toklas" tries to tell the story of the famous pictures, representing in careful detail the atelier adjoining the pavilion and housing the paintings:

> Against the walls were several pieces of large italian renaissance furniture and in the middle of the room was a big renaissance table, on it a lovely inkstand, and at one end of it note-books neatly arranged, the kind of note-books french children use, with pictures of earthquakes and explorations on the outside of them. And on all the walls right up to the ceiling were pictures. At one end of the room was a big cast iron stove that Hélène came in and filled with a rattle, and in one corner of the room was a large table on which were horseshoe nails and pebbles and little pipe cigarette holders which one looked at curiously but did not touch, but which turned out later to be accumulations from the pockets of Picasso and Gertrude Stein. But to return to the pictures. The pictures were so strange that one quite instinctively looked at anything rather than at them just at first. . . . The chairs in the room were also all italian renaissance, not very comfortable

for short-legged people and one got in the habit of sitting on one's legs. Miss Stein sat near the stove in a lovely high-backed one and she peacefully let her legs hang, which was a matter of habit, and when any one of the many visitors came to ask her a question she lifted herself up out of this chair and usually replied in french, not just now. (9)

Every detail contributes to Stein's calculated self-portrait, as "Toklas" struggles to assimilate an interior setting full of significant objects. The Renaissance furniture suggests the background of history and traditional culture which (according to the argument of *Paris, France*) makes possible the art and literature of the twentieth century; the inkstand and notebooks identify the atelier as a scene of writing, a place of creative productivity. The stove, tended by the faithful Hélène, figures as a sign of warmth and hospitality, while the oddments on the table—already treated as sacred objects—denote the intimate friendship between Gertrude and the great modernist painter. Stein portrays herself "peacefully" enthroned near the stove; guests must come to her, not she to them. She wields authority with the phrase "not just now," thereby declining to exhibit "drawings which were put away." She controls what can and cannot be seen—just as Stein the autobiographer determines what the reader can or cannot see of her life.

The celebrated paintings hang in full view, however, filling the walls "right up to the ceiling." Hemingway later likened the atelier to "one of the best rooms in the finest museum," but "Toklas" finds the canvases so "strange" that at first she averts her eyes, a gesture mirrored textually by the repeated deferral of her account of the paintings. She mentions them in passing three times before promising, "This time I am really going to tell about the pictures" (10). The works are unsettling for two reasons. The fractured images and vivid hues do not resemble the forms and colors of the natural world; they defy the conventions of representation and shock those of genteel sensibility. The paintings indicate, moreover, that, among other similarities, Gertrude and Leo share an appreciation of the female form; the numerous nudes, so obviously pleasing to the sister, hint at her sapphic orientation (fig. 7). The pictures—or Stein's unblushing pride in them—may

Figure 7. The atelier at 27, rue de Fleurus, in 1913.

indeed have been Toklas' first clear intimation of her new friend's sexual affinities. Within the autobiographical narrative, the paintings in the atelier thus announce that Stein's space of activity is precisely the unconventional; she has surrounded herself with strange, defamiliarizing images which offer analogies to her own modernist projects.

Stein's decision in 1914 (about the time of Leo's departure) to connect the studio to the pavilion by means of a hallway marked more than an architectural change; by this renovation, she annexed the scene of the Saturday salons, claiming it as a room of her own, an extension of her personal domain. Descriptions of this setting recur throughout the *Autobiography*, fixing the atelier as a sign of identity, a projection of her personality, and thus a mode of placing the autobiographical subject. In one such passage, Stein constructs an almost Proustian image of herself holding forth in the studio, unaffected by the passage of time or the flux of visitors: "It was an endless variety. And everybody came and no one made any difference. Gertrude Stein sat peacefully in a chair and those who could did the same, the rest stood. There were friends who sat around the stove and talked and there were the endless strangers who came and went" (123–24). As the years roll by, one crowd disappears and another collects; a few older paintings give way to newer ones, mirroring the ebb and flow of Stein's enthusiasm for certain artists. But the effect of these substitutions is slight ("no one made any difference"); in this representation of self, identity reveals itself not in the passing of time but in the stable details of place, as the atelier provides a sign of Stein's defining presence (fig. 8).

To be sure, for many younger writers, artists, and composers, the studio finally became something of a pilgrimage site. Portions of the closing chapter of the *Autobiography* sound like a traffic report; "Toklas" describes a succession of clever young men (Bravig Imbs, Carl Van Vechten, Virgil Thomson, Georges Hugnet, and René Crevel) passing through the atelier in the twenties to pay homage to Miss Stein. In this feminized space, so clearly the expression of her modernist tastes and lesbian tendencies, Stein receives male aspirants eager to signify their association with the new and the modern. In the spatial dynamic of the narrative, this pattern marks a fundamental reversal of Stein's earlier quests into the workplaces of contemporary male painters. Instead of seeking acceptance in the privileged sites of modernist production, she now welcomes admirers drawn to *her* studio by the avant-garde compositions and conversational style which have already become legendary. By the twenties, the very room where Stein busied herself night after night "writing lesbian Modernism" (in Benstock's phrase) had become a cultural landmark, a site of instruction and convocation for young men—like Hemingway—bent on achieving brilliant things in Paris.[34]

If the apartment on the rue de Fleurus provided a locus of feminized identity separate from Paris, however, Stein was also bound emotionally and imaginatively to that larger world. The atelier proclaimed her ties to Parisian art circles even as the Saturday evening salons dramatized her social connections on both sides of the Seine. She was also attached to the physical environment of the city: the *Autobiography* alludes to eating honey cakes at Fouquet's, shopping at the bazaar on the rue de Rennes, walking the dog in the Luxembourg Gardens, and strolling along the Boulevard Raspail with Picasso. After she learned to drive, Stein loved to cross the city in her automobile and "made her way through Paris traffic with the ease and indifference of a

Figure 8. Gertrude Stein presiding over the atelier after her brother, Leo, moved out.

chauffeur"; she even claims to have done some writing "while [the car] stood in the crowded streets" (206). But mostly she loved to wander about the city on foot, absorbing the spectacle of daily life.

The experience of writing the *Autobiography* in Bilignin enabled Stein to recognize her own profound attachment to Paris. Two separate episodes—both recounting absences from the city— underscore the point. When "Toklas" remarks during a trip to Spain that she "must stay in Avila forever," her companion reacts sharply: "Gertrude Stein was very upset, Avila was alright but, she insisted, *she needed Paris*" (115–16, my emphasis). By implication, Stein depends upon the city for some elemental sense of security and well-being. When the two receive word in England that the German army has moved within shelling distance of the French capital, Stein falls into despair: "The germans were getting nearer and nearer Paris and the last day Gertrude Stein could not leave her room, she sat and mourned. She loved Paris, she thought neither of manuscripts nor of pictures, she thought only of Paris and she was desolate" (149). Her personal possessions seem insignificant compared to the potential destruction of the city, and upon her return, she rejoices to find Paris "beautiful and unviolated" (155). Such passages belie the notion that place did not matter to Stein, that she lived entirely within herself and her domestic sphere.[35]

Stein "needed Paris" for a plethora of reasons. The city had enabled her to create an identity as a modernist and to enter into an openly lesbian relationship—both of which would have been difficult if not impossible to achieve in contemporary Oakland, Cambridge, or Baltimore. She liked to explain that "France let you alone"; Paris insured her privacy and offered the comforting routine of everyday, traditional life, which in her opinion made possible the creation of twentieth-century literature. Her development as a modernist writer was also stimulated to an extraordinary extent by the painting that filled the exhibition halls, galleries, and studios of Paris. In *Everybody's Autobiography* Stein notes: "I went on looking at pictures all the time and it is one of the nice things about Paris there are such a lot of pictures to be seen just casually in any street anywhere, it is not like in America where you have to look for them, here you just cannot help seeing them and I do like to see them."[36] The profusion of art in Paris and, specifically, the works of Cézanne, Matisse, Picasso, Braque, and others who had revolutionized painting, challenged Stein to develop a new conception of language, to bring about what she later called a "recreation of the word."[37] Modern painting suggested formal projects—abstract portraits, verbal collages—but more importantly encouraged in Stein a relentlessly experimental attitude, an indifference to rules and a willingness to try new strategies and methods. In Paris she found herself "in the heart of an art movement" and quickly became a self-appointed literary participant.

Paradoxically, Stein also needed the linguistic otherness of Paris to discover an intimate and original relationship to her native language. She wrote in the *Autobiography:*

> There is for me only one language and that is english. One of the things that I have liked all these years is to be surrounded by people who know no english. It has left me more intensely alone with my eyes and my english. I do not know if it would have been possible to have english be so all in all to me otherwise. And they none of them could read a word I wrote, most of them did not even know that I did write. No I like living with so very many people and being all alone with english and myself. (70)

Stein was not, of course, "all alone" with English, even in Paris. At home, she spoke English with Leo and later with Alice; she socialized frequently with English-speaking friends and patronized English-language bookstores like Shakespeare and Company. But everywhere else in the great city, spoken French filled the air and determined the vocabulary and inflection of all conversations. Stein spoke colloquial French with ease though never with native fluency or correctness. Her labored correspondence *en français* to Georges Hugnet, for example, reveals her indifference to the subtleties of French grammar, and she discloses in the *Autobiography* that "she rarely read french newspapers, she never read anything in french" (143–44). Not surprisingly, Stein considered French essentially "a spoken language," while English was for her "a written one."[38] The fact that she wrote in a language incomprehensible to her neighbors gave Stein the heady sense of working in a secret code; the tension or difference between the "special" language of writing and the spoken language of Paris seemed essential to her work. Her continual preoccupation with words and sentences rather than with larger units of discourse may have been a direct result of her long immersion in a foreign environment. Surrounded by French, she experienced a double estrangement: the *langue étrangère* literally imposed a strangeness upon daily experience through its radical renaming of the phenomenal world; this renaming problematized the relationship between words and things and thus disclosed to her the previously imperceptible strangeness—the arbitrary formulations—of her native tongue. Only in the context of linguistic difference, perhaps, could Stein have become so responsive to the oddities of English usage or to the quirks of its grammatical structure.

She also needed Paris because it was foreign enough to seem unreal and extraneous. For Stein, who steadfastly maintained an American outlook, every detail of Parisian life, from architecture to fashion to food, expressed cultural difference; despite her long residence there, the city remained fantastical because it arose from an alien tradition and an inconceivable past. "That is what makes anything foreign," she observed in *Everybody's Autobiography,* "it looks just as you expect it to look but it does not look real." Writers could only function in a foreign country, she believed, because such unreal places could not obtrude upon the consciousness of the writer. The sense of separation or exclusion from the dominant culture ironically freed the writer from the burden of a literary past, creating a space for writing not already assigned and determined. Hence for Stein the unreality of Paris made it (again paradoxically) a real and therefore a habitable place. A famous quip places this contradiction in perspective: about her hometown in California Stein remarked, "What was the use of my having come from Oakland it was not natural to have come from there yes write about it if I like or anything if I like but not there, there is no there there."[39] There is no "there" because the city is real, familiar, and American; in Oakland, writing is an unthinkable activity. By contrast, Paris possesses distinctiveness as a place—a "there"—precisely because it is foreign, romantic, and unreal; it sustains and nurtures literary production. In the *Autobiography* Stein underscores this last point by observing of her 1903 arrival in Paris: "She immediately began to write" (84).

Finally Stein the autobiographer "needed Paris" to represent the transformation which led her to produce what Marianne De-Koven calls "the most substantial and successful body of experimental writing in English."[40] In the chapter "Gertrude Stein Before She Came to Paris," the author gives some account of her upbringing and of the "desperate inner life" of her youth; the chapter title implies, however, that she was a different person before "life in Paris began." In her premodernist phase, Stein was a lonely adolescent, a lackadaisical undergraduate, and then a bored medical student. But in France, at the age of twenty-nine, she began to assume a new identity; Paris was where "everybody had to be to be free." Her experience there was radically different from life in Baltimore; serendipitously, she had arrived during a decade of explosive artistic change, and she soon came in contact with the most vital currents of modernist expression. Just as the *Autobiography* meditates on the painterly problem of "the external and the internal" (or "inner and outer reality"), so her view of Paris involves a double perspective which shifts back and forth between the interior, personal domain of the rue de Fleurus and the exterior urban scene. By representing Parisian studios, galleries, and exhibitions, Stein dramatizes her penetration of the world of male modernism and her putative connection to the Cubist revolution; by characterizing the atelier and what James Mellow has called its "charmed circle," she illustrates the social force of her wit and intelligence and offers a guarded view of her private life as a woman. In effect the *Autobiography* shows Stein drawing the most brilliant elements of that external world—the painters and their paintings—into the intimacy of her salon. If it is hard to imagine how Stein, during the first decades of this century, could have become an avant-garde writer anywhere but in Paris, it is even more difficult to imagine how she could reconstruct her improbable transformation without sketching the crucial site of her self-becoming.

Stein's subsequent autobiographical writings bear further witness to this attachment. In *Everybody's Autobiography*, which largely narrates her return to the United States in 1934–35, she observes redundantly: "I like Paris and I like six months in the country but I like Paris. Everybody says it is not very nice now [in

1936] but I like Paris and I like to live there" (227). As she recounts the tour of America, Stein meditates obsessively on the question of identity. Though she wants to believe that a primal connection to homeland determines one's sense of self ("everybody is as their air and land is"), her American odyssey puts that theory in question. Cambridge, where she had gone to college, has changed so greatly that she feels as if she has never been there: "There was nothing there that had any relation to any place that had been there." She laments, "I lost Cambridge then and there" (187). In Oakland, her experience is even more disturbing; standing before the site of her childhood home (glimpsed in *The Making of Americans*), she visualizes the house and struggles with conflicting ideas of who she is and who she has been:

> Ah Thirteenth Avenue was the same it was shabby and over-grown the houses were certainly some of them those that had been and there were not bigger buildings and they were ne-glected and, lots of grass and bushes growing yes it might have been the Thirteenth Avenue when I had been. The big house and the big garden and the eucalyptus trees and the rose hedge naturally were not any longer existing, what was the use, if I had been I then my little dog would know me but if I had not been I then that place would not be the place that I could see, I did not like the feeling, who has to be themselves inside them, not any one and what is the use of having been if you are to be going on being and if not why is it different and if it is different why not. I did not like anything that was hap-pening. (291)

A disoriented Stein both confirms and denies that identity is rooted in a particular place. If she were not still the same self, she would not be able to imagine the big house ("the place that I could see"); but only by coming back to Oakland as another person can she register the palpable difference. The local scene has changed so drastically that Stein finally doubts her own memory of place: "I did remember that but it did look like that and so I did not remember that and if it did not look like that then I did not remember that." This convoluted passage reaches a skeptical con-clusion about the value of memory as Stein wonders, "What was the use?"

Her discovery of the ephemerality of American places and the impermanence of memory seems to have triggered the obsessive meditations on identity in *The Geographical History of America* (1936) and *Everybody's Autobiography*. The author's traumatic return to Oakland apparently also prompted the contradictory claim at the beginning of her 1936 lecture, "An American and France": "America is my country and Paris is my home town." Unlike Oakland, Paris had remained the selfsame place despite surface changes, and the rue de Fleurus had been her actual home for more than three decades. Stein apparently realized that her identity was grounded in the Parisian scene and literally in her Left Bank address. In *Everybody's Autobiography* she observed:

> It is a funny thing about addresses where you live. When you live there you know it so well that it is like identity a thing that is so much a thing that it could not ever be any other thing and then you live somewhere else and years later, the address that was so much an address that it was like your name and you said it as if it was not an address but something that was living and then years after you do not know what the address was and when you say it it is not a name anymore but something you cannot remember. That is what makes your identity not a thing that exists but something you do or do not remember. (71)

Stein says that an address is "like identity" but implies that the relationship is more than figurative. Although she can no longer remember the self who lived on Thirteenth Avenue in Oakland, her apartment at 27, rue de Fleurus has become "so much an address that it was like [her] name." Indeed, that famous address was for Stein the sustaining matrix of memory and identity.

But in early 1938, Stein and Toklas were obliged to vacate the pavilion they had shared for nearly thirty years; they relocated on the rue Christine in a spacious apartment once owned by the queen of Sweden.[41] Though she professed in letters to be happy with the new flat, Stein's long residence on the rue de Fleurus and her theory of addresses compel us to inquire into the personal consequences, even the psychosymbolic implications of that removal. Friends could scarcely picture Stein and Toklas in a different setting; Sherwood Anderson wrote that "it seems strange to think of you two in any place other than the beautiful rooms in the rue de Fleurus."[42] To complicate the adjustment, barely a year after the move Stein found herself entirely cut off from Paris by the threat of a German invasion. Her literary response to this enforced exile, *Paris, France,* may thus be seen as an imaginative reclaiming of both place and identity. Though she enjoyed the country life at Bilignin, she needed Paris to be fully herself, and the book enabled her to explore those associations with the city within which Stein located her own identity. In this sense, the various paradoxical oppositions attributed to the city (peaceful/ exciting, traditional/modern, fashionable/logical, changing/un-changing) may be read as autobiographical characterizations. Her idiosyncratic sketch of Paris proves at last to be a self-portrait; place has become a repository of identity.

In the only passage which contrasts Stein's old address with the new, she compares the recently built "barracks of ateliers" she and Picasso had once occupied with the "picturesque" and "splen-did" seventeenth-century houses they later inhabited "in the an-cient quarter near the river" (17). With this gesture she seems to turn her back on the rue de Fleurus and what it had come to represent about her mind and sensibility, claiming instead as her dwelling place an old house in an ancient quarter. But such a reading ignores the distinction between inner and outer reality; although Stein and Toklas had moved to a new address, they brought with them the furnishings and paintings from the old apartment. To their obvious relief these belongings came through the war intact: four months after the liberation, Stein and Toklas were "seized by a nostalgia for Paris" and made their way through floods and snowstorms back to the rue Christine. "The house was as we left it," Stein wrote, "dear house, dear Paris." Although the Gestapo had ransacked the apartment for blankets, linen, and dishes, they had not touched the paintings:

> But the treasures, they left them all there, all the youth of me
> and Picasso, everything was there. Picasso and I kissed and
> we almost wept together, all of his things were there, nothing
> was broken, not even a plaster bust that Picasso himself
> sculpted in our youth, no everything was there. Perhaps, said
> Picasso, perhaps if a thing is strong enough it can resist.

Vollard always believed that, said Picasso. As for myself, I wonder why during the time of danger I was never afraid, but now that it is all over, I have a posthumous fear ["une peur posthume"]. Yes, that's it. But even so, even so, even so, it is a miracle, yes, it is a miracle. Paris is still and always there.[43]

Like the plaster bust of Picasso, the city had endured the occupation and survived the war. For Stein the return to Paris seemed like the recovery of a life and a self which had nearly been lost. Her malapropism ("une peur posthume") suggests how much like death her five-year separation from Paris had been. And her closing line—"Paris est toujours là"—expresses her wonderment at finding the city as it was before the war, still and always itself, still and always the Paris she needed in order to be Gertrude Stein.

City of Danger:

Hemingway's Paris

FROM his first glimpse of Paris in 1918, Ernest Hemingway associated the French capital with the exhilaration of danger—with the physical risk of being hit by one of the Big Bertha shells the Germans were firing into the city and with the fleshly temptations which beckoned the young man from Oak Park, Illinois. In his earliest effort to describe the allure of Paris, Hemingway (then an eighteen-year-old enlistee in the Red Cross ambulance corps) provided his parents with a glib, reassuring account of his sightseeing at the Hôtel des Invalides, on the Champs-Elysées, at the Arc de Triomphe, and in the Tuileries. With more imagination than accuracy he reported: "Our hotel is right on the place D'La Concorde where they guillotined Marie Antoinette and Sidney Carton." Memories of *A Tale of Two Cities* obviously colored his perceptions; Hemingway was actually billeted at the Hôtel Florida on the boulevard des Malesherbes, near the Eglise Madeleine, where a German shell had just blasted the Greek façade and decapitated a statue. A man could lose his head in Paris in all sorts of ways, or so Mrs. Hemingway may have worried when her son wrote: "Ted and Jenks and I are having Le Grand Time. Tonight we went to the Follies Bergert."[1] Hemingway of course knew the racy reputation of the Folies Bergère and foresaw the reaction of his mother, Grace, who epito-

mized for him the high moral tone of Protestant, conservative
Oak Park; as if to forestall a lecture he simultaneously promised
to follow "ye straight and narrow." But he was in Gay Paree, on his
way to the Italian front, thousands of miles from that snug en-
clave of puritan values where he had been reared. While he wanted
to retain the approval of his parents, he also wanted them to know
that he was becoming a man and that he had a right to be interested in women. In this conflicted gesture of trying at once to
scandalize and to please, to invite and to resist temptation, we
glimpse a fundamental tension in Hemingway's emerging identity, a tension which would complicate his long relationship to
Paris and his later depictions of its beguiling doubleness.

Aside from a stint in Kansas City as a cub reporter and a
season in Toronto as the hired companion of a millionaire's son,
the only big city which Hemingway knew prior to his wartime
tour of France and Italy was nearby Chicago. Under his mother's
tutelage, he spent many Sunday afternoons at the Chicago Art
Institute, forming early notions of painting and sculpture. But
until he returned from the war, wounded first by a mortar shell
and then by a nurse's inconstancy, Hemingway had never spent
much time on his own in the city. Oak Park was an inviolate
world apart, a self-satisfied village built by its founders "to keep
their families safe from the city's vice, filth, and hazard of fire."
Despite his edifying visits to the Art Institute or the Field Museum of Natural History, Chicago figured in Hemingway's early
moral education mainly as a hotbed of vice and crime. To be sure,
for local boys (as Michael Reynolds notes) "the invisible walls
around Oak Park made the city all the more attractive."[2] If Chicago offered a taste of sin, his hometown epitomized the virtues of
industry, piety, sobriety (Oak Park was dry before Prohibition),
and rectitude; Dr. and Mrs. Hemingway subscribed unquestion-
ingly to the village orthodoxy and so instructed their children.

For the young Hemingway, escape to the nearby city figured
less in his personal formation than those recurrent journeys into
the wilds of northern Michigan, where the family spent long
summer vacations at Windemere cottage on Walloon Lake near
Petoskey. Even after 1921, when marriage to Hadley Richardson
ended his annual pilgrimages, the wooded country around Lake
Charlevoix and Walloon Lake possessed an almost magical impor-

tance: here from childhood onward Hemingway swam, hiked, fished, and boated with bosom friends, and here he underwent various initiations into adult pleasures and responsibilities. The terrain embedded itself deeply in his memory and unconscious; when he became a writer, this was the landscape which he sought to reconstruct, over and over, in the Nick Adams stories. As Reynolds observes, "The woods and water about Windemere, the Pine Barrens to the north, the Fox River, the Black—these places were his touchstones."[3] The symbolic importance of the Michigan woods may be gauged by a curious ratio: whereas Hemingway evoked the charmed topography of "the last good country" in roughly a dozen stories, he never used Oak Park as a major setting (unless the Oklahoma town in "Soldier's Home" offers a disguised glimpse) and, with the exception of a flashback in "Now I Lay Me," rigorously excluded the home scene from his fiction.

After his return from the war, Hemingway found a refuge from parental scrutiny in the Michigan woods. Apart from four months in Canada (where he began writing articles for the *Toronto Star*), he lived in Michigan more or less continuously from May 1919 until October 1920 and there began to contemplate a literary career, drafting a few local color sketches (titled "Cross Roads") and some hackneyed war stories. As implied in the unpublished conclusion to "Big Two-Hearted River," Hemingway associated northern Michigan with the origins of writing and with his early recognition that "it was hard to be a great writer if you loved the world and living in it."[4] In the Michigan woods he began to understand that writing required a strategic retreat from the world of immediate experience; living in a place might even prevent one from writing well about it.

After a turbulent summer at Walloon Lake, where he feuded with his mother, Hemingway moved to Chicago in 1920, got a job with a trade newspaper, met the woman who would become his first wife, and fell in with a lively crowd which included Sherwood Anderson. The older writer took an interest in Hemingway, encouraged him to simplify his prose, and provided a model of literary commitment. Perhaps more significantly, Anderson planted the idea of going abroad; after returning from a summer visit to France, he regaled Hemingway and his new bride with details of the trip, assuring them, "the place to go was Paris, where

pleasant rooms and good wine were cheap, the cathedrals beautifully crafted stone on stone, and the lovers all along the Seine
kissing unashamedly. Paris was the city for lovers, he told them.
In the public gardens and sidewalk cafés, Anderson said he was
able to write in his notebook; story ideas flowed, American stories that he saw clearly in that city of bridges."⁵ Two aspects of
this account probably captured Hemingway's attention: the argument that Paris was a productive place to write, a city filled with
writers who cared about their craft; and the intriguing suggestion
that one could as readily compose "American stories" in a foreign
place.

Whether Anderson pulled out his Paris notebook or simply
talked from memory, Hemingway must have been struck by the
older writer's eye for telling details, his interest in cultural differences, and his perception of France as "a place you don't [ever
fully] understand." Anderson had seen so many things that Hemingway missed in 1918, sights both beautiful and banal. He may
have told his protegé what it was like

> to sit in the far corner of the court late in the afternoon when
> everyone has gone away and look at Sainte-Chapelle, the spire
> of Sainte-Chapelle, seen at night from a bridge, [the Tour St.]
> Jacques in the early morning with women sewing in the little
> park and carts rattling past in the street, an old workman
> washing his shirt in the Seine, his bare back very strong, a
> beautifully dressed aristocrat among women who alighted
> from a motor, the Louvre at night, in the late afternoon, in the
> morning, the rose window on the side of Notre Dame that
> faces the river—this seen at night with the three ghostly
> stone figures stepping down from above, an old woman with a
> pipe in her mouth at the tiller of a barge on the Seine, the
> upper chapel of the S. C. [Sainte-Chapelle] in the early after-
> noon with the light flooding in . . . the singing of a nightingale
> at night in the city. To sit in a cafe drinking and reading, now
> and then to glance up at people passing.⁶

As he encouraged Hemingway to go to Paris, Anderson also taught
him how to see the city—how to discover its distinctiveness in
the features of everyday life. As Hemingway listened, he must
have felt not only an eagerness to return but also a humiliating
awareness that in 1918, while racing to the tourist stops, he had

failed to observe much of anything and missed those ordinary
scenes that made Anderson's Paris so irresistible. Whether Hemingway's mentor touched upon the hazards of expatriation remains unclear; perhaps he passed on the story of his encounter
with an American artist, long ensconced in Paris, who declared
that "a man is of no consequence who hasn't his roots deep in his
native soil." Yet when Anderson asked if the artist planned to
return to the United States, he replied: "Not now. I have blown
about too long. I'm an empty thing."[7] In 1921, neither Anderson
nor Hemingway could have grasped the portentousness of this
comment about exile and deracination.

Barely a month after their conversation with Anderson, the
Hemingways arrived in Paris. As a farewell gesture, the older
author had provided letters of introduction which gave the young
man an entrée into the community of American writers on the
Left Bank. Once in Paris, Hemingway used the letters to establish key connections with influential expatriates: Sylvia Beach,
whose Shakespeare and Company bookstore on the rue de l'Odéon
was the practical and symbolic hub of activity for exiled American
and British authors; Gertrude Stein, the avant-garde writer whose
atelier on the rue de Fleurus was filled with paintings by Matisse
and Picasso; and Ezra Pound, the generous, irascible poet on the
rue Notre-Dame-des-Champs, who had recently arrived from
London and was editing an extraordinary new poem by his friend
T. S. Eliot. Other sites on his mental map of Paris included the
Anglo-American Press Club on the Right Bank, Bill Bird's Three
Mountains Press on the quai d'Anjou, and Michaud's restaurant at
the corner of the rue Jacob and the rue des Saints-Pères, where he
often saw the family of James Joyce. At the geographical and
symbolic center of Hemingway's Paris lay the Luxembourg Gardens (fig. 9), that elegant expanse of lawns, trees, fountains, and
flowers stretching south from the seventeenth-century palace. It
is worth noting that his three eventual domiciles on the Left Bank
circumscribed the Gardens and plotted an increasing proximity to
its quiet spaces. Something of its psychic importance may be
inferred from his recollection in *A Moveable Feast* about finding
the gates shut: "It was sad when the park was closed and locked
and I was sad walking around it instead of through it."[8]

After two weeks in a hotel on the rue Jacob, Hemingway's

Figure 9. The Luxembourg Gardens, the symbolic center of Hemingway's Paris.

home base was a fourth-floor apartment at 74, rue du Cardinal Lemoine, in a working class section of the Latin Quarter not far from the Panthéon. As he explained to his friend Katy Smith, the flat was located "directly above a fine place called the Bal au printemps," a neighborhood dance hall which attracted a motley clientele. In a report to the *Toronto Star* (for whom he served as a foreign correspondent), he described the volatile ambience of the *bal musette* and noted that because its patrons were "young and tough and enjoy[ed] life, without respecting it, they sometimes hit too hard or [shot] too quick."[9] In an odd way, living over the dance hall was like living on the edge of danger, flirting with corruption. Passion was in the air, not only in the tempers which erupted at the dance hall but also in the ubiquitous moral laxity which fascinated Hemingway. Three years earlier, he had been living under Prohibition in a town which forbade both public lewdness and sexual education; now he inhabited a neighborhood filled with drunks, prostitutes, "apaches," and homosexuals in various guises. Hemingway idealized the seedy quartier around the place de la Contrescarpe perhaps because it represented the cultural antithesis of Oak Park: an unpretentious lower-class milieu marked by joie de vivre and an easy acceptance of creaturely appetites, a place where people tolerated personal differences. He enjoyed the looseness and the freedom it conferred, but he also felt occasional disgust—residual moral disdain—when he observed the derelicts hanging about the Café des Amateurs.[10]

A more obvious focus of Hemingway's scorn was the artificial paradise of Montparnasse, where the two great cafés—the Dôme and the Rotonde—drew hordes of artistic types who came to "just sit and drink and talk and . . . be seen by others." The "Quarter" (as it was simply called) had become fashionable during the war years, supplanting Montmartre as the focus of avant-garde activity; Picasso, Duchamp, and Tzara often patronized the cafés at the intersection of the boulevard Montparnasse and the boulevard Raspail. American expatriates—the would-be artists—likewise collected there, much to the disgust of Hemingway, who three months after arriving in Paris filed a scathing report to the *Toronto Star:*

> The scum of Greenwich Village, New York, has been skimmed off and deposited in large ladles on that section of Paris adjacent to the Café Rotonde. . . . It is a strange-acting and strange-looking breed that crowd the tables of the Café Rotonde. They have all striven so hard for a careless individuality of clothing that they have achieved a sort of uniformity of eccentricity. A first look into the smoky, high-ceilinged, table-crammed interior of the Rotonde gives you the same feeling that hits you as you step into the bird-house at the zoo.[11]

Hemingway evinced further contempt for the Rotonde bunch: "They are nearly all loafers expending the energy that an artist puts into his creative work in talking about what they are going to do and condemning the work of all artists who have gained any degree of recognition."[12] Flaunting his own work ethic, he ridiculed those "posing as artists" and—leaving no doubt which group he identified with—added that "the artists of Paris who are turning out creditable work resent and loathe the Rotonde crowd."

To some extent, Hemingway was himself an impostor: he had as yet published almost nothing of a literary sort, and his offhand allusion to "the good old days when Charles Baudelaire led a purple lobster on a leash through the same old Latin Quarter" betrayed as much pretension as ignorance. The poet with the pet

Figure 10. Hemingway in his bohemian phase,
pictured in Sylvia Beach's bookstore,
Shakespeare and Company.

lobster was actually Gérard de Nerval, and the Rotonde was not
located in the *Latin* Quarter, anyway. Above all else, though, his
tirade seems to betray an internal conflict; as a working journalist, he blasted the casual morality and bohemian idleness which
on another level he seems to have found deeply seductive. Reynolds observes that Hemingway possessed a ready "ability to see
in others what he most disliked, feared, or resented in himself"
and adds that less than two years later, "without visible means of
support," Hemingway himself had become an habitué of the
cafés, affecting an artistic appearance (fig. 10), "nursing his drink
and conspicuously writing."[13] Indeed, by degrees his Oak Park

stiffness gave way to complacency, to a curiosity about the sexual negotiations occurring in the cafés, and then to a preoccupation with innuendo, body language, glances, clothing—with what might be called the semiotics of desire. Such insights would eventually work their way into the Paris section of his first novel, *The Sun Also Rises*. Through a subtle and perhaps inevitable process, the young man from the Midwest became engrossed in the sensual, ambiguous night world of Montparnasse.

But initially, at least, that world was not his world. Perhaps still unconsciously cowed by his mother, he initially recoiled from the atmosphere of decadence and corruption which pervaded the Quarter. During 1922–23, the twenty-minute walk from the apartment on the rue du Cardinal Lemoine to Montparnasse marked a crossing of zones: from a working-class neighborhood around the place de la Contrescarpe to the glittering playground of an international leisure class; from a cobbled street, down which might come a herd of goats, to a bustling boulevard, filled with automobiles and taxis; from a milieu of modesty and simplicity to the garish scene of intrigue at the great cafés. Although he made nocturnal sorties with Hadley into this perilous space of pleasure, he preferred the drab rue du Cardinal Lemoine (fig. 11) with its more authentically Gallic ambience. Ever afterward he associated the street and surrounding neighborhood with his greatest happiness in Paris.

If Hemingway liked living in a blue-collar milieu, he soon discovered, however, that he could not work in the two-room apartment. There was no way to escape domestic distractions, no place reserved exclusively for writing. His solution was to set up a studio in an unheated, top-floor room just around the corner at 39, rue Descartes. The old hotel had propitious literary associations—Verlaine had died there—and the chamber offered a fine view of the rooftops of Paris. According to the somewhat mythical account in *A Moveable Feast*, Hemingway here learned to craft "true sentences" by eliminating "scrollwork or ornament" from his style; if so, he mastered his trade quickly, for in all likelihood (given his journalistic assignments in 1922) he leased the room only for a few months. One of his earliest exercises in stylistic economy was a sequence of six "true sentences," prose miniatures grouped under the title "Paris 1922." This work, only recently

Figure 11. The rue du Cardinal Lemoine, as seen
from the building where Ernest and Hadley
Hemingway lived from 1922 to 1923.

published, marks an effort to achieve a more experimental form,
perhaps reflecting the immediate influence of Stein; it displays
his effort to distill early perceptions of Paris into a composite
impression of place.

In his role as correspondent, Hemingway had since his arrival
been combing the city for stories, scenes, or incidents which
would make good copy.[14] He had begun to develop that eye for
revealing, essential detail which would inform his best fiction,
and he used this attentiveness to striking effect in the prose
miniatures:

PARIS 1922
I have seen the favorite crash into the Bulfinch at Auteuil
and come down in a heap kicking, while the rest of the field

swooped over the jump, the white wings jointed up their stretcher, and the crowd raced across the pelouse to see the horses come into the stretch.

I have seen Peggy Joyce at 2 a.m. in a *dancing* in the Rue Caumartin quarreling with the shellac-ed haired young Chilean who had long pointed finger nails, danced like Rudolph Valentino and shot himself at 3:30 that same morning.

I have watched two Senegalese soldiers in the dim light of the snake house in the Jardin des Plantes teasing the king cobra who swayed and tightened in tense erect rage as one of the tall brown men crouched and feinted at him with his red fez.

I have seen the one legged street walker who works the Boulevard Madeleine between the Rue Cambon and Bernheim Jeunes' limping along the pavement through the crowd on a rainy night with a beefy red faced episcopal clergyman holding an umbrella over her.

I have watched the police charge the crowd with swords as they milled back into Paris through the Porte Maillot on the first day of May and seen the frightened proud look on the white, beaten up face of a sixteen year old kid who looked like a prep school quarterback and had just shot two policemen.

I have stood on the crowded platform of a seven o'clock Batignolles bus as it lurched along the wet lamp lit street and the men who were going home to supper never looked up from their newspapers as we passed Notre Dame grey and dripping in the rain.[15]

Practicing the method of condensation which would generate the vignettes of *in our time* (1923), Hemingway repeated the phrases "I have seen" or "I have watched" to imply an observer who has studied the city at all hours and knows its obscure quartiers. (Actually, one or two of his sentences were suggested by newspaper articles rather than first-hand observation.) In each miniature he specifies a particular place, noting the time, date, weather conditions, or social circumstances. But here Hemingway moves beyond journalism, working through implication rather than explication, creating effects by omission rather than elaboration. He carefully resists the rhetorical posturing evident in some of his newspaper dispatches. Each glimpse instead contains an arresting incongruity or irony: the crowd at Auteuil ignores the fall of the favorite horse; the exotic Chilean commits suicide after dancing with a woman; the African soldiers mock death by teasing a cobra; the Episcopalian priest squires a one-legged prostitute on the street which leads to the church of the Magdalen; the lad with the look of a prep-school quarterback kills two policemen; the men on the bus prefer their daily newspapers to the timeless façade of Notre Dame.[16] This collage of images projects a frenzied, cosmopolitan city of violent contrasts and illustrates the degree to which Hemingway had internalized the spectacle of Paris. His prose poems mark a transition from the amateurish narratives he had been writing in Chicago to the disciplined, compressed prose he was learning to write on the rue Descartes.[17]

Another early effort to represent the Parisian setting took the form of a short story probably composed during the summer of 1922. Having spent several afternoons at the racetracks on the outskirts of Paris, Hemingway tried to turn the insights he had obtained at Enghien, Chantilly, Auteuil, and elsewhere into a narrative frankly imitative of his old mentor, Sherwood Anderson. The resulting work, "My Old Man," was (with "Up in Michigan") the only work from the first year abroad to escape Hadley's loss of manuscripts and typescripts en route to Switzerland to join her husband for the holiday season.[18] In a colloquial voice typical of Anderson's adolescent racetrack hands, Hemingway describes the city as massive and confusing in contrast to Milan, which Joe and his father, a jockey, have just left:

> We got into Paris early in the morning in a long, dirty station the old man told me was the Gare de Lyon. Paris was an awful big town after Milan. Seems like in Milan everybody is going somewhere and all the trams run somewhere and there ain't any sort of a mix-up, but Paris is all balled up and they never do straighten it out. I got to like it, though, part of it, anyway, and say, it's got the best race courses in the world.

Seems as though that were the thing that keeps it all going and about the only thing you can figure on is that every day the buses will be going out to whatever track they're running at, going right out through everything to the track.[19]

Arriving at the very station where, coincidentally, Hemingway's other manuscripts disappeared, Joe is plunged into geographical confusion. Only the buses provide a sense of security and order. The boy admits that he "never got to know Paris well" because he stayed at Maisons-Laffitte on the edge of the city. After his father wins money betting on fixed races at Tremblay, however, the two "sit out in front of the Café de la Paix" on the place de l'Opéra (fig. 12), flaunting their sudden prosperity at a fashionable establishment. "It's funny sitting there," Joe remarks, "there's streams of people going by and all sorts of guys come up and want to sell you things." The boy's bafflement at sidewalk hustlers and prostitutes anticipates his confusion later at the Auteuil track where his father suffers a fatal fall in a steeplechase event. In a conclusion reminiscent of Anderson's "I Want to Know Why," Joe hears two bettors discussing his father's corruption. The obvious imitation of Anderson's methods and materials raises the possibility that "My Old Man" amounts to an effort to match, outdo, or even parody the work of Hemingway's literary mentor.[20]

Beginning with the peace conference in Genoa which kept him away from Paris most of April, Hemingway's journalistic travels in 1922 made the room on the rue Descartes increasingly superfluous. Moreover, his need for a studio diminished as he took up the expatriate trick of composing in a "private café," an obscure establishment where a writer could go "to work, or to read, or to receive [his] mail." In the Latin Quarter, far from the fashionable cafés of Montparnasse, Hemingway found a spot where, for the price of a café crème, he could sit undisturbed for hours with his pencil and composition book.[21] In the sketch which opens *A Moveable Feast*, he commemorates the "good café on the Place St. Michel" as a scene of writing, the precise location where (according to his recollection) he composed a story "about up in Michigan." The anecdote may or may not be accurate; the story in question may or may not have been "The Three-Day Blow" (as implied by references to cold weather and to boys drink-

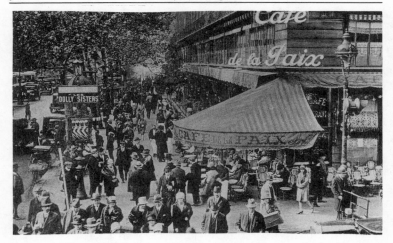

Figure 12. The Café de la Paix, where Joe and his father watch the passing
crowd in Hemingway's story "My Old Man."

ing). What seems fully plausible, though, is Hemingway's claim
that the "wild, cold, blowing day" in France recalled an autumn
storm in Michigan. Anderson had been right: you could write
about America abroad because the places that mattered, the ones
that framed and defined real experiences, were always fixed in
memory.

During his first years in Paris, Hemingway thought often
about the country around Lake Charlevoix and Walloon Lake and
the pine woods even further north around the Fox River; he corresponded with old fishing pals like Howell Jenkins and Bill Smith,
inviting them to join him in Europe; he tacked a map of northern
Michigan to the wall of his apartment; and he wrote story after
story—most apparently composed in Parisian cafés—evoking an
American landscape already lost to him as a playground or refuge.
The bitter conflict at the lake in 1920 and his marriage the following year had in fact sealed him off from those places of the heart.
"We can't ever go back to old things," he sententiously told Bill
Horne in 1923, "We have them as we remember them and they are
fine and wonderful and we have to go on and have other things
because the old things are nowhere except in our minds now."[22]
At the age of twenty-four, he realized that the lake and the life he
had known there were lost forever; the country that he had loved
existed for him now only in memory and imagination.

From 1922 to 1924, Hemingway wrote recurrently, even obsessively, about the northern places that he remembered, and, as
he explained to his father, "the country is always true—what
happens in the stories is fiction."[23] Through an irony of exile,
daily life in the gray, foreign city seemed to give sharpness and
immediacy to remembered images of lakes, streams, and woods.
Surrounded by a bustling, cosmopolitan scene utterly unlike the
American Midwest, Hemingway—in spite of his apparent eagerness to escape home and homeland—sought through the Nick
Adams stories to recover aspects of his own identity bound up
with the Michigan country. If the events in such stories as "Indian
Camp" and "The End of Something" were fictional, the places
that he represented were "true" in their consolidation of his experiences and perceptions. Elemental contrasts between day and
night, sun and rain, lake and shore, woods and sky expressed the
seeming clarity of nature in relation to the confusion of the human sphere where people deceived each other and relationships
went awry. If the landscape of these stories bears a legible inscription, it is that of Hemingway's nostalgia for simplicity, which
must be read against the emerging complications of his life in
Paris.

In his finest Michigan story, "Big Two-Hearted River," composed (according to the legend he generated) at the Closerie des
Lilas, Hemingway hints obliquely at these complications and
manifests his longing for the north country by projecting the
return to nature of a damaged Nick Adams. In the concluding
section deleted from the published version, we discover that his
protagonist has come back not just from the war (a retrospective
hint from Hemingway which has guided much interpretation) but
also from the expatriate literary milieu of the Left Bank. Allusions
to Pound, Joyce, Stein, Cummings, and Robert McAlmon connect
Nick to the scene of Hemingway's apprenticeship; moreover, in a
move which provisionally turns *In Our Time* (1925) into metafiction, Nick identifies himself as the author of "Indian Camp," "My
Old Man," and—by extension—the rest of the collection.[24] He
acknowledges an ambition to become "a great writer" and especially wants to "write about country" in the way that Cézanne has
painted it. He has also become an aficionado of the Spanish bullfights and misses his Michigan fishing buddies (who happen to

bear the names of Hemingway's friends): "Bill Smith, Odgar, the Ghee, all the old gang." As if to distance himself from his own fictional persona, however, Nick the writer tells us (in a phrase often simply attributed to Hemingway) that "Nick in the stories was never himself." He further observes that "the only writing that was any good was what you made up, what you imagined."[25] Through such equivocal declarations, Hemingway pursues a paradoxical strategy, implicitly disclaiming Nick as an alter ego while endowing him with a past life and a literary corpus identical to his own. Apparently, only through this contradictory scheme of exposure and concealment could Hemingway permit himself to stage the crisis of exile to which the discarded opening indirectly refers.

For as we see in the fragment published as "On Writing," the problem which oppresses Nick as he fishes the Big Two-Hearted River is not postcombat trauma so much as an agonizing consciousness that in getting married, becoming a writer, and moving to Paris, he has forfeited the halcyon world of northern Michigan. He misses "fishing in the bay, reading in the hammock on hot days, swimming off the dock, playing baseball at Charlevoix and Petoskey." Thinking about Bill Smith, Odgar, and the Ghee, he concludes that he "lost them all" because he "admitted by marrying that something was more important than fishing."[26] Yet was it? His own reflections call his decision—and Hemingway's—into question, and the most explicit reference to Nick's marital situation speaks of "discontent and friction." His expatriation has also contributed to a sense of loss; no one in Paris understands his passion for angling: "Ezra thought fishing was a joke. So did most everybody." By implication, he has not found among his Left Bank acquaintances the camaraderie that he felt with the old gang. Nick thus finds himself in a foreign city, caught in a troubled marriage, and cut off from a place and a way of life that he loved "more than anything." His main compensation for the lost happiness of fishing with friends is the solitary pleasure of writing, which Nick now believes to be "more fun than anything."

But he has paid dearly to become a writer, and the return journey of "Big Two-Hearted River" dramatizes the extent of his loss: Nick fishes alone not because he needs to transact private, existential business but because he no longer has pals to share the trip with him.[27] In this light, the trip becomes an exercise in nostalgic self-pity, which Hemingway in cutting the closing section recognized as a reductive sentimentalizing of his story. But "On Writing" nevertheless permits us to gauge, as no other Nick Adams material does, the intensity of Hemingway's psychic attachment to the Michigan country and the nature of his alienation from the Parisian milieu. Through a series of imaginative displacements, Hemingway (working in Paris) portrays Nick Adams in Michigan, thinking back to his life in Paris and—from that exilic perspective—remembering the Michigan that he has already lost. The suppressed fragment thus represents Nick as a jaded expatriate, already estranged from the familiar terrain to which he has returned.

Having exchanged the "last good country" for a "good café on the Place St. Michel," Hemingway used the perspective of exile to reconstruct various American settings linked to Nick Adams. Years later, recalling the cold autumn day in Paris which put him in mind of Michigan, he proposed a modest theory of the relation between place and writing: "I had already seen the end of fall come through boyhood, youth and young manhood, and in one place you could write about better than in another. That was called transplanting yourself, I thought, and it could be as necessary with people as with other sorts of growing things."[28] Near the end of his life, as he composed his Paris memoir in Cuba and Idaho, Hemingway perhaps saw his entire career as a series of transplantings. Moving from one place to another had provided vantage points which enabled him to discern those differences of flora and fauna, terrain, climate, and culture which distinguished one place from another and—in some inscrutable yet undeniable way—set one experience apart from another. Although he could not have imagined in the early twenties the travels and relocations which lay ahead, Hemingway already sensed that he could "write about country" better in Paris than elsewhere, perhaps because the intricacies and ambiguities of life in the cosmopolitan city sharpened his perspective on the simpler landscape of American innocence.

By the same principle of transplanting or relocation, Hemingway began his first extended portrayal of Paris while traveling in

Spain during the summer of 1925. In Valencia, Madrid, San Sebastian, and in the French border town of Hendaye, he worked furiously during July and August on a narrative based so closely upon
his recent experience at the fiesta in Pamplona that at first he did
not bother to change the names of the actual participants—Lady
Duff Twysden, Pat Guthrie, Donald Ogden Smith, Bill Smith,
Harold Loeb, a young bullfighter named Cayetano Ordoñez, and
the Hemingways, Ernest and Hadley. The story explored the male
rivalry excited by Duff, who while engaged to the alcoholic Guthrie had indulged in a brief affair with Loeb and then flirted provocatively with Hemingway. Soon after he started a notebook draft,
the author began changing the names and recasting the story to
depict the seduction of a handsome young matador first called
"Niño de la Palma" and then Pedro Romero. As the novel developed, the author paid increasing attention to the code of bullfighting and to the Spanish culture it typifies. Almost from the outset,
however, he recognized the need to write an opening section, set
in Paris, which would illuminate the emotional intrigue in Pamplona and establish a symbolic contrast with the traditional folk-
ways of provincial Spain. So while he was away from Paris, Hemingway began to imagine the noisy cafés of Montparnasse. It was a
scene that he had come to know intimately: since early 1924 he
and Hadley had been living in an apartment near the boulevard
Montparnasse at 113, rue Notre-Dame-des-Champs (fig. 13). As
he composed the novel, he perceived an important tension between the brazen intrigues of the Quarter and the natural simplicity of the Spanish countryside.

He acknowledged as much in the notebook draft of the novel's
opening chapters, which initially traced the geography of Montparnasse:

> To understand this situation in Pamplona you have to
> understand Paris. Not the Paris of Victor Hugo, or Murger, or
> of 1914–1919 or the Paris of France but the section of Paris
> bounded at one end by the Closerie des Lilas, which is quite
> outside the limits, so we had better make the boundary at
> that end Lavigne's restaurant—the Nègre de Toulouse, and at
> the other end by the Café Sélect. That is its east and west
> boundaries and the north boundary is the Cigogne and the

Figure 13. No prohibition in Paris: Hemingway takes a drink at 113, rue Notre-Dame-des-Champs.

south the Dingo and the Stix [Stryx] and the Hotel Istria. Inside the limits is the Café du Dôme which hardly figures and the Café Rotonde which might as well be in China. . . . This Paris is a very sad and dull place which has few permanent residents.[29]

From Spain, Hemingway sketched an idiosyncratic view of the Quarter, situating what had become his favorite workplace, the Closerie des Lilas, beyond its boundaries; discounting the importance of two major cafés, the Dôme and the Rotonde; and fixing as major points of reference the address of the photographer Man Ray, the Hotel Istria, and the bar where Hemingway had recently met Scott Fitzgerald, the Dingo. Although the author revised and then dropped this passage—along with an analysis of the Quarter and introductory portraits of Brett Ashley and Mike Campbell— the published novel nevertheless inscribes a study of Montparnasse within a view of Paris which renders local detail with scrupulous accuracy. To suggest the torment of his characters, Hemingway created a nocturnal city, a nightmarish whirl of bars, cafés, taxis, restaurants, and dance halls. At bottom, his Paris is a town without pity suffused by sexual ambivalence, inversion, masochism, and despair; a site of frenetic and seemingly random movement. When Hemingway claimed that "to understand this situation in Pamplona you have to understand Paris," he announced the relevance of comparative geography to the novel. Through his representation of the night world of Montparnasse, the author provided not only a key to the dilemma in Pamplona but also an index of the moral confusion of his generation and a hint of his personal uncertainties about Paris.

Near the beginning of the published novel, the ex-boxer (now expatriate) novelist Robert Cohn agonizes about "the feeling that all your life is going by and you're not taking advantage of it." When he proposes a trip to South America, narrator Jake Barnes ridicules his escapism and observes: "This is a good town. Why don't you start living your life in Paris?" Cohn replies, "I'm sick of Paris, and I'm sick of the Quarter."[30] While introducing the problem of how to live one's life "all the way up," this exchange also raises the related question of how different characters respond to Paris. We perceive a distinction between those worldly, self-reliant characters who enjoy the city and the dull, insecure figures who hate it. For Jake, it is "a good town," an opinion later shared by the bon vivant Count Mippipopolous, who says: "Paris is a fine town all right" (28). Brett Ashley refers mockingly to "this pestilential city" but concedes that "one's an ass to leave Paris" (75). The drunken Bill Gorton studies the darkened silhouette of Notre Dame and remarks, "It's pretty grand . . . . God, I love to get back" (77). Cohn, on the other hand, is "sick of Paris," and Jake speculates that he acquired his "incapacity to enjoy Paris" from H. L. Mencken, who reportedly "hates" the city (42). Georgette, the Belgian prostitute whom Jake takes to dinner at Lavigne's restaurant, also confides: "No, I don't like Paris. It's expensive and dirty" (19). As these comments imply, reactions to Paris provide a measure of one's ability to live fully and intelligently, getting one's money's worth.

In another sense, the novel dramatizes an array of positions rather than a simple dichotomy. David Zehr has delineated three main "expatriate attitudes" toward Paris: a superficial "tourist sensibility," a decadent surrender to the city's mystique, and a studied detachment from "the Parisian milieu." In this view Jake emerges as a balanced figure who both participates in the expatriate world and retains a clear-eyed, unsentimental affection for the city, resisting the mythifying of other exiles. "Through Jake's eyes," Zehr concludes, "we become conscious of a Paris separate from that of the Americanized bars of Montparnasse, a world neither limited nor adulterated by an expatriate consciousness."[31] There is much to be said for this reading: clearly, Jake's response to the city is more complicated and discerning than that of his friends. But as an instance of the "lyrical description" which conveys the narrator's "separate" vision of Paris, Zehr cites the reference to empty barges on the Seine at the beginning of chapter 6—yet misses the mordant irony of Jake's observation ("It was always pleasant crossing bridges in Paris") after he has been stood up by Brett at the Hôtel Crillon. Here, as elsewhere in Hemingway's writing, the narrator's seemingly neutral comment about landscape refers implicitly to inner turmoil: Jake feels as empty as the barges. If his relation to Paris thus holds the key to book one, his problem goes beyond a mechanical balancing of public and private attitudes. His troubled relation to the city derives from his simultaneous association with and antagonism for the expatriate group, as well as his perverse identification with the Montparnasse quarter, which he detests. Ultimately Jake's complex attachment to Paris and "the Quarter" reveals a contradiction within the narrator himself: his perceptions of locale disclose an agonizing personal conflict.

Although the narrator advises Cohn to "stay away from the Quarter" to cure his unhappiness, Jake ironically spends much of his time in that district. Hemingway establishes this point when a fellow newspaper correspondent poses a question:

> "What do you do nights, Jake?" asked Krum. "I never see you around."
>
> "Oh, I'm over in the Quarter."
>
> "I'm coming over some night. The Dingo. That's the great place isn't it?
>
> "Yes. That, or this new dive, The Select." (36)

Jake identifies himself with two favorite "dives," and indeed the Café Select figures significantly in his social habits. In what proves to be the defining pattern of the novel's first nine chapters,

the narrator sets out on nightly excursions only to be drawn back
to Montparnasse and the tables of the Select. One might contend
that this circular return merely confirms that Jake lives near the
Quarter and passes this way to get home; in chapter 4, after all,
the author maps the short walk from the Select, down the boulevard Montparnasse past Lavigne's Nègre de Toulouse, the Closerie des Lilas, and the statue of Marshal Ney to the narrator's flat
"just across the street, a little way down the boulevard St. Michel"
(29). This crossing, however, marks a subtle but important difference: living on the east side of the boulevard St. Michel, Jake
technically inhabits the Latin Quarter, the fifth arrondissement
(rather than the sixth and fourteenth which divide Montparnasse). Hemingway's precision here serves two purposes: it establishes a putative correspondence between the geography of Paris
and fictive world of the novel, and it implies Jake's marginal and
arbitrary relation to Montparnasse. He lives on the periphery of
the Quarter and on the fringes of its excitement. As in his relationship to Brett Ashley, Jake's situation is liminal; he is caught
between desire and disdain, perversely attracted by that which
sickens him.

In the two chapters cut in galley proofs at F. Scott Fitzgerald's
urging in 1926, Jake's underlying feelings about Paris and Montparnasse receive more explicit treatment. Introducing himself,
the narrator explains: "I am a newspaper man living in Paris. I
used to think Paris was the most wonderful place in the world. I
have lived in it now for six years, . . . and I still see its good points.
Anyway, it is the only city I want to live in." But while Jake prefers
to live in Paris, he is less enthusiastic about Montparnasse, noting
that he "never hung about the quarter much in Paris until Brett
and Mike showed up." With considerable acerbity he reports:

> The Quarter is sort of more a state of mind than a geo-
> graphical area. Perfectly good Quarterites live outside the
> actual boundaries of Montparnasse. They can live anywhere,
> I suppose, as long as they come to the Quarter to think. Or
> whatever you call it. To have the Quarter state of mind is
> probably the best way of putting it. This state of mind is
> principally contempt. Those who work have the greatest con-
> tempt for those who don't. The loafers are leading their own

lives and it is bad form to mention work. Young painters have contempt for old painters, and that works both ways too. There are contemptuous critics and contemptuous writers. Everybody seems to dislike everybody else.[32]

When we recall that the narrator lives near the Quarter and (now that Brett and Mike have arrived) spends considerable time there, this passage raises an interesting question: does Jake mean by this comment to distance himself from "the Quarter state of mind" or has he himself become a "perfectly good Quarterite" residing just beyond "the actual boundaries of Montparnasse"? His own contempt—reminiscent of Hemingway's 1922 *Toronto Star* sketch of the Rotonde—ironically seems to mark him as a "Quarterite" *malgré lui*. In Jake's estimate, everyone in Montparnasse is simultaneously scorned and scornful. As if to explain why anyone would inhabit such a neighborhood (as Hemingway did from 1924 through 1926), Jake—in a notebook draft of the preceding passage—explains: "Everybody in the quarter loathes almost everybody else and the quarter itself. They live on because there are so many people of their own kind and because no matter how low in their minds they may feel there is someone who can be sneered at."[33]

In the excised galley material, Jake tries to explain why Quarterites are unhappy, sneering first at local drunks who "eventually become depressed" and then at homosexuals, "the frail young men who go about together." The notebook draft reveals a more vicious allusion to "the Fairies" who "take flight like the birds and go off to Brussels or London or the Basque Coast" only to "return again even more like the birds." Despite his antipathy for flamboyant homosexuals, Hemingway confined himself in *The Sun Also Rises* to two sardonic but understated passages (set outside the Quarter), one depicting the crowd of young men with "newly washed, wavy hair" accompanying Brett to the *bal musette* and the other satirizing the young novelist with the English accent, Robert Prentiss, a fictionalized Glenway Wescott. Jake's tirade in the notebook draft goes well beyond satire, however, expressing virulent aversion; when the homosexuals leave, he says, Montparnasse becomes "quite pleasant," but one sometimes misses this pleasure by failing to note their departure:

"Once I remember they were all gone to Brussels for a week and were back before I had noticed that they were gone away and a week's worth of enjoyment of their absence had been lost." By omitting this jeering, Hemingway partially masked his prejudices; but traces of his angry fascination with homosexuality nevertheless remain.[34]

As these cancelled passages indicate, Jake (as originally conceived) despises Montparnasse—or at least certain aspects of its social scene. "There is nothing romantic about the Quarter and very little that is beautiful," he remarks in the notebook draft. A similar scorn pervades the early poem "Montparnasse," which Hemingway published in *Three Stories and Ten Poems:*

> There are never any suicides in the quarter among people
>   one knows
> No successful suicides.
> A Chinese boy kills himself and is dead.
> (they continue to place his mail in the letter rack at the
>   Dome)
> A Norwegian boy kills himself and is dead.
> (no one knows where the other Norwegian boy is gone)
> They find a model dead
> alone in bed and very dead.
> (it made almost unbearable trouble for the concierge)
> Sweet oil, the white of eggs, mustard and water soapsuds
>   and stomach pumps rescue the people one knows.
> Every afternoon the people one knows can be found at the
>   café.[35]

However unpoetically, this verse registers wry contempt for the unsuccessful suicides who hang around the café venting their unhappiness and conversing about stomach pumps. Hemingway subtly links despair and sexual practice: the Norwegian boy kills himself ostensibly after a feud with his homosexual companion; the model takes her life perhaps because she too is "alone in bed" without a lover. Life in the Quarter goes on—letters for the dead Chinese boy still arrive at the Dôme—but suicide remains a constant theme. Such occurrences seem on one level not to touch the speaker, whose rhetoric is flat and unemotional; yet on another level, they compel reflection on Montparnasse and "the Quarter state of mind."

The congruence between the author's cynical view of the Quarter and that of his fictional protagonist does not, of course, make the two figures identical. But it does call attention to Jake's contradictory attachment to Montparnasse, raising the question of Hemingway's strategy in thus positioning his tormented narrator. Though Jake finds Paris itself "a good town" and knows other quarters well, especially the Right Bank from the place de la Concorde to the Opéra, he returns continually to that section of Paris which he despises, as if to reenact his contempt for the expatriate crowd or, we begin to suspect, to exercise his latent self-contempt.

This circular movement, which may be seen as a geographical figure for obsession, reveals itself early in the novel. Following a preliminary sketch of Robert Cohn, chapter 1 closes with a scene in Montparnasse: Jake, Cohn, and Frances Cline dine at the Restaurant Lavenue (misspelled l'Avenue's), adjacent to the Gare Montparnasse, and afterward move to the Café-Restaurant de Versailles on the rue de Rennes for coffee and *fines à l'eau*. The scene ends with Jake's memorably sardonic remark about Cohn and his jealous "lady": "Evidently she led him quite a life" (7). But this ridicule reflects more clearly upon Jake's own insecurities than upon Cohn's, for as we shortly learn, a war wound has left the narrator sexually helpless, lustful but incapable of intercourse. By situating this episode in Montparnasse, Hemingway establishes a subtle but important connection between geography and gender relations. Impotent but voyeuristic (at one point admitting, "I have a rotten habit of picturing the bedroom scenes of my friends"), Jake frequents a quarter known for unconventional eroticism, for its acceptance of homosexuality, bisexuality, promiscuity, perversion, and prostitution. In Montparnasse, Jake surrounds himself with sexual activity and romantic intrigue; he comes back to this erogenous zone as if to participate vicariously in the circulation of desire. But the very movement by which he reenters this sphere of sensuality inevitably reconfirms his emasculation.

After the scene in the Café de Versailles, the action switches to the Right Bank, which Hemingway here associates with work, male camaraderie, and (implicitly) an escape from sexuality. At the end of the conversation set in the bar downstairs from Jake's office—where Jake ironically advises Cohn to "stay away from the Quarter"—the narrator then goes to the Café-Glacier Napolitain on the boulevard des Italiens, where he sits on the terrace watching the passing *poules*. Here, in an act of palpable self-torment, he engages Georgette, a "good-looking girl," for the sake of some company: "I had picked her up because of a vague senti-mental idea that it would be nice to eat with someone" (16). But instead of remaining on the Right Bank, Jake hires a horse-drawn cab and sets off with Georgette for the Left Bank, down the avenue de l'Opéra, into the rue des Pyramides, and through the Tuileries. Here, in front of the Louvre (fig. 14), the prostitute attempts to arouse Jake by a sexual touch that he rebuffs by explaining that he is "sick." The geographical movement suggests that Jake is "sick" in at least a double sense—genitally maimed yet driven to reenact the rituals of sexual encounter. The couple consequently crosses the Seine and heads for the Quarter, dining at Lavigne's Nègre de Toulouse on the boulevard Montparnasse. In this restaurant, re-called fondly by Hemingway in *A Moveable Feast*, Jake and his companion encounter the fatuous expatriate writer Henry Brad-docks (a thinly veiled Ford Madox Ford), leading the narrator to remark sotto voce that there are "too many" writers and artists on the Left Bank. Though the scene at Lavigne's seems formless rather than erotic, Braddocks gives direction to the evening by proposing that everyone meet later at a dance hall near the Pan-théon.

This expedition out of the Quarter and into the neighborhood that Hemingway had inhabited during 1922–23 leads to Jake's unexpected encounter with Brett. But what makes the staging so suggestive is a subtlety of locale: although the place to which Braddocks directs Jake reminds readers familiar with the Ford sketch in *A Moveable Feast* of the *bal* at 74, rue du Cardinal Lemoine, Hemingway actually alludes to a different site. He tells us, "the dancing-club was a *bal musette* in the rue de la Montagne Sainte-Geneviève. Five nights a week the working people of the Pantheon quarter danced there. One night a week it was the dancing club" (19). The address carries important implications, for the real Bal de la Montagne Sainte-Genevieve was no ordinary working-class dance hall. Describing the site as he photographed it in 1931, Brassaï wrote:

> A century before, the Bal de la Montagne Sainte-Geneviève had been a true popular dance hall, frequented by

250. PARIS (1ᵉʳ arrt.) — La Place du Carrousel et le Louvre   C. M.

Figure 14. The Arc du Carrousel and the Louvre. In *The Sun Also Rises*, Jake and Georgette probably enter the courtyard through the "dark gate" at the right edge of the photograph.

toughs and their girls from the nearby Rue Mouffetard. Gradually, however, the female element disappeared, the "toughs"
were transformed into "softs" and danced together—which
led to the establishment's being closed from time to time by
the cops. . . . In an attempt to mitigate the rather special
atmosphere of her dance hall, the owner—an ex-movie star-
lette—had had the clever notion of attracting a female clientele . . . but not just any kind of woman. Although butch
women repel male homosexuals and are not attracted to men,
homosexual men and feminine lesbians have always felt a
mutual sympathy, a kindness toward each other. In this
dance hall, Sodom and Gomorrah—or Lesbos, rather—got
along beautifully together.[36]

Why Hemingway chose to evoke the curious scene at the Bal de la
Montagne Sainte-Geneviève is not immediately clear, for he does
not depict same-sex dancing. Contemporary readers familiar with
Paris would have understood his allusion, however, as a prefiguration of the sexual ambivalence played out when Brett enters the
dance hall with group of male homosexuals.

For the narrator, the appearance of the woman with whom he
has been in love "off and on for a hell of a long time" (123) arouses
contradictory passions, for although Brett looks ravishing, Jake
cannot abide her companions: "I was very angry. Somehow they
always made me angry. I know they are supposed to be amusing,
and you should be tolerant, but I wanted to swing on one, any one,
anything to shatter that superior, simpering composure" (20).
Rather than jealousy toward male rivals, he feels outrage at their
epicene indifference to Brett's sexual allure. After his brief conversation with Robert Prentiss, Jake confides his disgust to Mrs.
Braddocks: "I just thought perhaps I was going to throw up" (21).
Jake is also nauseated by the presence of Robert Cohn, whose
immediate attraction to Brett adds a new sexual tension. Inten-
sifying the narrator's queasiness—and the sexual ambiguity of
the scene—is the spectacle of the "harlot" Georgette dancing in
the arms of the tall, dark homosexual called Lett. This travesty of
romance mirrors the impasse between Jake and Brett, who have
both arrived at the Bal with incongruous partners—attractive
persons of the opposite sex with whom lovemaking would be
impossible.

Given Hemingway's antipathies, his evocation of the Bal de la Montagne Sainte-Geneviève may thus refer to the sterility of homosexual relations. When Jake declares that "this whole show makes [him] sick," his repugnance seems grounded in the recognition of a similarity between his situation and that of the young men with wavy hair—both are incapable of satisfying Brett. Yet he is likewise conscious of a cruel difference: the young men possess the physical equipment he has lost, while he possesses the heterosexual desire they lack. But in the surreal ambience of the bal, sexual matters become even more problematic. Despite his hostility toward homosexuals, Jake notes approvingly that Brett (who refers to herself as "a chap") wears her hair "brushed back like a boy's." Later we find that she has been wearing a "man's felt hat." Brett's appropriation of masculine signs initially seems to emphasize her femaleness: "She was built with curves like the hull of a racing yacht, and you missed none of it with that wool jersey" (22). By suggesting Brett's androgyny, Hemingway— who once wrote of his wife Hadley, "She is the best guy on a trip you ever saw"—adds a new dimension to Jake's interest in his wartime nurse.[37] As we see later in the Pamplona episode, their relationship seems at times a model of male bonding (especially when the narrator initiates Brett into the complexities of tauromachy and makes her a fellow aficionado). Hence the scene at the Bal de la Montagne Sainte-Geneviève—that Left Bank conclave of Sodom and Lesbos—provides a revealing first glimpse of the sexual confusion at the crux of Jake's agony.

To escape the dance hall and the contradictions it embodies, Jake and Brett go to a nearby bar and call a taxi. Their destination is the Parc Montsouris, and with a few purposive details, Hemingway traces their route:

> The taxi went up the hill, passed the lighted square, then on into the dark, still climbing, then levelled out onto a dark street behind St. Etienne du Mont, went smoothly down the asphalt, passed the trees and the standing bus at the place de la Contrescarpe, then turned onto the cobbles of the Rue Mouffetard. There were lighted bars and late open shops on each side of the street. We were sitting apart and we jolted together going down the old street. Brett's hat was off. Her head was back. I saw her face in the lights from the open

shops, then it was dark, then I saw her face clearly as we came out on the avenue des Gobelins. The street was torn up and men were working on the car-tracks by the light of acetylene flares. Brett's face was white and the long line of her neck showed in the bright light of the flares. The street was dark and I kissed her. (25)

Their path traverses the poor neighborhood in which the Hemingways had recently lived, down the rue Descartes (the "dark street behind St. Etienne du Mont"), past the familiar place de la Contrescarpe, and into the rue Mouffetard, where the two lovers are literally thrown together by the cobblestones of "that wonderful narrow crowded market street" recalled in *A Moveable Feast*. This self-conscious trip down memory lane raises at least the possibility that Hemingway projected into the relationship between Jake and Brett not only his attraction to Duff Twysden but his growing indifference to Hadley. In this paragraph the deliberate alternation of darkness and light seems to convey the full ambivalence of the relationship between the narrator and his would-be lover. Both are, in Yeats' phrase, "sick with desire," but they are likewise restrained by an implicit sense of futility. When Brett moans, "Oh, darling, I've been so miserable," a reticent Jake studies her features "in the bright light of the [acetylene] flares" before kissing her in the dark. Again the author implies the psychic terrain through topographical detail: like the street, Jake and Brett are "torn up," but the problem between them, unlike the car tracks, cannot be repaired. The narrator's embrace causes Brett to turn away and ask not to be touched—a scene which, as many have observed, reverses Jake's earlier rebuff of Georgette's caress. The movement between light and dark ultimately reflects the delicate balance of this painful amour; caught between the erotic and the platonic, Jake and Brett alternately crave and resist each other. Though they yearn for physical intimacy, they know the frustration which must follow arousal. Brett expresses her sexual agony in a Dantesque metaphor: "I don't want to go through that hell again" (26).

Their journey to the Parc Montsouris thus reaches an emotional and geographical dead end: "We were sitting now like two strangers. . . . The restaurant where they have the pool of live trout and where you can sit and look out over the park was closed and dark" (27). At this nadir of desire, Brett suggests—perhaps to break the stalemate—that they go to the Café Sélect in Montparnasse. From the park, they descend the avenue Montsouris (now the avenue René Coty) to the place Denfert-Rochereau and enter the boulevard Raspail, where "with the lights of Montparnasse in sight," Brett asks Jake to kiss her again. In this journey from darkness back to light, Hemingway associates the Quarter with a resurgence of passion; though he does not describe the kiss, we learn that when the taxi stops, Brett's "hand was shaky" (28). Having briefly rekindled their love in the back of a taxi, however, both confront the reality of their situation. At the Select, Brett finds distraction from desire in her conversation with Count Mippipopolous, while Jake (after listening to Braddocks describe a commotion at the dance hall) develops "a rotten headache" and prepares to "shove off" after making a date to see Brett the next day—significantly, on "the other side of town" at the Hôtel Crillon.

On his way home, Jake pauses to gaze at the statue of Marshal Ney, who was executed on that site in 1815 for his support of Napoleon: "There was a faded purple wreath leaning against the base. I stopped and read the inscription: from the Bonapartist Groups, some date; I forget. He looked very fine, Marshal Ney in his top-boots, gesturing with his sword among the green new horse-chestnut leaves" (29). Since he has passed the statue hundreds of times before, Jake's stopping seems a peculiar act. Does he somehow link his own grotesque fate with Ney's defiance? Does he long for a martyr's death? Hemingway provides no answers, only a hint of pleasure in the deathless image set against the leaves. The particulars of place seem to condense the psychic content of experience.

The evening which began on the Right Bank culminates in Jake's return to the boulevard St. Michel. From the Café Napolitain to Lavigne's, the dance hall, the Parc Montsouris, and the Select, he completes a circuit which twice brings him into the Quarter, once with Georgette and once with Brett. But nothing happens, passion finds no outlet, and Jake comes home alone to confront his misfortune "in the mirror of the big armoire beside the bed." His perambulations suggest an effort to deny or evade the truth which the mirror inevitably throws back to him. In his room, the narrator strips off his clothing and his defenses, surrendering to "the old grievance," the repetition mechanism by which he relives his wounding and recuperation. Even in his bachelor's flat, however, he cannot escape the torment of desire; the now-drunken Brett intrudes into the space of misery to tell him about her new admirer, the count, giving a last, ironic twist to his evening. "This was Brett, that I had felt like crying about," Jake muses as he watches her climb into the count's limousine for a champagne breakfast in the Bois de Boulogne.

The next three chapters likewise trace a path which is both geographical and psychological. After his dark night of the soul (which is reenacted in Pamplona), Jake sets off for work, stopping at a café for coffee and a brioche. "It was a fine morning," he notes, and "the horse-chestnut trees in the Luxembourg Gardens were in bloom. There was the pleasant early-morning feeling of a hot day" (35). The sense of routine deeply etched in Parisian experience offers a singular comfort; by heading for the office, inserting himself into the busy, anonymous scheme of everyday life, Jake achieves a certain forgetfulness. He takes the "S" bus, descends at the Madeleine, and follows the boulevard des Capucines "to the Opéra, and up to [his] office." Jake remarks, "All along people were going to work. It felt pleasant to be going to work" (36). In the psychogeography of the novel, the Right Bank is the site of the super ego, the locus of responsibility and purpose; Jake knows that at work he can repress his libidinal dilemma. After a lunch at Wetzel's (where Robert Cohn reveals his interest in Brett), Jake works at the office until his five o'clock date with Brett at the Crillon. His decision to meet her at the place de la Concorde in a luxury hotel—and at a bar popular with working journalists— signifies his determination to avoid the expatriate crowd in Montparnasse and to receive her in a less eroticized setting. But Brett does not arrive, and after a consolatory drink with George the barman, Jake takes a taxi to the Select—again abandoning the Right Bank, the world of work, male companionship, and emotional detachment, for the sexual tumult of the Quarter.

On this journey, as noted earlier, Jake's observation about empty barges on the Seine mirrors his private anguish. Crossing to the Left Bank and following the boulevard St. Germain, he passes the statue of Claude Chappe, "the inventor of the sema-phore" (actually, the wireless telegraph)—a figure which literally calls attention to the Parisian landscape as a source of signs. As he reaches the boulevard Raspail, Jake perceives another topographi-cal correlative to his feeling of emptiness:

> The Boulevard Raspail always made dull riding. It was like a certain stretch on the P.L.M. between Fontainebleau and Montereau that always made me feel bored and dead and dull until it was over. *I suppose it is some association of ideas that makes those dead places in a journey.* There are other streets in Paris as ugly as the Boulevard Raspail. It is a street I do not mind walking down at all. But I cannot stand to ride along it. (41–42, emphasis mine)

Here the narrator makes explicit the connection between place and consciousness, acknowledging a tacit "association of ideas" with particular scenes to account for the feeling of numbness which overtakes him on the boulevard Raspail. Hemingway thus alludes to the principle of geographical correspondence which informs *The Sun Also Rises* and much of his early fiction. His omission of exposition—the so-called "iceberg" theory by which he submerged meaningful information—produced an almost sys-tematic displacement of emotional content onto the terrain of fictive experience.

The subsequent scene, which unfolds at the Select and the Dôme, associates Montparnasse with sexual rivalry and duplicity. At the Select Jake initially encounters the morose Harvey Stone, who personifies the dissolution of the Quarter and the potentially destructive consequences of expatriation. He then acts as an un-willing confidant to Robert Cohn's jealous mistress, Frances Cline. Suspicious of Cohn's behavior, Frances conducts Jake to the Dôme and there—in a scene which anticipates the age-beauty-money calculus of "The Short Happy Life of Francis Macomber"—laments the decline of her sex appeal and outlines strategies for holding on to Cohn. When they return to the Select, Jake witnesses a bitter exchange between the estranged lovers that exposes the history of their intimacy and suggests its cruel, naturalistic basis. Disgusted by the spectacle, Jake slips out a side door into the rue Vavin and back to the boulevard Raspail, where he catches a taxi

home. The quarrel at the Select has upset him because it dramatizes the power of jealousy (which he knows something about) and
the dark side of desire, the seething irrational force unleashed by
sexuality. But he has missed the great irony of the scene: as he
listens half-heartedly to Frances Cline's worries about her lover's
fidelity, his own love has already made plans to go to San Sebastian
with Cohn.

No sooner has Jake retreated from Montparnasse to the solitude of his flat than Brett once again intrudes, accompanied by
Count Mippipopolous. In this scene, Hemingway returns to the
problem of the sexual impasse between the would-be lovers. When
Jake earlier had remarked that being in love is "a lot of fun, . . . an
enjoyable feeling," Brett responded, "I think it's hell on earth" (27).
Whether or not the author knew Dante's story of Paolo and Fran-
cesca when he wrote *The Sun Also Rises*, the novel repeatedly
conjures up the idea that sexual pleasure entails hellish torment,
an unrelenting cycle of ecstasy and agony. Though apparently
untroubled by moral distinctions, Hemingway concludes that
love is hell because desire seeks satisfaction only in a continual
shifting of its object, in a pursuit of the unattainable. Appositely
Jake observes of Brett, "I suppose she only wanted what she
couldn't have" (31)—a comment which applies as well to his own
yearnings. In chapter 7, when she slips into his bedroom (leaving
the count to amuse himself), the half-dressed Jake moans, "Oh,
Brett, I love you so much" (54) and proposes that they could "just
live together." But she understands her own erotic compulsions
and admits, "I don't think so. I'd just *tromper* [deceive] you with
everybody. You couldn't stand it." In a controversial reading of this
bedroom scene, Kenneth Lynn argues that Hemingway implies
"an omitted action," sexual in nature, through his use of colons
before Brett's questions: "Then: 'Do you want me to send him
away?' . . . Then later: 'Do you feel better darling?' " (54–55). Brett's
second question indeed suggests a release; but no matter what
"degree of satisfaction" Jake momentarily experiences, he finds
himself at the end of the evening in the unhappy situation of
Frances Cline when Brett tells him, "I won't see you again" (65). Of
course she does, for like Dante's lovers, Jake and Brett seem
doomed to "go through that hell again" endlessly.[38]

The evening which begins with a lonely wait at the Crillon
and a tedious interlude at the Select leads to rounds of champagne

at Jake's flat, followed by dinner in the Bois de Boulogne and dancing at Zelli's in Montmartre. By reenacting Brett's encroachment upon the narrator's private space, Hemingway implies the insistence of desire; try as he might, Jake cannot escape Brett or the sexual longings she represents. In the much-examined elaboration of "the values," the count explains that he is "always in love" and that being in love "has got a place in [his] values" (61); but so do good cigars, well-chilled champagne, and excellent food. As a connoisseur, he thus regards love as a commodity rather than an irresistible force, an amusement rather than a fixation. Such is not the case for Jake and Brett: in the scene at Zelli's, when the two dance, their bodies pressed "tight in the crowd," Brett feels again the ache of desire and tells Jake, "I'm so miserable. . . . I just feel terribly." Her torment derives partly from her contact with Jake and partly from the guilt evoked by the black drummer's line, a reminder of sexual duplicity: "You can't two time . . ." (64). As the music plays on, the drummer's chant implies a recurrent erotic message. Unlike the earlier scene of sexual ambivalence at the Bal de la Montagne Sainte-Geneviève, at Zelli's Brett cannot deflect her longings by sporting with homosexuals. She asks to leave in order to escape her own libidinous nature and the consciousness that she will soon *tromper* Jake with Robert Cohn.

In Brett's absence, the narrator experiences relief from the problem of desire: "There was plenty of work to do, I went often to the races, dined with friends, and put in some extra time at the office." The arrival of Bill Gorton offers companionship and diversion as the two explore Paris. Together they walk down the boulevard St. Michel, past the statue of "two men in flowing robes" at the rue Denfert-Rochereau (now the rue Henri Barbusse). "I know who they are," Bill insists. "Gentlemen who invented pharmacy. Don't try and fool me on Paris" (72). In fact, the monument (melted down by the Germans during World War II) commemorates Pelletier and Caventou, the discoverers of quinine, but despite Bill's error, the statue depicting the two men functions as a sign of the healing effect of male friendship. Jake's temporary escape from libidinal torment is, however, once again interrupted by Brett, who pulls up in a taxi. She agrees to join the men for a drink and proposes the Closerie des Lilas, a café near Jake's flat and perhaps reflective of her desire to reestablish intimacy with him after her secret tryst with Cohn. At the Closerie, the conversation deals with cities real and unreal: " 'Vienna,' said Bill, 'is a strange city.' 'Very much like Paris,' Brett smiled at him, wrinkling the corners of her eyes" (74–75). Alluding both to her feeling for the French capital and—covertly—to her weekend in San Sebastian with Cohn, she adds: "I was a fool to go away . . . . One's an ass to leave Paris." Having insinuated herself into the company of men, Brett asks Jake and Bill to meet her later at the Select and hurries off to bathe in preparation for the arrival of her fiancé, Mike Campbell.

Thus reminded of yet another rival for Brett's affections, Jake takes Bill to dine at Madame Lecomte's place on the Ile St.-Louis. Their transit to the island figures as a bid to recover the stability of male solidarity, insofar as the restaurant's actual name, Le Rendezvous des Mariniers, signals their yearning for an all-male place. But while they enjoy a good meal, Jake grumbles as he had at Lavigne's about the horde of American tourists who have spoiled yet another spot in Paris. Ostensibly to avoid "compatriots," he sets out with Bill on a pedestrian tour which follows a route familiar to the author. In six paragraphs, Hemingway maps a walk around the Ile St.-Louis (which he knew from visits to Bird's Three Mountains Press and later to Ford Madox Ford's *transatlantic* office), across the Seine and up the rue du Cardinal Lemoine, past the site of his old apartment, through the place de la Contrescarpe and past the crowds at the Café des Amateurs, down the rue du Pot de Fer to the rue Saint-Jacques, and from there to the boulevard de Port Royal and the boulevard Montparnasse. The route thus connects those parts of Paris where Hemingway had lived and loosely follows the chronology of his own movements.[39]

But more significantly, this itinerary reflects Jake's unsuccessful effort to escape the contradictions of his sexual identity. For some time, the two friends stand on the Pont de la Tournelle, gazing down the river at Notre Dame "squatting against the night sky." Bill's simple declaration, "It's pretty grand," implies not only a response to the nighttime scene but a sense of communion with Jake; they share the cityscape, a mutual feeling for Paris, and an affection for each other. As they stand on the bridge, however, the narrator remarks that "A man and a girl passed us. They were walking with their arms around each other" (77). This notation of a commonplace image—lovers along the Seine—seems insignificant until we consider its ironic relation to Jake's situation. The lovers represent that world from which he has been cruelly excluded and yet can never wholly escape. Jake enjoys male companionship with Bill Gorton, and Hemingway's persistent use of the plural pronoun during their walk suggests this rapport. But Jake also has Brett on his mind, and his journey from the Ile St.-Louis to the Select, which begins as a reaffirmation of male comradeship, may be seen as an inexorable movement toward the irresistible female, the beguiling Circe.

As they reach the boulevard de Port Royal, Jake asks Bill almost casually, "What do you want to do? . . . Go up to the café and see Brett and Mike?" (78). Immediately upon his arrival at the Select, Jake notices Brett "sitting on a high stool, her legs crossed. She had no stockings on." This patently sexual image, an index of Jake's longing, introduces an erotically charged scene in which Brett's drunken fiancé, Mike, calls attention to her sensuality by referring to her six times as "a piece" or "a lovely piece" (79–80). Provocatively he suggests: "I say, Brett, let's turn in early." The sexually wounded narrator approaches the object of his desire only to witness Mike's lewd advances toward her. We see clearly what the evening holds for each of the four: Jake and Bill finally head off to see a prize fight—thus returning to the world of male solidarity—while Brett prepares to take her fiancé to bed. "Mike was pretty excited about his girl friend," Jake remarks, feigning indifference. This third scene in the Select crystallizes a meaning inherent in the previous two: that as a center of libidinal activity, a scene of erotic intrigue, Montparnasse recurrently forces upon Jake the realization that he is out of the game, relegated to a spectatorial role, excluded from the sexual play unfolding around him.

Jake's sense of exclusion from the world of desire becomes clearer when, in a final return to the Quarter, he locates Mike and Brett in the "new dive," the Dingo Bar. After making plans for the expedition to Pamplona, Jake learns from Brett that she has spent her sojourn in San Sebastian with Cohn. This conversation wounds Jake anew, and, as if to escape the carnality of Montparnasse, the next day he boards a train with Bill Gorton at the Gare d'Orsay and heads for Spain, where beside the trout stream and at the bullring he will try to forget the Quarter and his yearning for

Brett. Inevitably the strategy fails: Brett follows him to Pamplona, stirs up more rivalry among the "gents," and finally places Jake in the dubious position of sexual procurer. But the journey from Paris to Pamplona allows Hemingway to bring into sharper focus the nature of Jake's dilemma.

If, as the novel's opening suggests, the narrator's sexual wound is symptomatic of the "sickness" of the postwar period, Jake's journey to Pamplona also reflects a pervasive generational search for new values. In Spain he tests his belief that "enjoying living was learning to get your money's worth and knowing when you had it" (148). The fiesta exposes the arbitrary value of money and the absolute value of life through a ritualized wager with death. Both the *corrida* and the bullfights entail the deliberate risk of annihilation from which the fiesta derives its primal energy and its clarification of ultimate worth. Hemingway thus implies a contrast between the simple, natural truths revealed in Pamplona and the artificial values which obtain in Montparnasse. As Jake undergoes a crisis of values, he also gravitates toward the Church and feels an obscure religious longing. He visits the cathedral in Bayonne, prays alone in the cathedral at Pamplona, goes to mass "a couple of times, once with Brett," and later returns with her so that she can pray for Pedro Romero. Though he regards himself as a "rotten Catholic," Jake significantly assures Brett that "some people have God . . . quite a lot" (245). In the Pamplona section of the novel, the bullring and the cathedral mark two important centers of value, two alternative responses to the problem of desire, the former providing a catharsis through the symbolic slaying of brute passion, the latter offering sublimation through ritual.

In addition to the cathedral and the bullring, however, a third important site in the symbolic geography of Hemingway's Pamplona is the Café Iruña, where the expatriates drink incessantly and where Jake betrays his values as an aficionado by bringing Brett and Romero together. At the Iruña and in the dining room of the Hotel Montoya, Jake temporarily achieves forgetfulness through inebriation. Yet his drunken binge on the last night of the fiesta testifies more than anything else to the failure of his strategies of denial and to the final breakdown of his adopted value system. As he prepares to leave Pamplona, having violated its code by corrupting Romero, the narrator confesses to Mike and

Bill, "I'm blind" (224). Ostensibly a reference to his alcoholic
stupor, the comment also pertains to his moral and spiritual
condition. In effect, Jake's actions confirm the accuracy of Bill's
mocking assessment, delivered during their fishing trip: "You're
an expatriate. You've lost touch with the soil. You get precious.
Fake European standards have ruined you. You drink yourself to
death. You become obsessed by sex. You spend all your time
talking, not working. You are an expatriate, see? You hang around
cafés" (115). In Pamplona, Hemingway's protagonist discovers
just how much of the Quarter has remained with him. Carlos
Baker has remarked of the revelers that "wherever they go . . .
[they] carry along with them the neuroses of Montparnasse."[40]
Though Jake tries to become an aficionado, immersing himself in
traditional Spanish culture, his actions reveal a false commitment to "European standards." Try as he might to become an
insider, to enter the privileged world of tauromachy, Jake remains
an outsider, more responsive to Brett's sexual craving than to the
code of the bullring. Forsaking the Select for the Iruña, Jake continues to "hang around cafés," for (as Hemingway implies) the
madness of Pamplona is only an extension of "fiesta-ing" which
goes on continuously in Paris (232).

If *The Sun Also Rises* is finally a tale of two cities, an elaboration of cultural differences and comparative values, it also confirms the impossibility of escaping personal predicaments through
travel. In this sense, the narrative illustrates what Jake has known
from the beginning; in the novel's opening pages, he tells Cohn:
"Listen, Robert, going to another country doesn't make any difference. I've tried all that. You can't get away from yourself by moving
from one place to another. There's nothing to that" (11). On a
rational level, Jake perceives that geography has nothing to do with
unhappiness; he shares the Emersonian view that "traveling is a
fool's paradise" because it creates the false hope of transformation.
Yet emotionally, Jake hopes that Spain will provide an anodyne for
his sexual misery. By returning to a more elemental existence, to
fishing and bullfighting, to water and earth, to rituals of purgation
and catharsis, he seeks at least a momentary release from the
consciousness of his wound. But just as he cannot escape Brett, he
cannot free himself from the debility which determines his relationship to her. Neither can he shake the self-loathing his impo-

tence excites: one suspects that Jake's violation of the code stems not only from a pathetic desire to please Brett and wound Cohn but also from a deep-seated need to reinforce his self-contempt. By arranging the seduction of Pedro Romero, Jake betrays the trust of Montoya and ostracizes himself from the bullfighting circle. He leaves Paris for Pamplona, tries to insert himself into a ritualized, traditional order, but brings upon himself what amounts to symbolic banishment.

Significantly, in the novel's final scene, Jake finds himself again with Brett in the back of a taxi. They have just made reservations in Madrid to return to Paris on the Sud Express, and after a lunch at Botin's, Jake proposes that they "ride through the town." But Madrid barely figures in the scene; what matters here is not the city itself but the condition of displacement signified by the taxi ride. After Paris and Pamplona, Jake realizes that there is literally no place on earth where he can escape himself and the paradox of his frustrated longing. The taxi becomes the emblem of his condition; he is perpetually in transit, shuttling between distractions. "Oh, Jake . . . we could have had such a damned good time together," Brett tells him. But Jake knows that all taxi rides with her lead toward disillusionment: "Yes. . . Isn't it pretty to think so." He remains a man in motion, unable to find refuge or grounding. Indeed, his consciousness of the futility of movement ("you can't get away from yourself by moving from one place to another") makes his association with taxicabs, trains, and buses and his incessant journeys all the more ironic. At novel's end, Jake prepares to return to Paris and the circular inferno of inextinguishable desire.

By the time he composed *The Sun Also Rises*, Hemingway knew something about the complexities of desire. Two years in Montparnasse had provided an education in temptation and seduction; as Reynolds notes, "Fornication among those he knew appeared as casual as a shared drink," and everywhere in the Quarter provocative women signaled their availability.[41] Hemingway's flirtation with Duff Twysden in 1925 nearly provoked a marital crisis, and even before he finished revising the new novel, he had become entangled in a complicated amour with Hadley's new friend, Pauline Pfeiffer. While the novel scarcely amounts to

a staging of the author's predicament, surely Hemingway's ambivalence toward Montparnasse—his fascination with and contempt
for its dissipations—and his conflicted feelings about Hadley enabled him to portray Jake's dilemma with added insight. His
representation of the city as a whole conveys an even broader
ambivalence, for the distinction between Right and Left Bank
virtually mirrors the growing split in his own life between professional discipline and café revelry. In the final analysis, the city of
the novel seems transparently a geographical emblem of Hemingway's quarrel with himself during the mid-twenties.

Even as he was writing *The Sun Also Rises*, Hemingway
voiced a growing distaste for the French capital, announcing to
Jane Heap in August 1925: "Paris is getting shot to hell. Not like
the old days."[42] Through a kind of geographical projection, his
mounting irritation with the city paralleled his marital discontent, and in November 1925 he dashed off a savage little book
which prefigured both his divorce from Hadley and his subsequent return to America. Written mainly to extricate himself
from a contract with Boni and Liveright, *The Torrents of Spring*
parodied Sherwood Anderson's treatment of expatriate life in
Dark Laughter by recollecting Paris from the unlikely vantage
point of Petoskey, Michigan.[43] Yogi Johnson, one of the two main
characters, has fought in the Great War and entertains periodic
visions of "the gay city where he once spent two weeks." He
recalls the Left Bank and mocks the repetition of its best known
experimental stylist:

> There was a street in Paris named after Huysmans. Right
> around the corner from where Gertrude Stein lived. Ah, there
> was a woman! Where were her experiments in words leading
> her? What was at the bottom of it? All that in Paris. Ah, Paris.
> How far it was to Paris now. Paris in the morning. Paris in the
> evening. Paris at night. Paris in the morning again. Paris at
> noon, perhaps. Why not?[44]

To explain his sexual dysfunction, he reveals how a beautiful
woman there once took him to a mansion and made love to him;
but on a subsequent visit, he finds her plying her trade with a
houseful of soldiers. "Since then," Yogi says, "I have never wanted
a woman," in a conclusion reminiscent of Anderson's "I Want to

Know Why." Curiously, Yogi associates Paris with seduction and sexual nausea; but after telling the story and exorcising his horror, he recovers his libido and goes off with an Indian squaw whose papoose perhaps already represents his paternal destiny.

In contrast to Yogi's lack of passion, the problem of the other main character, Scripps O'Neil, is concupiscence; he no sooner weds an elderly waitress than he falls in love with a "buxom, jolly-looking girl" named Mandy. The elderly waitress has also had a disturbing experience in Paris, awakening in a hotel to find not her "Mummy" but an aging French general sharing her bed. Whether a surreal fantasy or an instance of sexual guilt and denial, the episode triggers the girl's journey to America to become a waitress. Her rivalry with Mandy becomes the focus of the Scripps chapters, as Hemingway plays off the anxiety of the elderly waitress ("Could she hold him? Could she hold him?") against the breezy, self-assured style of the younger woman, who specializes in literary anecdotes. While Hemingway cranked out the story, Hadley and her emerging rival Pauline must have followed the plot with peculiar interest, for the parody offers a prophetic gloss on the author's domestic crisis. Indeed, Lynn contends that "the marital doom of both women is written on the wall for all to see in *Torrents*, along with some insulting reasons why they would be cast off."[45] Yogi and Scripps each embody aspects of the author's ambivalence: one is revolted by multiple sexual relations; the other collects and discards women. Seen in this context, Hemingway's bifurcated plot discloses both his complicated feelings about Paris (which is now already distant, the scene of past traumas) and his confusion about the two women then vying for his love.

By 1926, when he returned to the scene of Jake's scandal—the Café Iruña in Pamplona—the writer was deeply involved in a liaison with Pauline, who had joined the Hemingways in Spain (as she had on the Riviera and in Austria) to share the merriment and provide companionship. In addition to his understanding of desire and temptation, Hemingway by now possessed a working knowledge of deception and remorse. During the late summer of 1926 his first marriage was unraveling, and in the story "A Canary for One," he depicted the painful journey of an American couple returning to Paris by train "to set up separate residences." Sharing the same car is an American lady who has just rescued her daughter from a foreign suitor in Vevey; she adds inadvertent irony by insisting repeatedly that "American men make the best husbands." Her conversation leads the wife to recall Vevey as the "very lovely place" where she and her husband had spent their honeymoon. The morbid ironies of the journey culminate as the train approaches Paris; the husband observes three railcars near the Gare de Lyon which have been in an accident: "They were splintered open and the roofs sagged in." Commenting simultaneously on smashed cars and marital catastrophes, he announces the obvious: "Look, . . . there's been a wreck."[46]

With his marriage in ruins, Hemingway badly wanted to return to America, admitting to his editor Max Perkins: "In several ways I have been long enough in Europe." But after separating from Hadley he remained on the Left Bank, taking cover in Gerald Murphy's studio at 69, rue Froidevaux, simultaneously writhing with guilt and pining for Pauline, who had gone home to Arkansas. As Hemingway confessed in *A Moveable Feast,* "Paris was never to be the same again," and after the breakup his territorial patterns changed: he abandoned the cafés of Montparnasse, shifted his loyalties to the Brasserie Lipp and Deux Magots in St. Germain, and began cycling with Archie MacLeish in the Bois de Boulogne.[47] Early in 1927 his divorce became official, and in May he exchanged wedding vows with Pauline in the Eglise St. Honoré d'Eylau. The following March, they relocated in Key West, and though they spent most of 1929 at 6, rue Ferou, the experience only confirmed Hemingway's sense that he had somehow lost the Paris that he cherished just as he had lost the Michigan country.

During the ensuing decades he brooded recurrently on the Paris years. To be sure, he had lived in the city only intermittently from 1922 to 1927 and was away, on assignment or vacation, roughly five months out of every year. But as his later writings indicate, Paris had nevertheless changed his outlook and habits. On the Left Bank he became virtually another person, acquiring with fame quite a different sense of his identity and importance. He also confronted in that charged environment certain aspects of personality, temperament, and sexuality which had hitherto been latent or repressed. What happened to Hemingway in Paris involved more than the erosion of his Oak Park values, more than the acting out of a revolt against his mother, Grace, more than the waning of his love for Hadley, more than his succumbing to the general enticements of the Quarter and to the specific charms of Pauline Pfeiffer. In a variety of ways, life in France undermined his faith in simple feelings and permanent bonds; during those years he learned how emotions could become complicated, how desires could become ambiguous and relationships exhausted. In later years virtually every time he wrote about Paris—whether from the vantage point of Key West, Cuba, or Idaho—he implicitly calculated what had been lost and what had been gained during that decisive epoch.

More than anything else, his retrospective accounts of exile disclose aspects of a hitherto concealed danger, the allure of sexual ambivalence. In the short story "The Sea Change" (1931), Hemingway connects the Parisian setting with a conflict threatening the relationship between "a handsome young couple," presumably Americans. In an unidentified café, the two quarrel about the woman's lesbian affair; the man, Phil, manifests his hurt and disgust through biting sarcasm, while the "girl" (who sports blonde hair "cut short") reaffirms her love and asks for understanding. She reminds him that "for a long time" their relationship has been exclusively heterosexual; now, however, she feels compelled to "go off" with a woman. She asks, "Can't you forgive me? When you know about it?" The request angers Phil, who grumbles about "vice" and "perversion," yet he seems finally to accept the liaison when he asks her to "come back and tell [him] all about it." The moment marks a turning point: "His voice sounded very strange. He did not recognize it." After her departure he takes his place among the other males at the bar, announcing that he is "a different man" and that vice is "a very strange thing."[48] Here as elsewhere, Hemingway's title carries ambiguous force: in crossing the Atlantic to France the young woman has undergone a "sea change," awakening lesbian tendencies. Phil's more obscure transformation perhaps implies that he has decided to end his relationship with the girl; it may indicate that he acknowledges a strange interest in women who love women; or it may, as J. F. Kobler has suggested, reflect Phil's openness to a "homosexual affair" of his own.[49] Regardless of the precise meaning of his becoming "quite a different man," the title and locale imply that for the innocent abroad, life in Paris may produce unforeseen changes in psychosexual orientation.

By the time he composed "The Snows of Kilimanjaro" in 1936, Hemingway was still living in Key West with Pauline but on increasingly difficult terms. As the Paris years receded into the past, the city itself assumed a double identity, becoming associated with both the seemingly uncomplicated happiness of his first years in France and with the bitterness and corruption now linked to his later years there with Pauline. As noted earlier, "Snows" presents a montage of recollected images through which Harry, the dying writer, seeks some pattern or significance in his past life. In this context he recalls the poor neighborhood near the place de la Contrescarpe, the apartment over the Bal Musette, and the room in the cheap hotel "where he did his writing." His dying regret is that "he had never written about Paris. Not the Paris that he cared about." But against the radiant memory of that quarter where "he had written the start of all he was to do," Harry contrasts later Parisian experiences with his current wife, Helen, the "rich bitch" whom he blames (when he is not blaming himself) for the destruction of his talent. Unlike the modest apartment he shared with his unnamed first wife, Harry has stayed with Helen at two luxury hotels: the Crillon and the Pavilion Henri-Quatre in St. Germain-en-Laye. Helen's reminder that he "loved" the latter place prompts a bitter retort: " 'Love is a dunghill,' said Harry. 'And I'm the cock that gets on it to crow.' " His remark betrays more than self-contempt: he represents love as a site of filth, implying disgust with his own emotional and sexual tendencies. Later, he confesses that he has "demanded too much" from every woman whom he has loved and (in a flashback) implies that his abusive behavior stems from the traumatic loss of his first sweetheart. Although Harry's experience does not precisely mirror Hemingway's, the story communicates the insight that the writer has forfeited an earlier Paris through his compulsive libidinal quest for an irrecoverable and idealized lover: "every one he had slept with had made him miss her more."

During the thirties Hemingway visited Paris several times, including a ten-week stay in 1938 with his new interest, Martha Gellhorn, later to become his third wife. As a journalist he witnessed the liberation of the city in 1944 and described his first glimpse of Paris as his jeep reached the crest of a hill: "I had a funny choke in my throat and had to clean my glasses because there now, below us, gray and always beautiful, was spread the city I love best in all the world."[50] Hemingway's return to Paris evoked what would become a compulsive nostalgia. After the war, Hemingway (by then living in Cuba with his fourth wife, Mary Welsh) began working on two never-to-be-completed novels, *Islands in the Stream* and *The Garden of Eden*. Both texts manifest an insistent need to explore and clarify the Paris years, to sift through memories of that time and place for clues to the person he had become.

In the "Bimini" section of *Islands*, the painter Thomas Hudson reminisces about Paris in the twenties, recalling his friend James Joyce and "that flat . . . over the sawmill" where he lived with his oldest son Tom and with his first wife, Tom's mother. He remembers wheeling the child down the street to the Closerie des Lilas for a brioche and café au lait. For his half-brothers Andrew and David (who never lived in Paris) young Tom recollects outings in the Luxembourg Gardens:

> I can remember afternoons with the boats on the lake by the fountain in the big garden with the trees. The paths through the trees were all graveled and men played bowling games off to the left under the trees as we went down towards the Palace and there was a clock high up on the Palace. In the fall the leaves came down and I can remember the trees bare and the leaves on the gravel. I like to remember the fall best.[51]

Elsewhere young Tom reminds his father of trips to the Auteuil race track: "We used to ride back home in a carriage, an open one, do you remember? Out of the Bois and then along the river with it just getting dark and the burning leaves smell and the tugs towing barges on the river." (188).

When he is not fishing, Thomas Hudson mainly indulges in drink, remorse, and remembrance. He sees his marital past as a movement "from one disastrous error of judgment to another that was worse," and he particularly regrets having left his first wife. In the "Cuba" section, Hemingway stages a brief, romantic reunion between Hudson and his first wife, a movie actress serving during World War II with the USO. Read against the author's warm letters to Hadley in the early forties, their encounter seems a transparent gesture of wish fulfillment, a symbolic reconciliation with the woman who personified the early years in Paris. But despite his "untransferable feeling" for Hadley and his longing to recapture their past life, in *Islands* he also acknowledges the irreversibility of time.[52] He thus tempers Thomas Hudson's interlude with his former wife with the revelation—initially concealed by Hudson—that young Tom has just been killed in combat.

By this time the painter has already lost his other sons (and their mother) in a car accident near Biarritz; when his first wife flies off to join her current lover, he feels utterly bereft. His involvement in submarine hunting in the final section, "At Sea," seems a desperate ploy to save himself from the despair of loss. Shortly before he is wounded in a skirmish, Hudson takes a summary view of his life and focuses on the happiness he knew with his family in Paris:

> They were all happy, really, in the time of innocence and the lack of useless money and still being able to work and eat. A bicycle was more fun than a motorcar. You saw things better and it kept you in good shape and coming home after you had ridden in the Bois you could coast down the Champs-Elysées well past the Rond-Point and when you looked back to see what was behind you there, with the traffic moving in two streams, there rose the high gray of the great arch against the dusk. (448)

Although the painter's past differs slightly from Hemingway's, this evocation of the city's image as a stay against the confusion and unhappiness of the present seems a revealing gesture, indicative perhaps of the author's need to efface the memory of decadence and corruption by erecting his own myth of Paris in a blissful "time of innocence."

If Hemingway wished to idealize the city of memory as a "paradise lost," he also felt a compulsive urge, however, to analyze his attraction to dissipation and to what Phil (in "The Sea Change") calls "perversion."[53] In *The Garden of Eden*, he embarked in 1946 on his riskiest fictional undertaking: a novel about two expatriate couples in France who jeopardize marital happiness by pursuing androgynous experiments and multiple erotic

relationships. Their fixations with unisex hair styles and erotic
reversals indeed have a common origin: the influence of Rodin's
statue, the Metamorphoses of Ovid, housed in the former Hôtel
Biron on the rue de Varenne. Both couples have discovered in this
statue the inspiration for the sexual "changings" which they undertake independently. Though most of the subsequent action
unfolds in Spain, at Hendaye, and on the Riviera, Paris figures as
the symbolic point of departure for the American couples.

David and Catherine Bourne, whose sexual adventures alone
and with a girl named Marita animate the abridged 1986 edition of
The Garden of Eden, meet at the Crillon bar—where Jake waited
for Brett—and marry at the American Church (St. Joseph's) on the
avenue Hoche. Other references to Paris surface throughout the
chapters concerned with the Bournes, and in a bizarre, discarded
fragment, Hemingway suggests his protagonist's connections
with other "exiles of art" (as Malcolm Cowley called them) by
depicting a conversation in which David asks Richard "Dick"
Blake about American friends:

> "Did you see Scott in St. Raphael?"
> "I saw him."
> "Do you think he'll ever write a good book?"
> "Sure. He's writing one now. He isn't drinking since July. His
> wife got in a jam with a French Naval flyer. They fixed it up
> and he's working good. He made good sense when I saw him
> only he was sad. Why don't you go see him?"
> "I might break him out."
> "That's true. Maybe you better leave him alone. Nobody
> leaves anybody alone now. That's the crappy way it's got.
> "Have you seen Hemingstein?"
> "That son of a bitch went to Canada."
> "He came back though."
> "Sure. Then he went to Austria. They're living in the rue
> Notre Dame des Champs now. Around the corner from the
> Closerie."
> "That's where they were when I left."
> "I see them quite a lot since you left. They were in Spain this
> summer too. Didn't you see them?"
> "No. They were gone when we got there."

Blake subsequently mentions Waldo Peirce and Mike Strater, two of Hemingway's painter-friends from the twenties. This abortive scene suggests the tangled relationship between *The Garden of Eden* and Hemingway's experiences in France.[54] David not only knows the vicissitudes of Scott Fitzgerald but also represents himself as an acquaintance of the author who created him; he glibly refers to "Hemingstein," knows the apartment in Montparnasse, and seems familiar with Hemingway's movements during the mid-twenties. One wonders what urgencies prompted such an illusion-breaking scene; perhaps a nervous Hemingway wished to distance himself from his androgynous protagonist. The net effect, however, is a metafictional confusion of memory and imagination. Like *Islands*, *The Garden of Eden* discloses the author's growing fixation with his own past and his determination, despite an instinct for self-concealment, to create a recognizable portrait of the artist as a young man. David Bourne's struggle to maintain writerly discipline in the midst of domestic upheaval seems to draw its force from Hemingway's complicated situation in 1925–26.

The autobiographical subtext also reveals itself in the abandoned parallel plot, the story of Nick and Barbara Sheldon. who live in a tiny apartment on a cobblestone street in the Latin Quarter. Without waking his wife, Nick goes out one cold morning to buy a brioche for her:

> Brioche and bed, he thought. That's the presents we have. I wish I could buy her something really lovely but we have to give the things that don't cost money. He thought about what he had been thinking in the night. He bought a morning paper and walked fast back to the studio. The breath from the horses pulling a high wheeled cart made plumes in the sharp air and he could feel the cold of the cobble stones through the soles of his shoes. (422a–3, 6)

This passage, which sets hunger, poverty, and cold against the warmth of love, brings to mind (and indeed anticipates) the description of the old neighborhood around the place de la Contrescarpe in *A Moveable Feast*. But the social haunts of the Sheldons—the Brasserie Lipp and Deux Magots—correspond more closely to the places that Hemingway frequented during his St.

Germain period, 1926–28. Though he developed the Sheldon plot enough to show them meeting the Bournes in Hendaye, to imply a lesbian attraction between Catherine and Barbara, to sketch Barbara's affair with the writer Andrew Murray, and to project her suicide following the accidental death of Nick, he never fleshed out that story as he did the marital tangle involving David, Catherine, and Marita. The Left Bank milieu inhabited by the Sheldons thus receives only passing attention in the narrative, while Paris itself figures mainly as a scene of expatriate encounters, a base for European travels, and—through the Rodin statue—a symbolic source for the androgynous transformations which affect all the major characters.

Perhaps concluding that the novel was *inaccrochable,* both indiscreet and unpresentable, Hemingway set aside the manuscript during the early fifties. When he again took up the subject of expatriate life in the twenties, discretion guided his preparation of a self-portrait for public consumption. Whatever the autobiographical experiences informing *The Garden of Eden,* sexual ambiguity seems not to figure—initially, at least—in the remarkable sketches of *A Moveable Feast.* Impetus for the memoir came, apparently, from Hemingway's 1956 discovery in Paris of some early notebooks and manuscripts; the recovery of these materials produced a Proustian recollection of lost time and an urge to memorialize, as the dying writer in "Snows" never could, the "Paris that he cared about."[55] By temperament Hemingway had long resisted autobiographical reflection; his protagonists often struggle to repress the past—as when Nick Adams, on the Big Two-Hearted River, starts to recall the old days: "His mind was starting to work. He knew he could choke it because he was tired enough." But Hemingway's recovery of this material triggered memories which from the glum perspective of his last years seemed rife with implication. Almost miraculously, his recollections allowed him to throw off the slack, self-indulgent style of his later work and recapture one last time the spare, condensed prose which had made him famous.

Inevitably, the Paris of *A Moveable Feast* is an imaginary city, a mythical scene evoked to explain the magical transformation of an obscure, Midwestern journalist into a brilliant modern author. Almost every aspect of the city contributes to the making of the artist. Near the "cheerful, gay flat" where he lives with his lovely and supportive wife, the young writer has a top floor room that looks out "over the roofs of Paris" (12). Somehow the view bolsters his confidence; he simply gazes over the rooftops and remembers how to write. In this room he constructs "true sentences" and imposes upon himself the "severe discipline" inspired by Cézanne, whose paintings by happy coincidence hang in a nearby museum. His promenades through the Luxembourg Gardens or along the Seine likewise have a settling and clarifying effect after a morning of work. The young man also benefits from contact with literary mentors who enjoy his company and teach him important lessons about the language of modern literature. Almost by chance, he makes connections with editors of little magazines and finds outlets for his early work. He locates an American bookstore and lending library where he borrows the works of Turgenev, Tolstoy, Dostoevsky, Chekhov, Stendhal, and Flaubert. He can scarcely contain his euphoria: "To have come on all this new world of writing, with time to read in a city like Paris where there was a way of living well and working, no matter how poor you were, was like having a great treasure given to you" (132). Almost redundantly he concludes that Paris is "the town best organized for a writer to write in that there is" (180).

Even the physical milieu invigorates the young man's imagination by presenting vivid scenes which already seem arranged and painted: "When we came back to Paris it was clear and cold and lovely. The city had accommodated itself to winter . . . . and on the streets the winter light was beautiful. Now you were accustomed to see the bare trees against the sky and you walked on the fresh washed gravel paths through the Luxembourg gardens in the clear sharp wind" (11). At night the brown and saffron sewage wagons look like "Braque paintings" in the moonlight. The writer recalls the memorable perspectives he has shared with his wife: "We walked back through the Tuileries in the dark and stood and looked through the Arc du Carrousel up across the dark gardens with the lights of the Concorde behind the formal darkness and then the long rise of lights toward the Arc de Triomphe" (53). Beyond the Louvre, the two pause on a bridge (fig. 15) and gaze at the Ile de la Cité: "We looked and there it all was: our river and our city and the island of our city" (55). Through this sugges-

Figure 15. The Seine, looking toward the Ile de la Cité. The Louvre is visible through the trees at left, the Gare d'Orsay is on the right, and the towers of Notre Dame appear in the distance.

tive epiphany, the young man conveys a feeling of belonging, almost a proprietary satisfaction with his visual domain. He declares his triumph over a city that is comforting and familiar; this expatriate feels no estrangement or displacement. On the contrary, he insists: "All Paris belongs to me" (6). He thus ascribes to his city—Hemingway's textual construct—an imaginative plenitude: whatever he desires can be found there. Even scenes of debauchery (like the Café des Amateurs) have a certain charm; this Paris continually provides sensory pleasure and intellectual stimulation. It is the ideal place in which to pursue the literary life: a city that venerates arts and letters, that contains a cosmopolitan community of authors, and that offers innumerable settings for the solitary task of writing.

But in shaping this myth of his literary beginnings, Hemingway constructs a fantastic place and a selective, even distorted version of his literary apprenticeship. Though he notes occasional bad weather, he emphasizes clear days and moonlit nights, suppressing his private impression that "it rained nearly every day."[56] He neglects to say that he rented the top-floor writing room only briefly; that journalistic chores stalled his literary projects and often took him away from Paris; that he had but sporadic contact with Pound and Joyce and that he saw Stein less frequently than his narrative implies; that he worked at cafés to escape the cramped apartments he shared with Hadley; that his wife's trust fund nevertheless provided a steady income which spared the couple that poverty and hunger which figure so prominently in the memoir. Hemingway does recount the most serious setback of his early career—Hadley's losing the suitcase containing his manuscripts—but downplays the mistake and says about the manuscript of a youthful novel that "it was probably a good thing that it was lost." He also banishes from the memoir most of the disgust he felt in the twenties about the Quarter and the café crowds; and, with the exception of oblique references to his affair with Pauline, he largely represses the story (implicit in *The Sun Also Rises*) of his complicated response to the sexual dangers of Paris and to the conflict between temptation and restraint which culminated in passion and remorse.

The implications of Hemingway's omissions loom larger when we consider the memoir in relation to *The Garden of Eden*, the unfinished novel on which he resumed work in the late fifties. Manuscript evidence indicates that for a time, Hemingway moved back and forth between projects, on one occasion (at least) scribbling ideas for both on the same sheet of paper.[57] Similarities and differences between the two works raise an interesting question: should they be understood as discrete narratives generated by altogether different impulses or as separate but related versions of the same story—a young writer's fall from innocence into the complications of sexual ambivalence? Evidence supports the latter conclusion: a nineteen-page manuscript fragment links the two works and underscores a crucial connection between androgyny and the Parisian milieu.

Initially, the hero of the memoir—alternately "Hem" or "Tatie"—and the fictional protagonist, David Bourne, present a striking contrast. Young Hem in *A Moveable Feast* displays ostensibly orthodox, heterosexual inclinations as he fantasizes about a "very pretty" girl he sees in a café, celebrates lovemaking with Hadley, and approves of Pascin's *machismo*. Conversely he ridicules a whining homosexual named Hal, satirizes Fitzgerald's sexual uncertainties, and implies disgust with the lesbian practices of Stein and Toklas. Meanwhile, in *The Garden of Eden*,

David emerges as an epicene figure engaging in sexual role reversals with his wife Catherine, who assumes the name "Peter," mounts him, and calls him (curiously enough) "my girl Catherine."[58] He also submits to her scheme of effacing gender differences as the two dress alike and sport matching coiffures of short hair bleached pale blond.

Yet beneath these obvious differences we note important parallels between the two narratives. Both foreground the life of writing as an "enforced loneliness," and both explore tensions between writing and the distractions of the author's private life. In the novel, David rents a work room at Aurol's hotel to compose "simple declarative sentences," while Hem crafts "true sentences in his rooftop studio." Catherine's destruction of David's notebooks recalls Hadley's loss of manuscripts, and in both cases the experience devastates the writer. Both narratives call attention to "hunger" as a metaphor for desire, as when Hemingway in the "False Spring" section of the memoir speaks of ineluctable yearning:

> It was a wonderful meal at Michaud's after we got in; but when we had finished and there was no question of hunger any more the feeling that had been like hunger when we were on the bridge was still there when we caught the bus home. It was there when we came in the room and after we had gone to bed and made love in the dark, it was there. When I woke with the windows open and the moonlight on the roofs of the tall houses, it was there. I put my face away from the moonlight into the shadow but I could not sleep and lay awake thinking about it.[59]

In the opening chapter of the published version of the novel, David refers to "the sudden deadly clarity that had always come after intercourse" and recurrently alludes to the "hollow" feeling that he cannot escape. Hem's feeling of emptiness prompts him to remark in the memoir that "Paris was a very old city and we were young and nothing was simple there" (57). David likewise realizes that his relationship to Catherine is both "very simple" and "very complicated." In both narratives, a developing sense of complication attends the protagonist's fall from relative innocence into sexual adventure and duplicity.

But Hemingway enforces the distinction between autobiography and fiction by insisting on the difference between Hem and David. Conceived for public inspection, the memoir projects a hero seemingly certain of his libidinal preferences and his gendered behavior. The notorious episode, "A Matter of Measurements," in fact illustrates the operating assumption that one's primary sexual traits naturally determine both gender (the role one plays as male or female) and desire (sexual attraction or affinity). Hemingway takes for granted a heterosexual determinism and thus undertakes to restore Fitzgerald's masculinity, his sense of gender, by validating his sexual equipment in the bathroom of Michaud's restaurant. Virtually the only moment in which an alternate sexuality expresses itself is when Hem overhears the lovemaking of Stein and Toklas on the rue de Fleurus. He registers the voice of lesbian desire as unnatural ("I heard someone speaking to Miss Stein as I had never heard one person speak to another; never, anywhere, ever") and rushes away presumably to spare himself further embarrassment.

In *The Garden of Eden*, however, Hemingway seems to question the assumptions about sex, gender, and desire which inform the memoir. When the androgynous, bisexual Catherine celebrates her lovemaking with Marita—"It was what I wanted to do all my life and now I've done it and I loved it" (120)—he gives voice to the desire which scandalizes the narrator of *A Moveable Feast*. Indeed, when read against the sketch "A Strange Enough Ending," David's voyeuristic fascination with and tacit acceptance of lesbianism mark one of the most striking contrasts between the memoir and the novel. His experience seems an elaborate revision of Phil's predicament in "The Sea Change." David's participation in Catherine's erotic reversals—doing the "devil things"—perhaps indicates his *own* androgynous interest in the female experience of intercourse. Studying his new unisex haircut in the mirror, David enjoys the sensation of strangeness, even though sexually "he did not know exactly how he was" (85). Thus while the memoir portrays a writer secure in his gendered identity and advances a rigorously heterosexual view of relationships, the novel conversely explores the unstable terrain of sexual ambivalence, exposing the multiple forms of desire and the seemingly arbitrary nature of gender.

Thus despite several resemblances between *A Moveable Feast* and *The Garden of Eden*, one might conclude that the narratives tell quite different stories and that their respective protagonists have little in common except marital problems and literary ambitions. But manuscript evidence indicates that at some point in the composition of the memoir, the author began a sketch which would have connected young Hem to David Bourne and even to Nick Sheldon by tracing an experiment in androgyny undertaken by the Hemingways in Paris in 1924. An unfinished and unpublished sketch provides the missing link between the narratives. This holograph manuscript, clearly drafted for the memoir, provides a privileged glimpse into the secret activities of the young writer and his wife. The tone of wry reminiscence, the reconstruction of the life shared by Hem and Hadley in Paris, and the allusion to topics developed elsewhere in the memoir all point to a composition date of 1957 or 1958.[60]

As the fragment opens, Hem describes a tactic for avoiding the more expensive Right Bank: "I found out very quickly that the best way to avoid going over to the right bank and get[ting] involved in all the pleasant things that I could not afford . . . was not to get a haircut."[61] He suggests that long hair marked a man as a bohemian, an outcast shunned by newsmen working in the quarter around the Opera. When the young writer's hair reaches a questionable length, a correspondent warns him: "You musn't let yourself go, Hem." The narrator claims that he got the idea to grow long hair from the Japanese painters he met at Pound's studio; after three months without a trim, he says, "you would have a good start on the sort of hair cut Ezra's wonderful Japanese friends had and your right bank friends would think of you as damned" (insert to 2). This association between long hair and damnation forms a key motif. Hem confesses: "I never knew just what it was that you were supposed to be damned to but after four months or so you were considered damned to something worse. I enjoyed being considered damned and my wife and I enjoyed being considered damned together" (insert to 2).

Here the insistence on damnation associates long hair with a deeper iniquity. Although he does not specify their transgression, Hem makes an extraordinary confession about the couple's relationship in 1924 after returning to Paris from Canada: "We lived

like savages and kept our own tribal rules and had our own customs and our own standards, secrets, taboos, and delights" (4).
The principal evidence of this "savage" phase is a long dialogue
between Hem and his wife which discloses a plan to achieve
identical unisex hairstyles. Hadley broaches the idea, we learn, at
the Closerie des Lilas just after Hem has decided—now that he is
no longer a reporter—to let his hair grow long. In the ensuing
exchange, Hadley offers encouragement and proposes an androgynous project:

"It's growing wonderfully. You'll just have to be patient."
"All right. I'll forget about it."
"If you don't think about it maybe it will grow faster. I'm so
glad you remembered to start it so early."
We looked at each other and laughed and then she said one of
the secret things.
"That's correct."
"Tatie I thought of something exciting."
"Tell me."
"I don't know whether to say it."
"Say it. Go on. Please say it."
"I thought maybe it could be the same as mine."
"But yours keeps growing too."
"No. I'll get it just evened tomorrow and then I'll wait for you.
Wouldn't that be fun for us?"
"Yes."
"I'll wait and then it will be the same for both."
"How long will it take?"
"Maybe four months to be just the same."
"Really?"
"Really."
"Four months more?"
"I think so."
We sat and she said something secret and I said something
secret back.
"Other people would think we are crazy."
"Poor unfortunate other people," she said. "We'll have such
fun Tatie."
"And you'll really like it?"

"I'll love it," she said. "But we'll have to be very patient. The way people are patient with a garden."
"I'll be patient. Or I'll try anyway."
"Do you think other people have such fun with such simple things?"
"Maybe it's not so simple."
"I don't know. Nothing can be simpler than growing."
"I don't care whether it's complicated or simple. I just like it."
(insert to 4, B–C)

While this passage generally recalls discussions of look-alike hair-styles in *A Farewell to Arms* and *For Whom the Bell Tolls*, it more explicitly parallels the text of *The Garden of Eden*. The plan to cultivate matching shoulder-length coiffures of course duplicates the project of Nick and Barbara Sheldon, and although there is no mention of an explicit gender change, the recurrent references to "secret things" (which echo the novel's "devil things") imply the sexual aspect of the experiment. Like David and Catherine, Hem and Hadley feel set apart from other people by an androgynous scheme which seems "simple" but may become "complicated." Hemingway metaphorizes the project by likening it to growing a garden and thus implicitly alludes to his unpublished novel. The reference actually elucidates the novel's title, positing an esoteric connection between hair growth and gardening—or between an-drogyny and Edenic happiness.

Mirroring the opening chapter of *The Garden of Eden*, the sketch moreover contains a scene in which Hadley returns from the hairdresser's to show Hem her newly cropped hair. "Feel it in back," she tells him, in a line which exactly echoes Catherine's request to David. Hem pulls Hadley close and feels their hearts "beating through [their] sweaters"; his fingers shake as he touches her hair:

"Stroke it down hard," she said.
"Wait," I said. Then she said, "Now stroke it down hard. Feel."
I held my hand against its silky weight and bluntness against her neck and said something secret and she said, "After-wards."
"You," I said. "You." (insert to 4, E)

This moment has its sequel in the novel, as Catherine instructs David: "Feel how smooth. Feel it in back." When David runs his fingers along the sides of her face, Catherine divulges her exciting secret: " 'You see,' she said. 'That's the surprise. I'm a girl. But now I'm a boy too and I can do anything and anything and anything' " (15). Although Hadley makes no such claim, she seems as obsessed as Catherine by the idea of unisex coiffures; she later gives Hem a trim to even the hair across his collar. Realizing that the experiment will demand patience, they vow to persevere and to resist criticism. "We'll just do it and not worry and have a lovely time," Hadley says.

Though the fragment subsequently slides into self-parody, its very existence raises two compelling questions: Why did Hemingway draft this sketch, and why did he then discard it as "worthless"? The second question seems easier to answer, for had the reminiscence been included in *A Moveable Feast*, it would have subverted the masculine image of young Hem, who would have been in no position to certify Fitzgerald's virility, to ridicule the effeminacy of Hal (in "Birth of a New School"), or to feign disgust at the lesbianism of Stein and Toklas. But given the difficulties which publication of the sketch would have created, we must also consider what Hemingway hoped to achieve when he composed it. Was he merely trying to recycle ideas from *The Garden of Eden*, or was he toying with the disclosure of a long-guarded secret? The long-haired Hem of the fragment indeed seems to manifest the author's covert desire to throw off the burden of a hypermasculine gender role and to adopt a more androgynous self-image. As Kenneth Lynn and Mark Spilka have argued in recent studies, Hemingway's early upbringing produced conflicting notions of masculinity, sometimes obliged him to play the role of a girl, and left him with a literally irrepressible urge to cross the gender line and assume an alternate female identity.[62] Yet aside from suggestive hints in earlier works, he did not address this impulse overtly until he began composing *The Garden of Eden*. Over the space of a dozen years and seventeen hundred manuscript pages, Hemingway struggled to exorcise his secret and potentially scandalous desire. Androgyny was thus much on his mind as he began *A Moveable Feast*; however, the idea of constructing an acknowledged self-portrait ultimately induced him to discard the "worthless sketch" about gender transformations in Paris.

The discovery of this fragment nevertheless places the memoir in a new light, enabling us to perceive hints of gender ambivalence—or its active repression—elsewhere in the text. Hem's unsuccessful attempt (in "A False Spring") to recall "the whole story about the wisteria vine" told by his homosexual friend Jim Gamble may mark one such moment of denial, particularly in a sketch which subtly contrasts male friendship with his marital relationship. Likewise Hem's reaction to the lovemaking of Stein and Toklas may be read as a displaced anxiety about the making public of his *own* fetishes, "secret things," and taboo practices. A revisionary reading might also attach new importance to Hemingway's allusion (in "Ezra Pound and his Bel Esprit") to the long-haired Japanese painters and to his nervous fascination (in "Hawks Do Not Share") with Zelda Fitzgerald's presumed bisexuality. The vicious portrait of Scott Fitzgerald similarly assumes a different aspect in relation to young Hem's presumed secret; when we read that Fitzgerald had "very fair wavy hair, a high forehead, excited and friendly eyes and a delicate long-lipped Irish mouth that, on a girl, would have been the mouth of a beauty" (147), we recognize the androgynous appeal that forced Hemingway to add: "The mouth worried you until you knew him and then it worried you more." By imputing a homosexual tendency to Fitzgerald, Hemingway attempts to disclaim the attraction he feels to a man "who looked like a boy with a face between handsome and pretty." Fitzgerald proves to be the perfect androgyne, the man-woman who is both handsome and pretty, and the balance of the sketch displays the working out of Hemingway's ambivalence, his alternate affection and hostility, for this incarnation of his own conflicted desire.

By juxtaposing *A Moveable Feast* and *The Garden of Eden*, we gain a new perspective on the relationship between Hemingway's gender trouble and his attachment to Paris. The fragment linking these works ties the experiment in androgyny—the unisex hair styles and "secret things"—to the Closerie des Lilas, to Pound's Japanese friends, and to the bohemian affectations of Montparnasse. Preparing his memoir for publication, Hemingway decided to discard the story of how he and Hadley had risked "damnation" by trying to erase gender differences. But the very existence of the fragment alerts us to other traces of sexual ambivalence concealed by macho posturing. It moreover reminds us of the salient point—obscured by the anecdotal pungency of *A Moveable Feast*—that living in the eroticized Quarter exposed Hemingway to the multiformity of desire and raised troubling questions about sexuality itself. If Paris provided auspicious conditions in which to become a writer, it also aroused in Hemingway certain anxieties about his gendered identity. As the memoir confirms, places change us; in different locations we become other people.

From Hemingway's first visit, the atmosphere of peril added to the enticement of Paris. As an inhabitant of the Left Bank, he savored the emotional risks and hazards which made him feel that he was living his life "all the way up" like a bullfighter. Yet even as Paris was changing him, he harbored a contempt for expatriate life in Montparnasse, and through his fictional character Bill Gorton he mockingly condemned his own profligacies and his concessions to "fake European standards." By the mid-thirties, when he wrote "The Snows of Kilimanjaro," Hemingway recognized both the influence of Paris in his literary formation and its role in his corruption. By the forties, he found himself caught between the urge to sentimentalize a place of memory and the need to reckon with disturbing changes which had begun in France. Temperament, creativity, and sexuality had all been affected, and in *The Garden of Eden* he traced the "changings" of his American couples back to the statue which had triggered their various experiments. In effect Hemingway asks us to regard Rodin's "Metamorphoses" as an emblem of the transformations of exile. His portrayal of the expatriate's loss of innocence carried him toward some of the most daring fiction he ever produced.

But it was a story, he must have concluded, that could not be told. Instead, he represented the Paris years in *A Moveable Feast* as a period of happiness, luck, and love. The city is a writer's paradise in which young Hem circulates with seeming impunity, witnessing the iniquity of others (like Ralph Cheever Dunning in "An Agent of Evil") without ever slipping himself. Yet his memoir is also suffused with a sense of loss, for in projecting this younger self, the aging Hemingway already knows the outcome: his first marriage breaks up; friendships go sour; he leaves Paris, becomes famous, makes money; he suffers two more marital disasters; sustains injuries in accidents; loses his health and his confidence as a writer; becomes bitter, alcoholic, and depressed. When Hemingway composed *A Moveable Feast*, he obviously foresaw the end of his career; he reflected on his apprentice years as if to consolidate the myth of his origins and to recover, by an act of identification, his earlier relationship to writing.

Closing the memoir, Hemingway summarizes his attachment to Paris and comments tellingly on the connection between place and self. Acknowledging certain "wicked" activities he has resumed "back in Paris" after a skiing holiday, he writes:

> Paris was never to be the same again although it was always Paris and you changed as it changed. . . . There is never any ending to Paris and the memory of each person who has lived in it differs from that of any other. We always returned to it no matter who we were or how changed it was or with what difficulties, or ease, it could be reached. Paris was always worth it and you received return for whatever you brought to it. But this is how Paris was in the early days when we were very poor and very happy. (208–09)

This apparently simple valediction compresses several insights. Hemingway suggests that the revisited city is never identical to the remembered city, even though "it was always Paris," always recognizable as itself. It can never be "the same again" because places, like people, undergo constant transformation. Thus, by implication, the concept of place always designates an absence, a set of conditions irrecoverable *as such*. Only in remembrance, perhaps, does place exactly coincide with itself; but of course each person remembers a different Paris because what remains in memory is the residue of consciousness, the trace of a subjective relationship to place. For Hemingway, Paris was more than a geographical location; it was the scene of a dramatic metamorphosis. His recurrent visits were "always worth it" because that place most resembled the terrain which persisted in the dreaming part of his mind, the topography of that fabulous city where he had become a famous writer but had lost in the process a "lovely, magic" marriage and an ingenuous, younger self. Paris became at last the complex, fetishized sign of his personal losses. Behind the image of that great good place he concealed the story of his attraction to danger and "damnation," reflecting instead on the precariousness of innocence and happiness, which perhaps in the end amounts to the same story.

CHAPTER FOUR

The Secret Paris of Henry Miller

UNTIL the "ten glorious years in France" (1930–39) that launched his career, Henry Miller regarded Brooklyn as his necessary sphere of being. Even in *Black Spring,* composed in exile in 1933, he styled himself a "patriot" of the Fourteenth Ward and conceded: "The rest of the United States doesn't exist for me except as idea, or history, or literature."[1] Since childhood his own existence had been so bound up with the life of Brooklyn streets and neighborhoods that when schemes for wealth or self-improvement lured him to other parts of the country—to California, Florida, or North Carolina—he floundered badly, as if unable to function in strange settings. In Brooklyn, he had become streetwise, versed in the tactics of survival, but outside the New York milieu he felt confused and paralyzed. A week in Jacksonville reduced Miller to a homesick vagrant; in National City, California, as Jay Martin notes, he lapsed into a fugue state: "His mind went blank. Around him people moved back and forth, strangely unreal and without purpose, like weird Chinamen walking across the Brooklyn Bridge. He didn't know where he was or who he was."[2] Martin's last comment—which underscores the elemental relationship between place and self—points to the crisis of identity which culminated when Miller (then thirty-eight) cut his ties with America, leaving behind a history of marital and occupational disasters to make a belated bid for literary renown in Paris.

Although he had some acquaintance with the city from a 1928 visit, Miller's expatriation posed personal risks, for the pattern of escape, collapse, and return which had previously confirmed his attachment to the Brooklyn scene revealed a deeper and more insidious dependency. Through an unconscious logic, he associated his hometown with a series of powerful female figures, caregivers who could likewise induce panic by denying approval or gratification. Away from Brooklyn—away from his scornful mother; his early lover, the maternal Pauline; his testy first wife, Beatrice; or his second wife, June, the seductive taxi-dancer—he seemed as disoriented and vulnerable as a lost child. Though he had learned the shifts of the poor and inured himself to hardship, he retained an enervating need to please Mother, or the mother-figure in his life.[3] When he was cut off from this source of direction and approval, he scarcely knew what to do. In Paris he faced not only the anxiety of separation from a maternal presence but the unrelenting problem of physical survival in a foreign place.

In a psychological sense, as Martin observes, Miller had "always been lost in New York," whether reeling from the childhood humiliations inflicted by his mother, the fierce moodiness of Beatrice, or the indignities imposed by June (who, for example, forced him out of his own apartment while she entertained male clients). Beyond the chaos of his emotional life, he was also lost vocationally; he had tried a score of odd jobs, including his father's tailoring trade, and for several years had acted—improbably and insouciantly—as a personnel manager for Western Union. What Miller wanted most to do, however, was to write. But even his first manuscripts, such works as *Clipped Wings* and *Dion Moloch*, betrayed through their self-conscious tone a deep confusion of purpose. By 1929, as the stock market crash heralded the Great Depression, he had reached a point of emotional and psychic debility; reduced to panhandling, discouraged by lack of progress on a third book (alternately titled *Lovely Lesbians* or *Crazy Cock*), and agonized by June's incessant affairs—with forty-two different men and sixteen women, he reckoned—Miller was clutching at straws. When June urged him to go off to Paris to do his writing and then produced the steamship ticket which would make it possible, he was just desperate enough to comply.[4]

Though he could not have realized it at the time, that voyage marked the great turning point in his life, as Miller distanced himself from dominating women, past failures, and the American cult of wealth and success. His solitary journey carried the "Brooklyn boy" toward an alien landscape and, inexorably, toward a decisive change in his way of thinking about himself. "By being alone," Martin contends, "he could, possibly, discover a self that his parents, his friends, his jobs, his loves, his life in America had long suppressed."[5] Miller's search for that liberated self indeed provided the imaginative impetus for *Tropic of Cancer* (1934), his first published book. When he left New York harbor with ten dollars in his pocket, however, he had no inkling of the hardships that lay ahead, only the bitter realization that little of definite importance lay behind him. For nearly a decade he had been hearing about writers and artists who had gone abroad, lived well, produced new work, and advanced their careers; but as the ship steamed into the Atlantic, carrying Miller toward exile, that phase of easy expatriation had already ended. As Malcolm Cowley remarked, "Paris was no longer the center of everything 'modern' and aesthetically ambitious in American literature."[6] If Miller suspected the belatedness of his own European sojourn, he may have enjoyed the sardonic reflection that, however bleak, his prospects in Paris seemed bright compared to the debacle of his American past.

Although *Tropic of Cancer* purports to tell the story of Miller's first years in Paris—and indeed contains little that is not rooted in first-hand experience—that book nevertheless advances a fictionalized version of events, designed to underscore certain conceptions of history, culture, and consciousness while presenting a particular image of the author-in-exile. A more immediate and veridical account of Miller's Parisian ordeal emerges, however, in his richly detailed correspondence with Emil Schnellock, the New York commercial artist who was Miller's longtime confidant and mentor. In the recently published *Letters to Emil*, editor George Wickes has made available the most revealing of Miller's reports from Paris.[7] Taken together, the letters (especially those written during the first two years) portray a critical stage in Miller's transformation, a prolonged trial which, by his own account at least, brought him close to madness. Examining the correspondence—which includes material later revised for *Tropic of Cancer*—one discovers a parallel narrative with its own preoccupations and revelations. These separate missives form a surprisingly continuous record of Miller's struggle to adjust to the unfamiliar Parisian scene, to resolve fundamental questions of voice and style which complicated his writing, and to construct an essentially new, expatriate identity. As he composed his letters to Schnellock, he explored the volatile tensions which link place and writing to the radical problem of self.

Among other disclosures, we learn in the correspondence that Miller's relation to Paris was more conflicted than *Tropic of Cancer* suggests and that, until his liaison with Anaïs Nin seemed to settle the issue in 1932, he wrestled recurrently with the idea of returning to the United States. Apart from the ongoing problems of food and shelter—which handouts from friends, wages from odd jobs, and checks from June relieved intermittently—Miller also experienced a persistent sense of displacement. Though determined to know Paris by heart, to achieve a mastery of its intricate topography, he recognized that his vision of the city was "a chimera" (29), an illusion created by his own ignorance of language and customs. The more he learned about Paris, the more deeply he felt the marginality and precariousness of his situation; even after two years there he had to confess about the city: "It's like my home now, though I am still a foreigner and always will be" (95). But despite the awareness that much of Paris remained sealed off from him, Miller nevertheless acquired a more intimate and extensive knowledge of the city than any other American writer.[8]

The impetus for his wide-ranging and unsystematic exploration of Paris derived, oddly enough, from a travel book about New York City by the French author Paul Morand. Although the newly arrived Miller probably picked up Morand's *New York* in a moment of homesickness, that book ultimately shifted his thoughts from New York to the immediate, foreign scene, suggesting a new focus for his literary work. The guide evoked American sites familiar to Miller, but more importantly, it sharpened his sensitivity to those elements of the Parisian cityscape which made it

different from New York—or any other place that he had visited.
He reasoned that if Morand, a Frenchman, could write knowl-
edgeably about New York's various districts and neighborhoods,
then he, as an American, could just as readily produce an illuminating overview of Paris. A few days after his arrival, these
notions cohered into a plan of action:

> I will write here. I will live quietly and quite alone. And each
> day I will see a little more of Paris, study it, learn it as I would
> a book. It is worth the effort. To know Paris is to know a great
> deal. How vastly different from New York! What eloquent
> surprises at every turn of the street. To get lost here is an
> adventure extraordinary. The streets sing, the stones talk.
> The houses drip history, glory, romance. (17–18)

The exuberant Miller imagined his life divided between two complementary activities: reading and writing. Paris would be both
the "book" he read by day and the work he composed by night; his
studies would require energy, diligence, and sturdy shoes. Even as
he noted parallels between New York and Paris, he celebrated the
"vastly different" aspects of the latter, exulting in the notion of
the city as historical text. From the outset, Miller recorded his
promenades and perceptions, noting as well his acquaintance
with other expatriates who helped him to survive in the French
capital.

Comparisons between New York and Paris helped Miller to
allay his initial confusion and apprehension; he perhaps also
hoped to lend an immediacy to his letters by using references
more familiar to his old pal (who had not seen Paris since 1921).
He thus wrote to Schnellock of the area around Les Halles: "Off
the Market are crooked streets, ill-lit, very dilapidated in character, and full of refuse. There is a powerful stench in the air—so
powerful, in fact, that it steeps through to the Metro station. At
first it seems like stale urine, then it changes to fish, and then to
cheese and leeks. It brings back tender memories of Delancey
Street Bridge, under the span on the New York side" (34). Around
the St. Germain quarter on Sunday mornings he felt "a fever in the
streets" and ventured that there was "nothing like it anywhere,
except perhaps on the East Side" (41). The suburban town of St.
Cloud, perched on the Seine, seemed "a little bit like Sheepshead

Bay" (36), whereas the red-light district around the rue Blondel recalled "certain vague areas off Chatham Square" and the lively rue Montmartre presented "scenes reminiscent of Bedford Avenue near the Fountain" (33, 84). In the immigrant neighborhood around the place d'Italie, he also felt a sense of déjà vu: "You look down one street and it seems like the end of the world is at hand; down another and you feel that you are standing at Eastern Parkway near Atlantic Avenue, Brooklyn; down another and it is Bensonhurst or Ulmer Park" (40). While one avenue stretched toward impending disaster, others appeared to recede into the past, into the drab but familiar terrain of Brooklyn; Miller saw his liminal situation, between two lives and two cultures, mirrored in the topography of Paris.

In his wandering he confronted the need to "place" himself in Paris, to conduct the mapping which would enable him to circulate there as easily as he had in New York. Although his personal life was in disorder, Miller interiorized his new habitat in a systematic way. "The first thing any man ought to do in a foreign country is to buy a map—and study it," he wrote Schnellock, adding that he often spent an hour "poring over the map" before striking out for some new section of the city. "Paris is like a wheel," he observed, "and if you keep the hub in mind the spokes take care of themselves."[9] Another geographical aid Miller employed was the planimeter found at major intersections:

> The map of Paris is circumscribed by a circle. In the middle of the map is a knob to which a pointer is attached. Along the pointer are letters and kilometers. Below the map on a roll is a coil of paper with the names of the streets alphabetically arranged. You want to find the rue de Lappe, or the rue Blondel? Turn to L on this big ticker tape and you see opposite the name of the street a letter and a figure. You point the pointer to the figure indicated, which runs around the circle of the city, and then look down your pointer for the letter. There precisely is the street you want to find, and the distance from the center of the finder, which is the Place du Carrousel. Very very simple and very ingenious.[10]

This meticulous explanation reflects his compulsive concern for map-reading and orientation, for locating "precisely . . . the street

you want to find." Though in later life Miller preferred the panorama of the Pacific coast, during his Paris decade he was—in
Poe's phrase—a "man of the crowd," a being drawn irresistibly to
the streets and alleys of the city to study the passing throngs and
to absorb the complex, changing spectacle of urban life. Part of his
interest was pragmatic: opportunities for meals, drinks, sexual
encounters, or overnight flops could be discovered only on the
street. But Miller also derived intellectual and aesthetic stimulation from the physical environment of the city.

Initially, he seems to have been entranced by romantic images; near the end of his first Sunday in Paris, he stopped on the
Pont du Carrousel to contemplate the "ghostly" form of Notre
Dame: "I am on the verge of tears. The beauty of it is suffocating
me and there is no one to whom I can communicate even a
fraction of my feelings" (25). On another evening, he was overcome by the sight of the city's most famous street: "The Champs
Elysées . . . gets me by the throat. I had never believed it to be so
beautiful" (33). Typically Miller—who had ambitions as a water-
colorist—responded to the visual charm of the city by composing
verbal tableaus for his artistic mentor. Even an ordinary nightfall
might produce a remarkable scene:

> It is winter and the trees do not obscure the sky. One can look
> between the naked boughs and observe the colors changing
> from rust and purple to lilac, to Payne's gray and then to deep
> blue and indigo. Along the Boulevard Malesherbes, long after
> the crepuscular glow of evening, the gaunt trees with their
> black boughs gesticulating, stretch out in infinite series,
> somber, spectral, their trunks vivid as cigar ash. (27)

Through such passages, Miller tried to preserve evanescent Parisian images; such compositions enabled him to consolidate his
impressions of place and to appropriate the city streets as imaginative material—to possess the landscape, as Emerson once put it.

For Miller one facet of the city's enchantment was the strangeness of the French language; though his pronunciation at first
baffled native speakers, he enjoyed conversation in bars and cafés,
read Gide and Proust to expand his vocabulary, and went to movies
to sharpen his ear for slang.. He announced his determination to
write in French, adding that he loved "the way the adjectives pile

up, and the modifying clauses, the swing, the sonority, the elegance, the subtlety of it" (50). He elsewhere assured Schnellock: "When one has a feeling for words, when one sleeps with a dictionary by one's side, how puny are the difficulties of a strange tongue." Miller commented in the same letter on "the abracadabra of the signs" which identified bars and restaurants and insisted that French made "even the names of the streets sound divine." He mused, "Maybe I will stroll along the Rue de l'Ancienne Comédie, or in the street of the old dove cotes Rue du Vieux Colombier."[11] On another occasion he pondered a walk "on the street of the Mauvais-Garçons, or Le Roi-de-Sicile, or Les Quatre-Vents" (65), flaunting his knowledge of quaint place names in the inner city. Perhaps influenced by Proust (who dilated on the spell of place names), Miller contemplated the etymologies of street names as clues to a buried past.

Curiously, his letters contain several antiquarian reflections and fantasies. At the Lutetian arena in the Latin Quarter, he imagined that the "ghosts of the slain" rose up out of the mist at midnight; on the rue St. Denis, said to be the oldest street in Paris, he traced the route of the Roman legions, of the Knights Templar, and of the martyred St. Denis himself (38, 47). Along the quai des Célestins, he followed the footsteps of the scorned and censured Rabelais, and at the Hôtel St. Paul he mused "long and ruefully" on the fate of Charles the Silly (Charles VI), perhaps identifying with the royal fool garbed in rags and "eaten by ulcers and vermin" after his "shameless" wife had betrayed him (46). Seen in the context of American expatriation from Washington Irving to Henry James, Miller's antiquarianism seems initially to partake of that nostalgia for tradition which motivated many nineteenth-century travelers to return to the Old World. But he responded to French history chiefly insofar as it recorded instances of injustice; from the outset Paris was for him both a colossal emblem of human misery and, increasingly, a symbol reflective of his own sufferings. In its geographical configuration and its historical landmarks, the city embodied reminders of cruelty and death. Miller would express this idea even more trenchantly in *Tropic of Cancer*, projecting the city as a veritable site of blood sacrifice, a scene of trial and torture.

Although Miller was dazzled by "the glamour of the city" (25), he took a deeper interest in the squalor and ugliness of Paris. The ancient quarters exerted an irresistible fascination: he sought out the "frightfully crooked, dismal, and narrow" streets of the St. Antoine quarter where the "scum" seemed to thrive; he cataloged the deformed types near the boulevard de Sébastopol, where he observed a breed of "demented" old women with mangy hair, prowling about "in carpet slippers, their clothes in tatters, soiled with garbage and filth of the gutters" (46). Some insight into Miller's preoccupation with wretchedness emerges from his sketch of a dingy neighborhood around the rue de l'Ouest in the fourteenth arrondissement:

> Always in these squalid districts the streets reveal the grotesque aspects of humanity. The imbecilic dwarfs of Velázquez, the wretches and cripples of Fantin-Latour, the idiots of Chagall, the monsters created by Goya—all these pass now in review, brush up against one in filthy tatters, mumbling to themselves, singing or cursing, staggering under heavy burdens or stopping to pick a crust from the gutter. It is cruel, no doubt, to call this glorious, but I must confess that in contrast to these sights the glitter of the grands boulevards seems pale and lifeless. This is humanity in the raw, the endless procession of that prolific spawn at the bottom on whose backs the boulevardiers climb in greed and lust. (23)

Miller's interest in the "squalid districts" of Paris sprang not from sympathy for the masses but from a practical sense that such purlieus offered more material for the writer. If the "glitter" of the boulevards typified the lifeless bourgeois preoccupation with material display, the twisted figures of the Paris poor expressed a more interesting struggle for dignity and survival. Yet in calling the spectacle of dwarfs and cripples "glorious," Miller also betrayed a certain aloofness, perhaps symptomatic of his anxiety that these unfortunate types in "filthy tatters" might just prefigure his own Parisian fate.

Day after day Miller checked his notebook for new places to investigate, consulted a map, and then sallied into the streets to scout nondescript areas like the warehouse district at Bercy or offbeat attractions like the dog cemetery at St. Ouen. He tracked down odd exhibits and tiny galleries; he attended a meeting of the

Club de l'Ecran and listened to a heated debate—in a language he then scarcely understood—on French cinema. He also developed a preoccupation with the shabby red-light districts of Paris and kept careful notes on his nocturnal forays. "Around Réaumur-Sébastopol station on the Metro things begin to look up," he wrote. "It gets thick. It gets rotten. Whores dive out from the hallways and cafés" (33). With Hemingway's journalist friend Guy Hickok, he sought out the tiny (and now nonexistent) rue Asselin, "a street packed with the lowest dives where the Algerians and the Arabs get their hump" (49). His *recherches* by day and night soon led to the discovery of a mysterious city of strange sights and esoteric revelations—virtually the same Paris that Brassaï (later to become his friend) was then photographing.[12] Miller had located this secret Paris, however, through his own investigations, and he listed for Schnellock some of the curiosities that he meant to write about: the legend of the *pissoirs,* the ham and iron fair, the *abattoir hippophagique* (horse slaughterhouse), the mummies at the Trocadéro museum, the "Mussulman's" cemetery in Père Lachaise, toilets on the Right Bank and toilets on the Left, the lesbians at the Jockey Club and the "fairies" on the rue de Lappe. He also named several streets and squares which held a peculiar fascination: the boulevard Richard Lenoir, the Villa Malakoff, the place Violet and the place Vauban, the rue Blomet, and the rue Mademoiselle (48). Miller's perambulations etched the topography of the city into his consciousness; of his urban epiphanies he later wrote: "There are scarcely any streets in Paris I did not get to know. On every one of them I could erect a tablet commemorating in letters of gold some rich new experience, some deep realization, some moment of illumination."[13]

Mapping this private world in copious letters to Schnellock, Miller seems to have followed the example of the surrealists who had—with the publication of Aragon's *Le Paysan de Paris* (1926) and Breton's *Nadja* (1928)—begun to treat Paris itself as a kind of master text, a repository of cryptic signs and visionary images.[14] Almost as soon as he arrived in Paris, Miller had fallen under the influence of surrealism, first through Buñuel's film *Un Chien Andalou* and then through Soupault's *L'homme coupé en tranches* and the second manifesto of the surrealist group. He alluded frequently in letters to new surrealist works and confided to

Schnellock: "I believe in [surrealism] with all my heart. It is an emancipation from classicism, realism, naturalism, and all the other outmoded isms of the past and present" (28). We cannot be sure whether Miller had read either *Le Paysan de Paris* or *Nadja* when he was conducting his investigations of 1930, but the surrealist emphasis upon the spontaneous eruption of dreamlike, revelatory images unmistakably affected his perception of certain Parisian scenes.[15]

One evening in St. Germain, for instance, he came upon the secluded Square de Furstenberg, which he described in hallucinatory terms as

> A deserted spot, bleak, spectral at night, containing in the center four black trees which have not yet begun to blossom. These four bare trees have the poetry of T. S. Eliot. They are intellectual trees, nourished by the stones, swaying with a rhythm cerebral, the lines punctuated by dots and dashes, by asterisks and exclamation points. . . . It is very, very Lesbienne here, very sterile, hybrid, full of forbidden longings (42)

On two separate occasions he was taken aback by the nightmarish sight of butchered horses hanging in the marketplace, "enormous carcasses . . . still dripping blood" and swinging "in a dazzling, eerie light, all stiff and cold" (34). He remarked that "it is only when the horse is seen split open, and hung from a peg, that one realizes what a big animal it is" (23). On another outing, he had a sudden vision (at the Jaurès metro station) of an unreal city: "The rails fall away into the canal, the long caterpillar with sides lacquered in Chinese red dips like a roller coaster. It is not Paris, it is not Coney Island—it is a crepuscular mélange of all the cities of Europe and Central America" (42). Miller found this sight so arresting that he repeated the passage almost verbatim in *Tropic of Cancer*, just as he included other signs of his passion for surrealism.

These random excursions broadened Miller's knowledge of the city so markedly that by early August he assured Schnellock: "I know Paris now like I know the dictionary" (61). In accumulating practical, local information, he had at the same time acquired a vast array of new ideas for writing. Indeed, Miller perceived the stimulating effect of his topographical inquiries: "Each day I go out nets me at least ten or fifteen pages" (47). His rounds in fact yielded so many provocative insights that he fretted about getting them all down on paper. In one letter he pictured himself in a café, jotting his notes on a paper tablecloth: "I get so damned chockfull of ideas that I am afraid they will dribble away before I get back to the [typewriting] machine" (42). Wickes has aptly remarked that for Miller, "Walking in the city was a creative act in itself. He was forever composing in his head as he walked, the writing as vivid to him as if he had put it down on paper."[16] The experience of discovering Paris gave Miller the confidence that he could "turn out a book a month" (43), and by mid-June 1930 he was working at such a feverish pace that he reported (in a crudely ambiguous simile): "The stuff is pouring out of me like diarrhea" (58).

But even as Miller discovered new material for writing, he continued to struggle with the problem of his not-quite-voluntary exile. Personal hardships forced him to confront repeatedly the question of why he was in Paris—and whether he ought to remain there. After dispatching a handful of supplicatory telegrams to America, he admitted to Schnellock: "It is very hard when you are three thousand miles away and there is nothing but a vast ocean and a vast silence separating you from home" (44). The anxiety of exile, of being estranged from home and homeland, caused Miller to feel more keenly his own marginal status. While claiming an exhaustive knowledge of Paris, he also conceded that he knew "all the places—from the outside" (62). His comment discloses both a persistent sense of exclusion from some quintessential Paris— perhaps accessible only to the native speaker—and a frank acknowledgement of the difficulties of assimilating a complex urban scene. Miller found himself in a paradoxical limbo, prohibited from penetrating the real Paris yet unable to leave its precincts. June paid a five-week visit to Paris in the fall of 1930, but that reunion only seemed to exacerbate Miller's anxieties. At times he saw himself as a virtual "prisoner" (44, 63), and in November 1930, after eight months in France, he informed Schnellock: "I have decided to try to return [to the U. S.]—despite everything. Can't stick it any more—a life more miserable than a dog's. . . . Believe me, I didn't want to return but I simply must. I'm worn out with the daily struggle for meals, with the uncertainty of a room, etc." (66). Just as Miller was about to give up, though, his luck changed: Richard Galen Osborn, Michael Fraenkel, and Alfred Perlès successively provided lodging, and Miller landed a job in 1931 as a copyreader at the *Herald Tribune*. But his insecurities erupted later that year, after another tumultuous visit from June; Miller refused to be "stranded" in Paris and woefully remarked: "Two years of vagabondage has taken a lot out of me" (87).

While Miller was working out the problem of place, resolving the question of which city to call "home," he was simultaneously undergoing a crisis of confidence and identity which spilled out in his correspondence to Schnellock. The sense of failure which had haunted his life in Brooklyn now dogged him in Paris, and at the end of one letter he broke out bitterly: "Why does nobody want what I write? Jesus, when I think of being 38, and poor, and unknown, I get furious. I refuse to live this way forever" (37). Although he had learned much about Paris, he reluctantly admitted: "I know everything but how to earn a living—tant pis! In other words, I am the same miserable failure as always" (61). Poverty and obscurity both seemed to deny the self-worth that Miller wished to assert; he felt himself "always living on the edge of disaster," coming apart psychologically (71). Recurrent allusions to Van Gogh betray his identification with that deranged artist: "Something's got to happen soon—or it will be the end. I'll be cutting one of my ears off, or a nose, and sending it on as a Christmas gift," he jested darkly (89). One year after his arrival in Paris he characterized himself as "always on the border of insanity, due to worry, hunger, etc." (79). We cannot know how close Miller came to actual madness; probably he exaggerated his mental distress to elicit Schnellock's sympathy. But lack of food and shelter did force Miller to rely upon his own resources, contriving strategies for survival. His precarious situation also raised basic questions—about his ongoing sense of displacement, his aims as a writer, and his need to create (like his hero, Walt Whitman) an identity or persona commensurate with his robust ambition.

In 1931–32, these issues began to converge in ways which illuminate the intricate relation of place to self and writing. As the project of mapping the city generated a plethora of ideas, impressions, and episodes, Miller began to conceive of "a rollicking book" which might emerge from the notes piling up "like

dirty linen" (53). He would convert his discoveries about Paris
into a pungent narrative of expatriate life. But to do so, he recognized the urgent need to purge his literary style: "Out with the
balderdash, out with the slush and drivel, out with the apos-
trophes, the mythologic mythies, the sly innuendoes, the vast and
pompous learning" (64). The task of revising *Crazy Cock* in 1930
had made him conscious of the "sentimentality" and "crap" in his
writing; he finally realized that in striving for rhetorical effect, he
had not yet found his own voice. "What I must do, before blowing
out my brains," he concluded, "is to write a few simple con-
fessions in plain Milleresque language" (65). That is, he suddenly
grasped the necessity of writing *as himself*, of adopting the first-
person pronoun and the candid, personal style he had been using
in his letters to Schnellock. He would, moreover, inscribe "con-
fessions," autobiographical revelations, rather than projecting
stories about fictional characters. In various ways, the city itself
had proved conducive to this reconsideration of purpose. "Here in
Paris," he wrote, "I have done more deep, serious thinking about
writing than ever before in my life" (73). By early 1931, Miller had
become disgusted with his overdetermined novel-in-progress and
looked forward to the revolutionary work to follow: "This book,
[*Crazy Cock*], has been so carefully and painstakingly plotted out,
the notes are so copious and exhaustive, that I feel cramped,
walled in, suffocated. When I get thru I want to explode. I will
explode in the Paris book. The hell with form, style, expression
and all those pseudo-paramount things which beguile the critics.
I want to get myself across this time—and direct as a knife thrust"
(72). As this passage indicates, Miller was on the verge of a major
breakthrough. But his reconstruction of writing—his decision to
represent himself, to speak in his own voice, and to work from
lived experience—also led to a disturbing realization: "Certain
things are beginning to clarify in my mind. I think I know the
direction I want to take. Unfortunately, it is a direction that will
further alienate the reader. It's almost as though I had made up my
mind to prevent people from liking me" (73). If he allowed himself
to "explode"—to express subversive or blasphemous opinions, to
use forbidden, obscene language, and to represent illicit sexual
acts—he might also get himself expelled from France. Yet Miller
had become convinced that not only his literary prospects but

also his sanity and selfhood depended on writing the revolutionary text that he had in mind. On 24 August 1931 he defiantly
vowed: "I start tomorrow on the Paris book: first person, uncensored, formless—fuck everything!" (80).

During the nine months which marked the gestation of the
first draft, Miller felt himself undergoing a rebirth. By the summer of 1932, with a manuscript of the "Paris book" in hand, he
could observe: "I have gone thru the most important period of my
life these last two and a half years" (101). The writing process had
effected a dramatic new relation to his own experience; from the
misery of his first year in Paris he had constructed an earthy
narrative of survival. The unshackled first-person perspective enabled him to voice his own "barbaric yawp" and to project a
persona liberated from worry, a figure at once cynical and exuberant, flaunting his appetite for food, sex, art, literature, and life
itself. Looking back on the project he wrote:

> The great importance of *Tropic of Cancer*, as I now see it, lies
> in the fact that it summed up (alas, all too incompletely for
> my satisfaction) a whole period of the past. I suppose, nay I
> am quite sure, I shall never write another book like that. It
> was like a surgical operation. And out of it I emerged whole
> again. Though when I embarked on it, it was with no inten-
> tion to cure myself of anything—rather to rid, to divest my-
> self of the horrible wounds that I had allowed to fester in me.
> (116)

Miller immediately realized that in creating the book he had recreated himself. He began to affect the defiance of poverty and
despair expressed by the ebullient rogue of the narrative. As with
Stein and Hemingway, the experience of exile had simultaneously
jarred Miller's sense of self and created the freedom to invent a
fundamentally new identity. His narrative obliged him to relive
and reimagine the ordeal of his first two years in Paris, yet the task
effected a kind of writing cure, healing psychic wounds and, by
bringing the book itself into existence, relieving him of the burden of literary failure.

Even as he was inscribing a new self in *Tropic of Cancer*,
Miller was also entering into a relationship that accelerated his
personal transformation. In late 1931 Richard Osborn introduced

him to Anaïs Nin, and by early 1932, Nin (who had already endured her own struggle with displacement) was providing financial support as well as intellectual and libidinal satisfaction. Under the happy influence of Nin's interest in his career, Miller flourished. "Now my whole life is opening up," he reported, "there is some kind of exfoliation going on" (106). Among other results, the liaison facilitated an extraordinary literary exchange: the two shared an enthusiasm for D. H. Lawrence, and as Miller's treatment of sexuality in *Tropic of Cancer* stimulated Nin's composition of erotica, her diaries opened him to the power of autobiographical reflection. Nin's generosity also permitted Miller to resolve his longstanding ambivalence about exile by relieving the want which had complicated his feelings about Paris. On a practical as well as an emotional level, Nin made the city habitable for Miller, just as Beatrice, June, and his mother had made Brooklyn finally unlivable. If Nin became, as Ferguson suggests, his "shadow wife and shadow mother," she played the maternal role in a way which gradually freed Miller from emotional dependence.[17] "Since I know Anaïs my life in Paris has become almost a dream," he remarked in Germanic fashion in October 1932 (107). As a displaced writer who had finally adapted himself to a foreign place, he declared: "I don't want to return to America. Nothing but a catastrophe can make me go back. This is my world, and I knew it long, long ago, and I only regret it took so long to make the decision" (93).

Paris had become Miller's "world" through personal privation and through arduous geographical reorientation. By April 1932 he had begun to think of himself as an "expatriate" and pointedly declared: "I am no longer an American" (94). Thus the revolution of writing in *Tropic of Cancer*, which signaled the emergence of a new, cosmopolitan self, also produced a psychological detachment. By 1932 he was ready to let go of his American identity, to proclaim himself a man without a country. "I feel free of all cults, isms, movements, countries, latitudes, and philosophies," he announced (152). But Paris nevertheless remained his point of reference, the city which sustained his intellectual freedom: "Whenever I make a journey," he conceded, "it will always be Paris that I want to think of coming back to—not New York" (95). Although Miller still retained a vestigial attachment to Brooklyn (in 1933

Figure 16. Henry Miller in Paris, around 1932.

he requested a photo of the Driggs Avenue house where he had been raised), he realized just how instrumental his adopted city had been in his personal transformation (fig. 16). In a letter to Schnellock he posed a question which summed up the relation of place and self: "What would I have been," he asked, "without Paris?" (108).

The book written to explain the city "for all time" (119) was no mere travel guide; Miller carried out his threat to "explode in the Paris book" by producing a text which even today retains its power to offend and disturb. Radical in almost every respect, the book resists generic categorization, sliding between novel and autobiography when not veering into poetry or philosophy. Leon Lewis calls it "a mutant of sorts, a journal that resembles a diary, a packet of sketches, a rough collection of essays, an assemblage of anecdotes."[18] Its apparent formlessness defies readers to locate plot or design, as episodes unfold in a seemingly arbitrary sequence. Miller creates the impression of random experience and impromptu composition, an unstudied narrative of everyday banalities, interwoven with fantasies and diatribes which erupt suddenly and terminate ambiguously. Attention shifts from the narrator to friends and acquaintances whose obsessive schemes skew the book's focus. On another level, Miller further violates literary decorum with unabashed obscenities; he revels in sexual transactions with whores, whom he depicts reductively as mere "cunts." He imagines his work as a "gob of spit in the face of Art," a repudiation of genteel literature and its puritanical avoidance of human creatureliness. Scatology thus figures significantly; one episode concludes with the narrator contemplating "two enormous turds" floating in a bidet. "There is only one thing which interests me vitally now," he declared, "and that is the recording of all that which is omitted in books."[19] He wanted to thrust before the reader shocking, previously unprintable words and images. Miller saw his book as a revolt against the taboos of polite, commercial fiction; he wanted to write the "last book," which would speak the raw, unspeakable truth of the human situation.

Influenced by Michael Fraenkel and Walter Lowenfels, self-styled prophets of entropy, Miller further railed against the deadening effects of religion and morality, perceiving (with Spengler) the decline of the Western world in the aftermath of the Great War. Miller's work was also darkened, as Lowenfels later pointed out, by a consciousness of the war to come, by a sense of the pathetic inevitability of a new cycle of mass destruction.[20] *Tropic of Cancer* unleashes a torrent of anger against official high culture and institutional religion; Miller thought that the world was "rotting away, dying piecemeal" and conceived of his book as a bomb which might blow the established order "to smithereens" (26). Opposing traditional Western aesthetics, in which (as Joyce's Stephen Dedalus reminds us) beauty manifests itself as wholeness, harmony, and radiance, Miller advanced a counteraesthetic of disintegration, chaos, and ugliness. The prevailing metaphor of disease, epitomized by cancer, conveys the grotesque, moribund condition of modern life. As Ihab Hassan has observed, Miller's "images of decay burst into apocalyptic visions."[21] In the exhaustion of the present era Miller foresees the emergence of a "new world, a jungle world in which the lean spirits roam with sharp claws" (99). Following Nietzsche, he praises the inhuman; following Rabelais, he admonishes, *"Fay ce que vouldras!"* (Do what you want to!) In the face of a lifeless world he shouts his credo: "Do anything, but let it produce joy. Do anything, but let it yield ecstasy" (252).

The formal discontinuities of *Tropic of Cancer* seem well suited to the author's anarchical vision. As in the work of Joyce, Woolf, Faulkner, and other contemporaries, the decentered structure of Miller's text and the willed incoherence of certain passages project a global, metaphysical breakdown. Yet the book nevertheless possesses a focal consciousness, a narratorial presence. Within its disorganization and dissonance, Miller composes a Whitmanesque song of self: "I am going to sing for you, a little off key perhaps, but I will sing," he promises (2). His song is poignant but elusive, defined as much by its silences as by its outpourings. At irregular intervals, however, his refrain breaks through narrative and declamation to reveal intimate desires, resentments, and anxieties. Miller alludes in these isolated passages to a private dilemma nearly obscured by the escapades of friends or by his narrator's fulminations against the sickness of the age.

In fact this strain is less a song of self than an expression of certain qualities which differentiate the narrator of *Tropic of Cancer* from the living writer who corresponded with Emil Schnellock. Jay Martin underscores this point by remarking that "at the time of his writing the main character of the book and Miller were not at all identical."[22] Unlike the "Brooklyn boy" who wrote affectionately to his old friend, this expatriate persona taunts the reader by declaring: "I will sing while you croak, I will dance over your dirty corpse" (2). Although Miller at times waxes sentimental in the letters, the protagonist of *Tropic of Cancer* writes to shock and to offend. More self-reliant and self-possessed than Schnellock's correspondent, the narrator exults: "I have no money, no resources, no hopes. I am the happiest man alive" (1). Within this paradox he articulates the absurd, existential freedom he possesses. Indeed, his narrative proceeds from the assumption that he has already become an artist. In contrast to Miller, who during his first two years in Paris worried incessantly about food and shelter and considered returning to the United States, the hero of *Tropic of Cancer* hopes "never to leave" France. The author underscores this difference when the maladjusted Van Norden (Wambly Bald) asks the narrator: "Listen, Joe, don't you ever get homesick? You're a funny guy . . . you seem to like it over here" (106). Though Miller alludes to the multiple relocations of 1930–31, his protagonist—whom we may for the sake of convenience identify as "Henry"—rarely expresses concern about displacement. In a rare moment, when Boris (Michael Fraenkel) is trying to rent the room Henry uses at the Villa Borghese (18, Villa Seurat), the narrator complains, "How the hell can a man write when he doesn't know where he's going to sit the next half-hour?" (32). But typically he celebrates his freedom to move about at will, as when he parts company with Serge: "It's as though I had been released from prison. I look at the world with new eyes" (72). Even hunger—which bedeviled the living writer—figures more often as phagomania than as pain; the narrator's food fantasies provoke the wry observation that if life consists of what a man is thinking all day (as Emerson declared), his own life is "nothing but a big intestine" (69). Repeatedly the protagonist of *Tropic of Cancer* rises above the indignities of Miller's own experience through mockery which implies a Nietzschean transcendence of suffering.

Yet in one significant respect the expatriate persona seems more vulnerable than his flesh-and-blood counterpart. Whereas the author who corresponded with Schnellock evinced only passing concern about June and rarely indulged in self-pity, the book's narrator exposes his emotional scars. At crucial junctures Henry details the suffering inflicted by his estranged wife, Mona, and alludes to episodes with her which have conditioned his experience of Paris. Curiously, though, she figures in *Tropic of Cancer* more as an absence than a presence. For long stretches the narrator's ribald adventures occupy his attention and occlude his memory. The textual evidence of her power lies partly in the narrator's avoidance of her name and memory (he speaks directly of Mona in only a half-dozen scattered passages) and partly in an extraordinary confession which occurs past the midpoint of his account. In a real sense, Henry's separation from Mona and his struggle to break her spell form the obscure yet essential context of *Tropic of Cancer*. At the outset he acknowledges: "I was sent here for a reason I have not yet been able to fathom" (1). Miller thus frames the narrative as an inquiry into this problem, an attempt to discern the purpose of Henry's European banishment; he has been "sent" by Mona for reasons associated with her mysterious erotic life, yet he senses as well the operation of some cosmic destiny and seeks by writing the book to clarify the meaning of his painful and joyous exile.

Miller's isolated reflections on Mona provide a vital perspective on the narrator's Paris exploits, limning a treacherous relationship which explains his cynical view of others' infidelities and suggests a rationale (if not an excuse) for his callous treatment of women. At the end of his opening section—Miller avoids the convention of formal chapters—the narrator contrasts two separate occasions when he has been in Paris with Mona. The first alludes to a visit in 1928, a period when Paris meant little to him; he was "fed up with cathedrals and squares" and consumed by jealousy over Mona's interest in an artist named Borowski (transparently, Ossip Zadkine). At a café Henry acts out his anger by "dancing with every slut in the place"; he tries to have sex in a bathroom with an American "cunt" and ejaculates on her "beautiful gown," all the time expecting, even hoping, that Mona will come "to fetch [him]." This exhibition unfolds, significantly, between nearly identical references to untouched notebooks and lifeless manuscripts; hence the narrator concludes his evening performance by vomiting in the hotel room all over "the suits and gowns and the galoshes and canes and the notebooks [he] never touched and the manuscripts cold and dead" (18), thereby implying a connection between literary impotence and sexual frustration.

The second scene, a year or so later, finds the narrator waiting for a visit from Mona; when she fails to arrive at the Gare St. Lazare (fig. 17), he strolls back to Montparnasse and discovers her sitting at the Dôme. Despite their previous difficulties, he immediately succumbs to her: "I hear not a word because she is beautiful and I love her and now I am happy and willing to die." After intercourse, however, old anxieties emerge: "How good to feel her body again! But for how long? Will it last this time? Already I have a presentiment that it won't" (20). As if probing the origins of his mistrust, Henry recollects the snowy day he left New York: he recalls Mona at the window, waving goodbye, while across the street a heavily jowled man looked on. Because this suspicious observer—"a fetus with a cigar in its mouth"—is actually Mona's secret admirer and benefactor, the memory of her blank expression at the window haunts the narrator as a sign of her deceit. In the Paris hotel room, he feels the "miracle" of her presence, but he also notices the bedbugs in her hair, the thinness of her dress, and the compulsiveness of her behavior ("Must have a bath. Must have this. Must have that. Must, must, must."). When money runs short, moreover, he understands the meaning of her cable to the cigar-sucking "fetus" (21).

After this disquieting visit, Mona seemingly vanishes from the narrative; in the next hundred pages her name appears only briefly, when Henry in a symbolic gesture starts to wear his wedding ring on his pinkie finger (54). By shifting his attention to the activities of Boris, Cronstadt (Walter Lowenfels), Sylvester and Tania (Joe and Bertha Schrank), Carl (Alfred Perlès), Marlowe (Samuel Putnam), and Van Norden, the narrator signals his immersion in an expatriate milieu and his determination to forget the woman who sent him to Paris. In the midst of a long section on the sexual fixations of Carl and Van Norden, however, he reveals that "now and then" he still gets cablegrams from Mona announcing her passage on the next boat. Yet she never arrives, nor do her promised letters, leading Henry to confide: "I haven't any more expectations in that direction" (152). Insisting that time and distance have dimmed his memories, he sorts through ambivalent feelings about Mona and feels released from old bonds:

> There are days, . . . when the sun is out and I get off the beaten path and think about her hungrily. Now and then, despite my grim satisfaction, I get to thinking about another way of life, get to wondering if it would make a difference having a young, restless creature by my side. The trouble is I can hardly remember what she looks like, nor even how it feels to have my arms about her. Everything that belongs to the past seems to have fallen into the sea; I have memories, but the images have lost their vividness, they seem dead and

desultory, like time-bitten mummies stuck in a quagmire. If I try to recall my life in New York I get a few splintered fragments, nightmarish and covered with verdigris. It seems as if my own proper existence had come to an end somewhere, just where exactly I can't make out. I'm not an American any more, nor a New Yorker, and even less a European, or a Parisian. I haven't any allegiance, any responsibilities, any hatreds, any worries, any prejudices, any passion. I'm neither for nor against. I'm a neutral. (152–53)

This declaration marks an apparent turning point in the narrator's experience. He senses that in crossing the Atlantic he has jettisoned his own past and that his "proper existence" as an American citizen has ended. Celebrating his escape from emotional loyalties, he styles himself a "neutral" and defines his situation in terms of absolute displacement.

The narrator's declaration of independence from his hometown and native land may of course be understood as a reaction to Mona's cruelty. But his refusal here to assume a provisional Parisian identity—to insist, rather, on his expatriate status—indicates a curious relation to the city of exile. Only in a later passage do we learn that his experience of Paris has likewise been tainted by his involvement with Mona. At last he concedes what his long silences have already implied—his desperate need to repress the thought of her powerful presence: "I couldn't allow myself to think about her very long; if I had I would have jumped off the bridge. It's strange. I had become so reconciled to this life without her, and yet if I thought about her only for a minute it was enough to pierce the bone and marrow of my contentment and shove me back again into the agonizing gutter of my wretched past" (177). He admits the long history of his obsession with Mona and confesses that Paris presents continual reminders of their tempestuous encounters: "Sometimes when I feel that I am absolutely free of it all, suddenly, in rounding a corner perhaps, there will bob up a little square, a few trees and a bench, a deserted spot where we stood and had it out, where we drove each other crazy with bitter, jealous scenes" (178). Even as the narrative itself registers his attempt to forget Mona, Henry's walks through the streets of Paris conversely trigger recollections of her. Place has been contaminated by memory.

Indeed, the narrator subsequently confesses that he can go nowhere in Paris without confronting his own terrible longing for Mona; he imagines that the very buildings and statues have been "saturated with [his] anguish." Whereas Mona would forget their walks together, Henry recalls each site through specific, indelible associations: "She wouldn't remember that at a certain corner I had stopped to pick up her hairpin, or that, when I bent down to tie her laces, I remarked the spot on which her foot had rested and that it would remain there forever, even after the cathedrals had been demolished and the whole Latin civilization had been wiped out forever and ever" (179). The consequence of this fetishizing is that, for the narrator, Paris itself enters into the imaginary; his longing has transfigured the city, incorporating its streets and squares into the symbolic scheme of his desire. He acknowledges the existence of a secret Paris "whose *arrondissements* are undefined," a fantastic metropolis constructed by his loneliness and hunger for Mona. He further concedes, "This Paris, to which I alone had the key, hardly lends itself to a tour, even with the best of intentions; it is a Paris that has to be lived, that has to be experienced each day in a thousand different forms of torture, a Paris that grows inside you like a cancer, and grows and grows until you are eaten away by it" (179). Here the narrator makes a crucial revelation: through the power which Mona holds over him, even the city of exile has been transformed into a site of "torture," a zone of sickness. Though he struggles to forget Mona, he discloses that his separation from her has profoundly affected his relationship to Paris. *Tropic of Cancer* hinges in effect on his effort to reclaim the city as a habitable space uncontaminated by memory, to construct an expatriate identity and a new relationship to place.

This predicament of exile without escape helps to account for the violent contradictions of Miller's view of Paris. The narrator's representation of the city fuses conflicting images which express the paradoxical extremes of his obsession for Mona. Yet such a reading oversimplifies his projection of place, for the expatriate persona inscribes a cityscape which manifests not only his personal psychodrama but also his complex response to the crisis of modernity. Like *The Waste Land*, *Tropic of Cancer* crystallizes the collective experience of the modern age; like the "unreal city" of Eliot's poem, Miller's Paris is "a crepuscular melange of all the cities of Europe and Central America" (4). It condenses the wreckage of Western culture, providing graphic evidence of the moral and spiritual rot infecting its urban centers. But if Paris reflects the morbid condition of the global order ("the world is a cancer eating itself away"), it also possesses an extraordinary fertility as a source of signs. As represented by Miller's narrator, the metropolitan scene provides a myriad of tropes; these metaphors associate the city with profusion rather than depletion. Through the shifting figurality of place which conveys the multiplicity of urban experience, Henry strives to discover and articulate the reason for his exile in Paris. In short, the figure of the city as a social and geographical entity, as an emblem of cultural collapse, and as an embodiment of hunger and longing enables Miller to connect public and private crises, to merge the historical and the confessional.

The changing images of Paris also suggest the sometimes conflicting aims of Miller's narrative method. In one sense *Tropic of Cancer* displays the urge to achieve a radical realism, to expose the actual conditions of everyday life in the city. This impulse generates interior scenes of squalid simplicity like the hovel of Eugene and Anatole, where the butter is "hidden away in the commode" and the bed is "crawling" with insects (61–62), or the sordid hotel room in which Van Norden satisfies his sexual cravings (128). It also produces numerous topographical references to streets, cafés, and restaurants frequented by the expatriate narrator. Thus, for example, Henry reports: "The Rue Amélie is one of my favorite streets. It is one of those streets which by good fortune the municipality has forgotten to pave. Huge cobblestone spreading convexly from one side of the street to the other. Only one block long and narrow. The Hôtel Pretty is on this street. There is a little church, too, on the Rue Amélie" (66–67). The allusion seems purely documentary; but by describing a little street near the Invalides, the narrator also signifies his knowledge of the city and his preference for obscure neighborhoods over tourist sites. The persistent notation of street names in *Tropic of Cancer* in fact enables the reader to plot the narrator's movement, even as it discloses Miller's own obsessive concern for mapping.

Yet concrete topographical detail recurrently slides into surreal impression. That is, extravagant figurality pushes the narrative toward hallucinatory or dreamlike perception. When Henry traces his route home from the newspaper office "through the court of the Louvre, over the Pont des Arts, through the arcade," he arrives at the Quarter haunted by that other distracted newspaper man, Hemingway's Jake Barnes:

> In the blue of an electric dawn the peanut shells look wan and crumpled; along the beach of Montparnasse the water lilies bend and break. When the tide is on the ebb and only a few syphilitic mermaids are stranded in the muck, the Dôme looks like a shooting gallery that's been struck by a cyclone. Everything is slowly dribbling back to the sewer. For about an hour there is a deathlike calm during which the vomit is mopped up. Suddenly the trees begin to screech. From one end of the boulevard to the other a demented song rises up. It is like the signal that announces the close of the exchange. What hopes there were are swept up. The moment has come to void the last bagful of urine. The day is sneaking in like a leper. (161)

Dimly recalling the imagery of Eliot's "Fire Sermon," this passage exposes the hideous unreality which looms on the far side of realism and which pervades the secret Paris of Miller's narrator. The spectacle reveals the disease, dissipation, and madness beneath the surface glamor of Montparnasse; even trees "screech" in unnatural agony. Henry's surreal fantasies thus serve a double purpose, making tangible the grotesque form of his private suffering as they exhibit the deformity of modern experience. At another such moment, the narrator imagines himself in a room lined with "maps and charts"; from a window overlooking the Seine he observes "mud and desolation, streetlamps drowning, men and women choking to death, the bridges covered with houses, slaughterhouses of love." He has a vision of entropy in which "the universe has dwindled" and concludes of Paris (as had Eliot about London) that "the people who live here are dead" (64). This phantasmagoria merges psychic trauma with cultural disintegration to disclose the congruence between Miller's personal nightmare and the nightmare of history.

In another rhetorical move, the expatriate narrator attempts to cast his ordeal in mythic rather than historical terms, thus

transcending the problem of modernity by associating his exile
with archetypal experience. One obvious pattern is the descent
into the underworld: in this scheme, Paris figures as Henry's
"inferno," and (as in *The Waste Land*) Dante provides a recognizable model for the journey into darkness and suffering.[23] But a
more immediate influence is Strindberg's *Inferno*, which Miller's
narrator evokes in confessing his own struggle with despair. Recalling that Mona was at one time "saturated with Strindberg," he
decides to stop at the Pension Orfila to see the room in which the
dramatist wrestled with private demons. The visit allows Henry
to realize that he himself has "not yet come to the end of [his]
rope"; yet further reflection also enables him to grasp the mythic
import of Strindberg's Paris sojourn and (by extension) the possible object his own exile:

> I began to reflect on the meaning of that inferno which Strind-
> berg had so mercilessly depicted. And, as I ruminated, it began
> to grow clear to me, the mystery of his pilgrimage, the flight
> which the poet makes over the face of the earth and then, as if
> he had been ordained to re-enact a lost drama, the heroic
> descent to the very bowels of the earth, the dark and fearsome
> sojourn in the belly of the whale, the bloody struggle to
> liberate himself, to emerge clean of the past, a bright, gory sun
> god cast up on an alien shore. It was no mystery to me any
> longer why he and others (Dante, Rabelais, Van Gogh, etc.,
> etc.) had made their pilgrimage to Paris. I understood then
> why it is that Paris attracts the tortured, the hallucinated, the
> great maniacs of love. I understood why it is that here, at the
> very hub of the wheel, one can embrace the most fantastic,
> the most impossible theories, without finding them in the
> least strange; it is here that one reads again the books of his
> youth and the enigmas take on new meanings, one for every
> white hair. . . . Here all boundaries fade away and the world
> reveals itself for the mad slaughterhouse that it is. (181–82)

This lengthy passage conveys both the necessity of the poet's
odyssey and the inevitability of Paris as the exile's destination.
With Joyce's Stephen Dedalus, Henry suggests that the life of
writing requires "pilgrimage" and "flight," a deliberate forsaking of the known and familiar to embark on a quest that is at

once geographical and psychic. That is, the horizontal movement through space and the vertical plunge into the inferno imply a concomitant exploration of self, a probing of one's deepest needs and anxieties. Yet this "fearsome journey" into uncharted territory also creates an opportunity for change, for emerging as "a bright gory sun god cast up on an alien shore" or, alternatively, as a fabulous artificer. The departure from homeland entails both peril and possibility—the danger of annihilation and the prospect of radical transformation.

In its basic figurality, then, the trope of the hero's journey into the underworld and his subsequent reemergence among the living complements the other mythic pattern inscribed in the narrative, that of rebirth. Joseph Campbell makes explicit the frequent conjunction of these motifs in myth and legend.[24] As we have seen, Miller characterized the composition of *Tropic of Cancer* as a transformative process; not surprisingly, imagery of pregnancy or childbirth abounds. Yet the immediate uses of the trope vary dramatically. Early in the book, the narrator rhapsodizes about Tania as his personal "chaos" and declares to her: "I am still alive, kicking in your womb" (2). Later, he imagines *himself* "pregnant" with the narrative he is composing and insists that "the book has begun to grow inside [him]," causing him to "waddle awkwardly" as he walks the streets "big with child" (26). Then, in an extended allusion to childbirth, Miller writes that "Paris is . . . an obstetrical instrument that tears the living embryo from the womb and puts it in the incubator. Paris is the cradle of artificial births" (29). Exactly who or what the "living embryo" might be seems ambiguous until we discover that it refers to those expatriate writers who have been somehow reborn in Paris and thus paradoxically enabled to contemplate (and write about) their native cities: "Rocking here in the cradle each one slips back into his soil: one dreams back to Berlin, New York, Chicago, Vienna, Minsk. Vienna is never more Vienna than in Paris. Everything is raised to apotheosis" (29). In Miller's complex metaphor, one must go to Paris in order to recover an imaginative perspective on the place from which being and identity have first emerged. Yet the very passage entailed by exile produces a rebirth, creating a new self which can reflect upon the old precisely by virtue of this difference from itself.

These various formulations of the trope of rebirth, which generally assert Miller's sense of having reinvented himself through the writing of *Tropic of Cancer*, lead to a final, intimate reflection on the narrator's problems with women, which are rooted (he suspects) in the trauma of his own birth and in his inveterate longing for the maternal womb:

> Going back in a flash over the women I've known. It's like a chain which I've forged out of my own misery. Each one bound to the other. A fear of living separate, of staying born. The door of the womb always on the latch. Dread and longing. Deep in the blood the pull of paradise. The beyond. Always the beyond. It must have all started with the navel. They cut the umbilical cord, give you a slap on the ass, and presto! you're out in the world, adrift, a ship without a rudder. (287)

Placed in the context of Miller's enduring resentment of his hypercritical, rejecting mother, this confession helps to account for both the narrator's obsession with female genitalia (which erupts in a three-page meditation on the vagina) and the ferocity of his sexual conquests. Here Henry intuits a vital connection between "dread and longing": his "fear of living separate," deprived of a nurturing maternal presence, has produced the "misery" of intractable desire, the satyriasis which manifests itself in sexual exploitation, in futile attempts to achieve through violent, indiscriminate penetration a reentry into the paradisal womb. This confession also helps to explain Henry's conflicted response to Mona, who in sending him to Paris has reenacted the outrage of abandonment. The narrator protests: "She left me here to perish" (250). Her picture on the wall apparently triggers his angry disquisition on "the riddle of that thing which today is a called a 'crack' or a 'hole'" (249). And the confession finally suggests why the narrator's symbolic rebirth in Paris carries such dramatic significance. The engendering of an expatriate self through "artificial birth" produces a myth of personal origins which sublimates the trauma of natural birth and maternal rejection.[25]

In view of this sexual conflict, it is curious to note that Miller's narrator in several key passages metaphorizes Paris as female or associates it metonymically with prostitution and seduction. Henry represents the female body as urban topography when he describes intercourse with a "cunt" named Llona: "You entered on the Boulevard Jules-Ferry and came out at the Porte de la Villette. You dropped your sweetbreads into the tumbrils—red tumbrils with two wheels, naturally. At the confluence of the Ourcq and Marne, where the water sluices through the dikes and lies like glass under the bridges. Llona is lying there now" (7). In a metaphor calculated to explain the psychic hold of the city, he compares Paris to a "lovesick bitch who'd rather die than let you get out of her hands" (172). A later section opens with the observation that "Paris is like a whore. From a distance you can't wait until you have her in your arms. And five minutes later you feel empty, disgusted with yourself. You feel tricked" (209). This figurality persistently links Paris with predatory females; in the Faubourg Montmartre, he tells us, "they attach themselves to you like barnacles, they eat into you like ants" (158). Yet the narrator makes it clear, as in his portrait of Germaine (42–47), that he appreciates the directness of the prostitute. Metaphorized as whore, Paris is a counterimage of the rejecting mother: the available female who permits the narrator to satisfy his desperate need for intimacy. Interestingly, though, when he reflects on Paris as "an obstetrical instrument," he avoids altogether the attribution of gendered identity. Instead, the city figures in this symbolic parturition first as a mechanism of delivery and then as a "cradle," the nurturing space (Plato's chora) within which development might occur. In effect, Miller's narrator also conceives of Paris as his "incubator," the artificial environment which has enabled him to flourish in the absence of maternal care.

Whatever charm Henry may see in the physical scene, however, he refuses to sentimentalize his attachment to the city and later remarks (in explicit reference to Paris) that "the cradles of civilization are the putrid sinks of the world, the charnel house to which the stinking wombs confide their bloody packages of flesh and bone" (182). This imagery—which evinces more disgust with female nature—reminds us that however instrumental Paris has been in the narrator's rebirth or self-transformation, its nurturing power derives in part from a paradoxical negativity, from the city's concentration of malignant influences. Miller metaphorizes these qualities as disease: Paris itself is the tropic of cancer. He observes that "the city sprouts out like a huge organism diseased in every part, the beautiful thoroughfares only a little less repulsive because they have been drained of their pus" (40). Sickness and deformity surround his narrator; at each turn Henry sees evidence of universal contagion:

> In every Metro station there are grinning skulls that greet you with "*Défendez-vous contre la syphilis!*" Wherever there are walls, there are posters with bright venomous crabs heralding the approach of cancer. No matter where you go, no matter what you touch, there is cancer and syphilis. It is written in the sky; it flames and dances, like an evil portent. It has eaten into our souls and we are nothing but a dead thing like the moon. (185)

Insofar as Paris is a "putrid sink," a "charnel house," or a cancer ward, it exemplifies the corruption of the Western world and its loss of passion. In this way, the loathsomeness of the city strips away all illusions about "humanity," forcing the narrator to confront the problem "of living separate, of staying born." The very absence of a secure, sustaining environment compels him to face the problem of dependency which has long delayed his self-creation and deformed his erotic life.

This paradoxical nurture by torment and deprivation helps to explain how Paris could be for the narrator both an inferno and a site of rebirth. Explaining why other exiles of art ("the tortured, the hallucinated, the great maniacs of love") have made a pilgrimage to Paris, Henry likens the city to a madhouse; the "cold, indifferent faces" of the city's inhabitants "are the visages of one's keepers." In this place of hysteria and delusion, however, fundamental truths become clear: "The world reveals itself for the mad slaughterhouse that it is." This descent into a living hell clarifies the existential terms of being: "Not an exit sign anywhere; no issue save death" (182). Reaching this degree zero of cynicism, the narrator also confronts the fact of his personal mortality ("clearer than all I see my own grinning skull") and discovers in his creaturely condition—literally in his own "slime" and "excrement"—a connection with that vital current which breeds life exuberantly, mindlessly in the face of extinction.

Through this insight, Henry recognizes his relationship to

that other species, "the inhuman ones, the race of artists," whose task has always been "to overthrow existing values, to make of the chaos about [them] an order which is [their] own, to sow strife and ferment so that by the emotional release those who are dead may be restored to life" (253). In this gesture of identification, which confirms the purpose of his misery in Paris, the narrator finally discerns the origins of the self begotten in the city of exile:

> Today I am aware of my lineage. I have no need to consult my horoscope or my genealogical chart. What is written in the stars, or in my blood, I know nothing of. I know that I spring from the mythological founders of the race. The man who raises the holy bottle to his lips, the criminal who kneels in the marketplace, the innocent one who discovers that *all* corpses stink, the madman who dances with lightning in his hands, the friar who lifts his skirts to pee over the world, the fanatic who ransacks libraries in order to find the Word—all these are fused in me, all these make my confusion, my ecstasy. (255–56)

That is, Miller's narrator denies his biological origins, his own "blood," to avow his consanguinity with those lunatics and outcasts, those poets and artists, who are "always clutching and grasping for the beyond, for the god out of reach" (255). This genealogical account corroborates Wallace Fowlie's claim that Miller was essentially a "seer and prophet" who found "the peace of the world" in Paris because there, more readily than anywhere else, he was able to achieve wholeness as an artist.[26]

Thus, despite the dark skepticism borne of the narrator's vertiginous descent into the depths of the inferno, an unexpected peace and harmony prevail in his concluding paragraphs. Following a bitter sojourn in Dijon, Henry returns to Paris to witness the crackup of Fillmore (Richard Galen Osborn), an American who has given him lodging. After arranging Fillmore's passage back to the States (and pocketing the money intended for his mistress), Henry strolls through the city and exults: "Paris had never looked so good to me." He then makes a deliberate circuit by taxi through the Bois de Boulogne to the Pont de Sèvres, where along the banks of the Seine he too considers returning to America: "I asked myself—'do you want to go?' There was no answer." The American scene has faded from view, and Mona is now little more than an afterthought: "I wondered in a vague way what had ever happened to my wife" (318). Once, her hold had been so powerful that Paris itself seemed contaminated by her memory, the narrator now finds himself in imaginative possession of the urban terrain. On the rim of the great city, the prospect fills him with a sense of transcendence:

> Here, where the river gently winds through the girdle of hills, lies a soil so saturated with the past that however far back the mind roams one can never detach it from its human background. Christ, before my eyes there shimmered such a golden peace that only a neurotic could dream of turning his head away. So quietly flows the Seine that one hardly notices its presence. It is always there, quiet and unobtrusive, like a great artery running through the human body. In the wonderful peace that fell over me it seemed as if I had climbed to the top of a high mountain; for a little while I would be able to look around me, to take in the meaning of the landscape. (317–18)

This last line indeed comments upon the entire narrative, which insistently explores "the meaning of the landscape." Henry's relation to the landscape of Paris ultimately discloses the purpose of his exile in that artificial birth which could only occur though a "bloody struggle" in the very "bowels of the earth." The radiance of the final scene implies the narrator's emergence from his "dark and fearsome sojourn in the belly of the whale"; he has at last reached the shores of light, changed by his suffering and possessed of a new consciousness of his status: "A year, six months ago, I thought that I was an artist. I no longer think about it. I *am*" (1). Reflecting on the necessities which sustain human beings, Henry concludes that "more than anything they need to be surrounded with sufficient space" (318). Paris has provided the psychic, experiential field within which he has confronted the contradictions of his past life and has composed, in the textual gesture of the narrative itself, an alternate identity. The Seine, which flows through the city "like a great artery running through the human body," seems now to course through his own being, nourishing his creativity and sustaining that new self conceived in the "sufficient space" of Paris.

When detained en route to London in 1932 by British customs officials curious about a manuscript called *Tropic of Cancer*, Miller blustered that "this happens to be about geography."[27] Though he feared deportation as a pornographer, the author told the truth more fully than he imagined. His first book constructed a geography of the imagination, the complex rendering of a personal struggle worked out on the level of symbolic topography. Representing the narrator's effort to survive in Paris and to discover the reason for his exile, the account contrasts the harrowing, vitalizing foreign scene with fleeting recollections of "cold, glittering, malign" New York, a city "erected over a hollow pit of nothingness" (68). Whatever indignities or horrors he has suffered abroad, the narrator attributes to his descent into the Parisian inferno that revolutionary sense of vocation which infuses the section depicting the artist-writer as a connoisseur of chaos (227–33).

But while he acknowledges the "deep wish" never to leave France and concedes that Paris gives even the beggar "the illusion of being at home," the narrator explicitly resists this at-homeness himself and underscores his radical alienation by insisting that he is neither an American nor a European but instead a "neutral" (68, 153). In effect, *Tropic of Cancer* explores the consequences of this indeterminacy in the narrator's experience of place. Henry projects his metamorphosis as an escape from America and from that cult of material success exemplified by the "beautiful white prisons" of Manhattan. George Wickes points out that "for him the United States represented 'the air-conditioned nightmare' of technology without a soul."[28] Though the narrator interiorizes the geography of Paris as an imaginary construct ("the Paris whose *arrondissements* are undefined"), he nevertheless remains an outsider, a stranger for whom the city possesses imaginative power precisely by virtue of its strangeness. His formulation of a new, expatriate self thus manifests both a denial of his American identity and a resistance to some factitious bohemian identification with Paris and the "lost generation." In 1934 Miller wrote to Schnellock: "I am alone, a man, an artist, by Jesus, and I want nothing to do with these sap-heads—[Samuel] Putnam, [Abraham

Lincoln] Gillespie, and [Wambly] Bald, etc. *Cripes!* Nor with Pound or Eliot or Joyce."[29] In his first published book, the author imagined a homeless, undaunted figure, a subversive writer, who derives his sense of self from the situation of exile, even from the delirium of dislocation.

In his second book, however, the expatriate reconstructed his Brooklyn childhood, juxtaposed those memories against his life abroad, and conjectured about the nature of the self. Under the title *Self-Portrait* Miller had already begun working on the manuscript in early 1933 when he advised Schnellock: "I hope to let off that effluvia which ordinarily went into my letters. . . . I want to get in a lot of that *street* stuff—the physical, sensuous Paris—plus my warped moods, introspection, ghosts, etc. Follow me? Above all, the captivating, motivating idea is *'marginal'* thoughts."[30] This determination to register "cracked" notions, hallucinations, and odd, liminal perceptions increases both the fascination and difficulty of the work he finally titled *Black Spring*, a series of ten impressionistic sketches ranging from the sentimental to the surreal. The manuscript possibly served as a receptacle for ideas left over from *Tropic of Cancer*, since the occasional "street stuff" extends Miller's survey of that secret Paris composed of obscure streets and unreal scenes. Another link to the first book resides in the numerous dream sequences ("Into the Night Life," for example) which reinforce the impression of an apocalyptic end-time— the collapse of civilization into the "universe of death." When he began the second manuscript, Miller planned to divide it into four parts corresponding to the four seasons; but he never got past the vision—implied by his title—of a dark springtime of corruption and decay.

Although Paris figures in only a few sections of *Black Spring*, the book merits attention here because Miller self-consciously explores place, time, and memory. In his opening pages he signals the influence of Proust:

> Suddenly, walking down a street, be it real or be it a dream, one realizes for the first time that the years have flown, that all this has passed forever and will live on only in memory; and then memory turns inward with a strange, clutching

brilliance and one goes over these scenes and incidents perpetually, in dream and reverie, while walking a street, while lying with a woman, while reading a book, while talking to a stranger . . . suddenly, but always with terrific insistence and terrific accuracy, these memories intrude, rise up like ghosts and permeate every fiber of one's being.[31]

Like Proust, whose *Albertine Disparue* he apparently read during this period, Miller sought to explore the relation between the remembered self and the remembering self. If *Tropic of Cancer* stages an escape from the American past and a nearly successful suppression of memory, *Black Spring* marks a concerted exercise in remembrance. Miller's *recherche du temps perdu* proceeds, however, not as a linear narrative with calculated flashbacks but rather as disparate reveries which shift back and forth unpredictably between Brooklyn and Paris, between past and present, between dream and reality.

Declaring himself at the outset a "patriot of the Fourteenth Ward, Brooklyn," Miller in several sketches sifts through recollections of his boyhood home, the old neighborhood, and the friends of his youth. His longest sketch, "The Tailor Shop," represents his father's business place just off Fifth Avenue in Manhattan—the longtime employees, "the old man" who always "raised hell with everybody," and the regular patrons—"all these old farts we catered to" (79). The piece also reconstructs the ambience of family gatherings, the painful journey with Tante Melia to an insane asylum, and his father's drunken carouse with Tom Jordan. Miller suggests that these recollections "form the black flowing river which keeps the axis of [his] world in constant revolution" (115). He acknowledges the effect of nostalgia—the dream-memory of *nostos*—on the older writer; each morning the river "overflows its banks," leaving upon the margins of consciousness a psychic residue, "all the rinds of a dead universe," upon which the writer must re-create the world each day (116). Through the retrospective sketches of *Black Spring* Miller tries to assemble a portrait of the artist as a young man but concedes that "this is a self-portrait which yields only the missing parts" (29).

In this sense the book meditates upon both the origins of creativity and the difficulties of representing the self. It does so through a largely implicit contrast between American places embedded in the writer's consciousness and the immediate Parisian scene, which in its foreignness comprises "just the right world" in which to write. This contrast becomes fully explicit in the sketch "Walking Up and Down in China," in which Miller juxtaposes memories of New York and Brooklyn with impressions of the city of exile. "Paris is France and France is China," he writes, explaining that China epitomizes the unfamiliar and "incomprehensible" within which he has discovered a paradoxical "peace and security . . . where a man [can] be himself" (185). Paris is thus the quintessential "China," a place so imageable (as Kevin Lynch might say) that it evokes its own fantastic double in the unconscious. The author alludes to this doubled, imaginary city as he reconstructs an epiphany on the rue Caulaincourt:

> I look to the right of me and there on a slanting street is precisely the Paris I have always been searching for. You might know every street in Paris and not know Paris, but when you have forgotten where you are and the rain is softly falling, suddenly in the aimless wandering you come to the street through which you have walked time and again in your sleep *and this is the street you are now walking through.* (199)

Beyond the actual city lies an idealized place, a locus of desire, which recurs in dreams. This illumination recalls similar moments in the surreal narratives of Breton and Aragon, but for Miller it triggers the thought of walking along this very street and seeing a dead man in front of a butcher shop. Whether this is nightmare or memory remains uncertain; the ambiguity compels the writer to wonder whether he is dreaming or insane, even whether he himself might be "the man on the sidewalk, the man with arms outstretched" (201). The fantasy of encountering his own corpse on a Paris street connects with the notion—expressed variously throughout *Black Spring*—that one is "born and reborn over and over" (185), leaving behind outworn bodies and prior selves.

This motif of course links the work to *Tropic of Cancer* and its metaphors of gestation and rebirth. But Miller goes further in *Black Spring:* he projects not a single, exilic self but a myriad of selves, a succession of identities, each associated with different sites. Positing an engaging theory of the relation of self and place, he offers a Whitmanesque inventory of eighty-four locations (mostly cities in America and Europe) which have changed him. "In each and every one of these places," he writes, "something happened to me, something fatal. In each and every one of these places I left a dead body on the sidewalk with arms outstretched" (202). The corpse of self lying before the butcher's shop in Paris is but one of many bodies Miller has left behind. By implication, his "self-portrait" consists of a series of postmortem identifications, prose examinations of the remains of previous selves—autobiography as autopsy. Place determines this process, insofar as each town marks a death: "Each city I walked through has killed me— so vast the misery, so endless the unremitting toil. From one city to another I walk, leaving behind me a grand procession of dead and clanking selves" (205). By ascribing to place a virtual fatality, Miller inverts the Platonic notion of chora; but he does so to imply that the body, the physical self, does not pass through space untouched by its environment. Rather, he contends that the self internalizes place, acquiring through this subtle incorporation a new body which quite literally dis-places the old. He suggests that we actually become different persons in different settings; we experience place in the flesh, sensually and kinesthetically, as a force which acts upon us, entering our blood and bones (as well as our conscious and unconscious thoughts) to change us radically and irreversibly. In Paris, this revelation comes to Miller in a first-class compartment on the Métro: *"l'homme que j'étais, je ne le suis plus"* (the man I was, I no longer am) (31).

If the individual is truly "born and reborn again and again" in a continuous state of becoming, different places inevitably become associated (as Hemingway hints in "The Snows of Kilimanjaro") with certain phases of life and with specific incarnations. By shifting his perspective back and forth from Europe to America, from the streets and cafés of Paris to the old neighborhood in Brooklyn, Miller positions himself to observe the various bodies he has inhabited. But he goes still further, contending that the proliferation of selves is not only diachronic but synchronic: "There was never any time when I was living *one* life, the life of a husband, a lover, a friend. Wherever I was, whatever I was engaged in, I was leading multiple lives" (28). Figuring himself a "corporate entity" (41), Miller brings together in *Black Spring* fragments of dreams and memories belonging to the various selves he has been, successively and simultaneously. His relentless contemplation of prior habitations, which returns obsessively to Brooklyn and the houses of his own childhood, bears out Lloyd Kramer's characterization of exile and of the writing which it generates:

> The experience of living among alien people, languages, and institutions can alter the individual's sense of self about as significantly as any of the traumas known to psychologists. The referents by which people understand themselves change dramatically when they are separated from networks of family, friends, work, and nationality. Although this separation affects each individual somewhat differently, the resulting disorientation commonly provokes important changes in self-perception and consciousness. Intellectual exiles frequently respond to their deracination by describing home (idealistically) or rejecting home (angrily) or creating a new definition of home (defiantly); in any case they almost always explore problems of national and personal identity in new ways and write about their conflicts in texts that can become unusually rich revelations of both conscious and unconscious needs, motivations, and anxieties.[32]

Miller's reconstruction of his American past exhibits both nostalgia and anger. Though he recalls with evident fondness the old neighborhood and the local characters (205–10), he also calls America "a black curse upon the world" and declares (apropos of the Seine and the *banlieue parisienne*): "I have such a sense of being at home that it seems incredible that I was born in America" (37). *Black Spring* mirrors all of the contradictions of the author's sense of home and all of the multiplications of identity which arise from his changing self-perceptions. Indeed, the very multiplicity of selves which Miller associates with his peripatetic existence seems at last to express—ironically—an American conception of identity, an assumption of the unlimited possibilities of self-creation implicit in unfettered movement across the landscape: "Pawtucket, Wilmington, Coogan's Bluff, North Beach, Toulouse, Perpignan, Fontenay-aux-Roses, Widdecombe-in-the-Moor, Mobile, Louveciennes" (202).

Near the end of *Black Spring* in the sketch "Burlesk," a dizzying evocation of bars and strip joints along Broadway culminates in a symbolic return to Miller's childhood home: "I go back over the Brooklyn Bridge and sit in the snow opposite the house where I was born. An immense, heartbreaking loneliness grips me" (224). Like Gertrude's Stein's visit to Oakland, recalled in *Everybody's Autobiography*, Miller's journey to the site of childhood memory produces a numbing sense of loss and disconnection.[33] After a night of erotic stimulation which has left him "desperate and lonely," he feels a sense of "the grotesque and the void" as he contemplates his old house. On one level the episode appears to disclose a residual craving for the bliss of intimacy denied him by his mother, a figure curiously excluded from the memoir; on another, it manifests a traumatic confrontation between the real and the imaginary, between Miller's conscious perception and his subliminal memory. Gaston Bachelard contends that "there exists for each one of us an oneiric house, a house of dream memory, that is lost in the shadow of the beyond of the real past." He calls this dream dwelling "the crypt of the house we were born in," implying a radical distinction between the physical place—which undergoes change, even destruction—and the "oneiric house," the enduring unconscious image, which is at once the repository of the past and the sign of its absence.[34] As he sits in the snow before the house of childhood, Miller imagines himself as not yet conscious of the Parisian experience which he has in fact already undergone: "I don't yet see myself standing in Freddie's Bar in the Rue Pigalle" (224). In this complex moment, the older author visualizes himself as a desperate younger man, revisiting a place associated with a still earlier self and a happier epoch. This reflection on remembrance implies that a single place can mark the juncture of different selves—which is of course the discovery Wordsworth made a few miles above Tintern Abbey. But Miller gives this insight a modern turn by suggesting that the loneliness he experiences before the house in which he was born is itself characteristic of "the lonely man of the city surrounded by his inventions, the lost seeker drowning in the common identity" (244). In *Black Spring*, problems of "national and personal identity" indeed recur obsessively; Miller suggests that by returning in dream or memory to the places in which his "multiple lives" have been grounded, he discerns the corpses of his former selves and, in this reflexive gaze, also locates the writing self which momentarily claims the first-person pronoun, having found "just the right world" in Paris.

Aside from a six-month interlude in America in 1935 and a shorter visit in early 1936, Miller remained in Paris until the threat of war obliged him to leave in May 1939.[35] His decade in France had produced a handful of books published by Jack Kahane's Obelisk Press; more important, it freed Miller from chronic self-doubt and from the sense of failure which had long paralyzed him. Inevitably, over the years, the Parisian scene seemed less foreign, and the author lost the perspective of displacement which had infused his earlier representations of the city. After completing *Black Spring* in 1935, Miller produced only a few other works which consider Paris as place: *Aller Retour, New York* (1935), a long letter to Perlès, compares the vulgar, vacuous American scene with the sustaining ambience of the French capital; two pieces in *Max and the White Phagocytes* (1938)—"Max" and "The Eye of Paris"—show flashes of his earlier interest in the secret metropolis, its street life, and its esoteric revelations. But his major project of the late thirties, *Tropic of Capricorn* (1939), evoked memories of New York and the nightclubs associated with June as he first knew her. By the end of the decade, with France itself bracing for invasion, Miller perceived (as Martin notes) that "Paris was irredeemably altered for him"; after five months in Greece, he returned to the "air-conditioned nightmare" of America in early 1940.[36]

Back in New York, Miller tried to relieve the nausea of repatriation by writing *Quiet Days in Clichy*, a superficial account of his revels with a Montmartre prostitute and of orgies in the Clichy apartment he shared with Alfred Perlès.[37] As with the accompanying story, "Mara-Marignan," Miller offers fleeting glimpses of Parisian settings but seems mostly concerned with pornographic effects. A more thoughtful retrospective emerges in "Remember to Remember," a long essay-memoir composed just after the end of World War II. Here Miller (in his early fifties) reflects on "those ten glorious years in France" from a geographical and historical distance, speculating on the unconscious basis of his affinity for the country. With maps of Paris and France at hand, he retraces his travels and muses on the French genius for "beautiful, evocative names." As Stein does in *Paris, France,* he also meditates on the distinctive qualities of the French ("their native courtesy, their tolerance, their sense of discrimination, their keen ability to evaluate the essential and the significant") and on the abiding "Catholicity" of the country. He reconstructs mundane images of daily life in Paris and concludes: "No matter what I touched, what I looked at, my interest and curiosity were aroused. Nothing grew stale, not even the vegetables in the stalls." Perhaps the most revealing passage, however, is a long quotation (from Jakob Wassermann) which Miller uses to elucidate the relationship between a writer and his landscape:

> Any landscape . . . which somehow becomes part of our destiny generates a definite rhythm within us, an emotional rhythm and a rhythm of thought of which we usually remain unconscious and which hence is all the more decisive. It should be possible to recognize from the cadences of a writer's prose the landscape it covers as a fruit covers its kernel. . . . The landscape in which a person lives does not merely frame the picture; it enters into his very being and becomes a part of him. . . . Personality is engendered at the point where the inner and outer landscapes are contiguous, where the mythical and the permanent flow into limited time. And every literary work, every deed, every achievement is the result of an amalgamation of the tangible and the intangible, of the inner vision and the actual picture, of the idea and the factual situation, of conception and form.[38]

Through this citation Miller explains his own complicated attachment to France and to Paris. That distant terrain had inscribed itself in his unconscious (as "dream landscape") and had even insinuated itself into his prose and his personality. Miller understands—via Wassermann—that his expatriate self has emerged "at the point where the inner and outer landscapes are contiguous," in that textual space (*Tropic of Cancer*) where the city of exile—the geographical place—converged with its imaginary double, "the Paris whose *arrondissements* are undefined."

After a tour of the United States in 1940–41 and a stint in Los Angeles, Miller took up residence in 1944 at Big Sur, a coastal setting which answered his new need (following the visit to

Greece) for elemental, even primitive simplicity. "I found freedom in Paris and I found peace of soul in Big Sur," he wrote.[39] Far
from the city which had delivered him from his most disabling
anxieties, he found on Partington Ridge the serenity to complete
his three-volume narrative, *The Rosy Crucifixion*, as well as *Big
Sur and the Oranges of Hieronymus Bosch*. With the American
publication of *Tropic of Cancer* in 1961, the importance of Miller's first book (and his tribulations in Paris) became more widely
appreciated; yet even with the recent expansion of the American
literary canon, he remains curiously excluded from the major
anthologies. Kate Millett's observation two decades ago remains
accurate: "Official criticism perseveres in its scandalous and sys-
tematic neglect of his work."[40]

Among the fifty-odd volumes Miller produced, the early accounts of his metamorphosis in exile still seem the most ex-
plosively original. With foresight he wrote in the mid-thirties: "I
see now that I am leaving behind me a record of Paris which I have
written in blood—but also in peace and good-will. The whole
city—every arrondissement, every carrefour, every impasse, every
enchanted street. Through me Paris will live again, a little more, a
little brighter."[41] His *Letters to Emil, Tropic of Cancer*, and *Black
Spring* make the city live again as a source of imaginative profusion. Within that "sufficient space" Miller was able to imagine a
rambunctious, iconoclastic self, outraged by America and by his
ties to that colossal, senseless scene and yet unable to conceive of
himself as a Parisian or as a European. His experience defined the
dilemma of expatriation, of living between two worlds and belonging to neither, of working in the marginal space between
inner and outer landscapes to articulate a provisional identity.
The author outgrew his expatriate self, leaving its corpse behind
in 1939 when he left Paris; but that version of Henry Miller
continues to command attention, for his early narratives cap-
ture—as richly as any American ever has—the predicament of
the exiled, ungrounded writer searching for the city of writing.

CHAPTER FIVE

Modernism as Exile: Fitzgerald, Barnes, and the Unreal City

ERTRUDE Stein remarked that modernist writers and artists of her time had converged on the capital of France because "Paris was where the twentieth century was." The city not only incorporated within its diverse cultural life the most distinctive projects and features of modernism, but (as her claim implies) it had also become a geographical sign of the modern. Other European cities—notably Vienna, Berlin, and London—had harbored important avant-garde coteries during the two decades bracketing the turn of the century, but by 1910, Paris had achieved preeminence as a site of modernist production. Stein suggests that she became an exile in order to position herself at the center of a historical phenomenon—as if the temporal (the twentieth century) had suddenly assumed a spatial form which might be located and occupied. The conflation of time and space in Stein's observation itself reflects a distinctively modern tendency to problematize categories of thought and perception. New ways of conceptualizing time, space, form, distance, speed, and direction emerged, as Stephen Kern has shown, from revolutionary developments in art, philosophy, science, and technology during the years between 1880–1918. Kern demonstrates how these changes radically altered the general meaning of the past, present, and future as frames of experiential reference. His analysis also redefines aspects of modern consciousness in ways which seem especially apposite to the problem of exile, and his account of the interplay between material culture on the one hand and intellectual and aesthetic life on the other offers a fresh perspective on the narrative construction of identity and experience in the city where (as Stein believed) the twentieth century first revealed its distinctive qualities.[1]

To be sure, every age witnesses changes and marks transitions; even in apparently quiescent phases, culture on some level remains astir, dynamic. There is, moreover, another sense in which every period seems modern in relation to an earlier time; each era defines itself by its innovations, by its distinctive crises, and by its repudiations of outworn conventions, philosophies, and practices. Yet no previous "modern" age had ever brought such precipitous and sweeping change to everyday life and to human understanding. Within a few years, new technologies of communication and transportation changed the pace of daily activity, widened the horizons of personal consciousness, broke down geographical barriers, and made these changes instantly perceptible to a mass culture linked by electronic media. Writers variously expressed a recognition of unprecedented, fundamental transformations: Henry Adams believed that the year 1900 marked the onset of a new historical epoch; Virginia Woolf speculated with mock precision that "on or about December, 1910, human nature changed"; Charles Peguy declared in 1913 that "the world has changed less since Jesus Christ than it has in the last thirty years." Diverse as such claims may be, the peculiar urge to specify a date for the advent of the modern age reflects an awareness of new conditions of being, coinciding (very roughly) with the turn of the twentieth century. Whatever the discrepancy between the estimates of Adams, Woolf, and Peguy, their efforts to designate the exact moment at which the Western world entered into this phase testifies both to a consciousness of historical liminality—a sense of living (and writing) on the threshold of a new era—and to a recognition that this epoch had arrived abruptly rather than gradually, through cataclysm rather than through evolution.

The various inventions and technologies which helped to produce new forms of modern consciousness had, as Kern notes, manifold effects on literary and artistic expression. For example, the establishment of World Standard Time in the 1890s, the "universal diffusion of pocket watches" about 1900, and the introduction in 1916 of electric clocks all served to intensify the distinction between public time and inner, subjective time—the very distinction upon which Henri Bergson had developed his theories of duration. Thus, as Kern points out, Proust's *A la Recherche du temps perdu* and Joyce's *Ulysses* both entail deliberate though contrasting explorations of the psychological experience of time (16–18). Likewise the telephone enabled journalists of the late 1890s to report events unfolding almost as the paper rolled off the presses. This mind-boggling simultaneity of experience also occurred on the level of personal communication as long distance lines made possible direct conversations with far-flung acquaintances. Obviously, the consciousness of other peoples and cultures did not itself arise from the technological advances of the late nineteenth century; but the capacity to converse with those far away endowed the remote with a presence and tangibility it had never before possessed. As Kern speculates, this new consciousness of events unfolding at the same instant in different places probably influenced both Joyce's representation of a "temporally thickened present" in *Ulysses* and Stein's effort to expand the present moment with verbs in the continuous present and with successive reiterations of opening lines (85–86).

Concurrent developments in transportation had a comparable effect on the perception of space and place. In the 1890s the popularization of the bicycle and the subsequent introduction of the automobile stimulated leisure travel and altered basic conceptions of speed and distance, dramatically extending what might be called the proximate landscape while fostering an expanded sense of geographical contiguity. Motorized trams, subways, and elevators accelerated personal movement within urban spaces; high-speed passenger steamers plied the Atlantic in record time, and airplanes flew over topographical and national boundaries, dissolving notions of remoteness and separation while producing a new consciousness of global relations. Reflecting on the emerging "technology of speed," Octave Uzanne commented in 1912 that "the rapid movement which sweeps us in space and piles up a variety of impressions and images in a short time gives life a plenitude and a unique intensity" (128). After the Great War (which saw fearsome applications of the new technology), these forms of transportation produced a tremendous vogue for international travel which helped to spawn both the American expatriate movement and the great exodus of writers from Great Britain during the twenties and thirties. The ease and relative swiftness of international travel contributed to the notion of place as a commodity of tourism and as an arbitrary locus of experience. When Hemingway's Robert Cohn proposes to Jake Barnes that they abandon Paris for South America, he typifies the modern notion of travel as an easy collapsing of great distance to obtain (like some consumer product) a fresh view or a new range of possibilities. As a result of what Paul Fussell terms the "unceasing kinesis" of postwar travelers, the "travel sense of place" soon yielded to "the touristic phenomenon of placelessness," the perception of the external scene as an unreal spectacle.[2]

The various types of transportation and communication which emerged in the modern period thus produced new ways of conceiving and experiencing time and space. Rapid, incessant travel and immediate electronic contact with distant places and cultures broke down provincial perspectives and helped to generate a cosmopolitan consciousness which transcended national themes and issues. Malcolm Bradbury and James McFarlane argue that "the essence of Modernism is its international character," and this confluence of sensibilities promoted the formation of a synthetic culture infused with the sense of its absolute modernity. The inescapable multiplicity of twentieth-century experience— its inherently pluralistic, multicultural nature—seemed to substantiate Ortega y Gasset's concept of perspectivism which held, as Kern reminds us, that "there are as many realities as points of view" (151). Cubism provided a visual corroboration of sorts, breaking objects into geometrical shapes viewed, seemingly, from several perspectives at once. The idioms of modern painting from Impressionism to Fauvism and Cubism also suggested a corollary consequence of multiplicity: the dismantling of representation as the unitary function of visual art and the liberation of painting from a rational system of proportionality.

Everywhere the proliferation of theories and viewpoints bore out the realization that knowledge itself had become relative and problematic; one could no longer assume the existence of essential, objective truths behind surface phenomena. Alan Bullock has noted that "between 1895 and 1915 the whole picture of the physical universe, which had appeared not only the most impressive but also the most secure achievement of scientific thought, was brought in question and the first bold attempts made to replace it with a new model."[3] This intellectual upheaval caused a general disorientation in which the conditions of everyday life became suddenly defamiliarized by the collapse of assumptions once thought to be secure. McFarlane describes three discrete stages in what might be called the reformulation of reality under modernism:

> Initially, the emphasis is on fragmentation, on the breaking up and the progressive disintegration of those meticulously constructed "systems" and "types" and "absolutes" that lived on from the earlier years of the [nineteenth] century, on the destruction of belief in large general laws to which all life and conduct could be claimed to be subject. As a second stage . . . there came a re-structuring of parts, a re-relating of the fragmented concepts, a re-ordering of linguistic entities to match what was felt to be the new order of reality. . . . Finally, in its ultimate stages, thought seemed to undergo something analogous to a change of state: a dissolving, a blending, a merging of things held to be forever mutually exclusive. A sense of flux, a notion of continuum, the running together of things in ways often contrary to the dictates of simple common sense (though familiar enough in dream) alone seemed able to help in the understanding of certain bewildering and otherwise inexplicable phenomena of contemporary life.[4]

From a formalist perspective, these phases roughly correspond to the tendencies of modernist art which Roger Shattuck has identified as fragmentation, juxtaposition, and superposition.[5] But beyond such aesthetic implications, the stages outlined above suggest important correlations with expatriate experience and indeed permit us to regard modernism itself as a kind of exile.

In the first phase of modernism—a disintegration of intellectual systems and laws governing "life and conduct"—we see a loss of orienting structures comparable to the exile's renunciation of the functional security of homeland: the familiar geography, language, and customs which enable one to negotiate more or less unconsciously the routines of everyday life. The phase of restructuring, the assimilation of a "new order of reality," likewise corresponds to the experience of immersion in an alien culture and the metabolizing of differences at virtually every level of consciousness, beginning with the problem of renaming reality itself in the dominant language of the country of exile. In the third stage of modernism, marked by a strange dissolving of differences, a merging of conceptual opposites, and a dreamlike confusion of categories, we find an analogy to the bemusement of the expatriate for whom the foreign has become familiar while remaining paradoxically unreal. This third stage recalls Stein's comment that writers needed a second country that was "not real" yet "really there." Modernism effects displacement through "future shock" (in Alvin Toffler's phrase) when the rate of change in a customary environment exceeds one's capacity to assimilate change. Thus, insofar as exile marks a rupture with the past, a loss of the familiar, a relocation amid alien surroundings, and a persistent sense of estrangement, it thus provides a suggestive model for the experience of modernism.

In its dizzying third phase, this reformulation of reality produces disorientation both through the appearance of new forms and conditions and through the collapse of previous barriers, boundaries, and oppositions. McFarlane observes that under modernism, human nature could no longer be contained or explained by "vast and exhaustive inventories of naturalistic detail arranged and sorted under prescriptive heads" but instead revealed itself to be "elusive, indeterminate, multiple, often implausible, infinitely various and essentially irreducible."[6] Perhaps the most basic human distinction to be challenged and "demolished" by modernist thought was that between subject and object, between "man the observer and nature the observed." Just as Virginia Woolf wrote of Mrs. Ramsay (in *To the Lighthouse*) that she "became the thing she looked at," so other modernist writers explored the suddenly ambiguous relation between self and other, sometimes figured as a convergence of the internal and the external. As McFarlane notes, the philosopher Ernst Mach insisted on "an intimate interpenetration between things inner and things outer" in which the terms "within" and "without" no longer marked an absolute breach. In psychoanalysis as well as in quantum physics, entities once conceived as opposites—love and hate, matter and energy—proved to be interrelated, even indistinguishable. Influenced by Nietzsche, much of Western thought—certainly the domain of metaphysics—underwent a skeptical reexamination of its suppositions. Kern describes a corollary "breakdown of old forms" which "leveled hierarchies" and undermined a range of conceptual dichotomies: "solid/porous, opaque/transparent, inside/outside, public/private, city/country, noble/common, country-man/foreigner, framed/open, actor/audience, ego/object, space/time" (209–10). The crisis of modernity perhaps arose less from the fragmentation of reality into discrete phenomena than from the erasing of those distinctions which seemed to hold in place the conventional order of things. With some urgency Yeats asked, "How can we tell the dancer from the dance?" This blurring of traditional oppositions—social, moral, physical, and psychological—pervaded the culture of modernism and informed its most distinctive literary texts.

In one such work, *The Waste Land*, Eliot evokes a teeming "Unreal City" in which life and death have become indistinguishable; he thereby calls attention to the undeniably urban nature of modernism itself. The various transformations of culture bracketed by this concept of course first manifested themselves within the great cities of Vienna, London, Berlin, New York, and Paris. Reminding us of the metropolitan character of "experimental modernism," Malcolm Bradbury points out that with vast, heterogeneous populations, cities inevitably became "places of friction, change and new consciousness."[7] This multiplicity attracted a new kind of artist or writer seeking to escape regional influences, to absorb the diversity of cosmopolitan life, and through self-conscious displacement to achieve a more intimate involvement with art or writing. Raymond Williams has sketched the way in which the cities of modernism thus fostered a poetics of exile:

> The key cultural factor of the modernist shift is the character of the metropolis . . . in its direct effects on form. The most important general element . . . is the fact of immigration to the metropolis, and it cannot too often be emphasized how many of the major innovators were, in this precise sense,

immigrants. At the level of theme, this underlies, in an obvious way, the elements of strangeness and distance, indeed of alienation, which so regularly form part of the repertory. But the decisive aesthetic effect is at a deeper level. Liberated or breaking from their national or provincial cultures, placed in quite new relations to those other native languages or native visual traditions, encountering meanwhile a novel and dynamic common environment from which many of the older forms were obviously distant, the artists and writers and thinkers of this phase found the only community available to them: a community of the medium, of their own practices.[8]

Attempting to free themselves from the influence of familiar, native settings, writers and artists underwent dislocation to achieve a new relation to their work and to the verbal or visual language of its composition. The city of exile combined for them the strangeness of the foreign and the unreality of the modern, producing an alienation from the immediate environment while at the same time endowing it with the sort of imaginary power which only the unreal can possess. Works from the mid-thirties by Scott Fitzgerald and Djuna Barnes convey the unreality of Paris from this perspective of modernist displacement.

Whatever its residue of personal calamity, Fitzgerald's *Tender is the Night* (1934) stands as a tortured record of the psychic and cultural confusions of modernism. As Matthew J. Bruccoli has shown, this novel underwent twelve drafts in three separate versions, emerging over a period of nine frantic years spent mostly abroad.[9] In its portrayal of Dick Diver's disintegration and his wife Nicole's recovery from mental illness, the narrative also captures the reckless unreality of the twenties, a condition metaphorized throughout by allusions to movie-making and acting as the construction of illusion. Chaotic in its stylistic excesses, its bizarre episodes, its shifts of perspective, and its lapses of chronology, the novel betrays distraction even as it displays hard-won insight into the contradictions of desire and the ironies of American optimism. Most revealingly, the work depicts the situation of modernist exile as a struggle against deracination and historical discontinuity; Diver's collapse results both from the loss of his American roots (symbolized by his father's death) and from the destruction of fundamental certainties by the violence of the Great War. The novel finally suggests that expatriates of the twenties faced the double jeopardy of spatial and temporal dislocation.

Fitzgerald's biographers have provided an ample account of the author's four visits to Europe from 1921 to 1931. We know, for example, that his first extended stay (from mid-1924 through the end of 1926) grew out of a need to free himself from the Long Island social circuit—from what James Mellow has called "continuous and extensive weekend partying" and from resultant debt and emotional exhaustion.[10] Afflicted by a sense of his own "deterioration," Fitzgerald sailed for France with his wife and daughter to test his friend Edmund Wilson's theory that the cultural density of France made that country a more propitious place to complete his new novel, *The Great Gatsby*. "We were going to the Old World to find a new rhythm for our lives," Fitzgerald wrote, "with a true conviction that we had left our old selves behind forever." But if he believed that one could become a different person in another country, he nevertheless avoided the sort of cultural immersion that some of his contemporaries sought. André LeVot notes that Fitzgerald had

> very little communication with the French writers of the period and does not seem to have taken any interest in the literary movements (Dada, Surrealism) of the time. Unlike Hemingway, who shared for a while the life of the poor, his relationships with the French were those of a rich tourist who spoke the language badly and dealt mostly with paid employees—taxi-drivers, restaurant and bar waiters, servants, and nurses and policemen when things were getting out of hand.[11]

As a Minnesotan educated at an Eastern prep school and then at Princeton, Fitzgerald remained curiously indifferent to those aspects of daily life in France which intrigued Stein, Hemingway, and Miller. Part of this indifference may be attributed to the drinking which especially during 1925—the summer of "1000 parties and no work"—left him oblivious to a great deal of what was happening around him. Another factor was his essentially bourgeois conventionality; as Wilson had observed in 1921, he was "so saturated with twentieth century America, bad as well as good, . . . so used to hotels, plumbing, drugstores, aesthetic ideals and vast commercial prosperity" that he could not readily appreciate the ancient and foreign.[12] While Fitzgerald later assured Wilson that he had "gotten to like France," what he liked most was his relative affluence (in 1925 a dollar bought twenty-two francs), the availability of liquor (while America endured Prohibition), and the presence of lively American friends like Gerald and Sara Murphy.

The three later sojourns nevertheless produced inexorable changes in the Fitzgeralds. Their first extended stay witnessed Zelda's 1924 affair with a French aviator, Scott's completion of *Gatsby*, his acquaintance with Hemingway, his preliminary work on the book to become *Tender is the Night*, and his developing obsession with the Murphys, the original models for Dick and Nicole Diver. During this visit, the Fitzgeralds made merry in St. Raphaël, Rome, Capri, Cap d'Antibes, Juan-les-Pins, and for much of 1925 in a luxury flat (14, rue Tilsitt) near the Arc de Triomphe in Paris. During a five-month visit to France in 1928, they occupied an apartment (58, rue de Vaugirard) opposite the Luxembourg Gardens; Zelda studied ballet, Scott met James Joyce, and the Fitzgeralds plunged into social activities which included evenings at the sapphic salon of Natalie Clifford Barney (20, rue Jacob). Scott's work on the new novel sputtered, and "desolate" side trips to the battlefields at Verdun and Rheims did not relieve a domestic discontent rooted in his drinking, Zelda's compulsive dancing, and mutual suspicions of homosexuality.[13] The third excursion (March 1929–September 1931) began with a sodden summer in Cannes and culminated in Zelda's mental collapse in Paris in early 1930. While she received treatment for schizophrenia at a Swiss clinic above Lake Geneva, Fitzgerald weathered her confinement mostly in nearby towns, shuttling to Paris periodically to visit his daughter.[14] In such places as Vevey, Caux, and Lausanne, he grappled with despair over Zelda's illness and with his own concomitant guilt and self-pity.

He also worked on several short stories, including two which indicate progress toward the still-unfinished novel. In the first of these, "One Trip Abroad," Fitzgerald traces the effect of prolonged expatriation on a young, affluent American couple, the Kellys. The story unfolds over several years; in the first scene, set in Algeria, Fitzgerald contrasts the couple's innocence with the jaded attitude of an older couple named Miles. Mrs. Miles acknowledges what Fussell has called the "touristic phenomenon of placelessness" when she comments: "Every place is the same. . . . The only thing that matters is who's there. New scenery is fine for half an hour, but after that you want your own kind to see. That's why some places have a certain vogue, and then the vogue changes and people move somewhere else. The place itself never really matters." For such exiles, foreign settings are meaningless backdrops for social transactions, and soon Nelson and Nicole Kelly likewise succumb to the movement and merriment of an existence as unreal as it is enervating. After a Parisian scene in which they have been duped into hosting an expensive riverboat party on the Seine, Fitzgerald shows them at Lake Geneva, trying to recover their health as they confront in yet another young couple the mirror image of their own debauchery. To underscore the danger of placelessness, Fitzgerald remarks: "This is the story of a trip abroad, and the geographical element must not be slighted. Having visited North Africa, Italy, the Riviera, Paris and points in between, it was not surprising that the Kellys should go to Switzerland. Switzerland is a country where very few things begin, but many things end."[15] He thus locates in the itinerary of their travels a symptom of some underlying malaise.

As Fitzgerald came to recognize, the glamorous lifestyle of the expatriate leisure class concealed certain insidious risks, including not only the loss of innocence and optimism but also the danger of a pointless, ungrounded existence which might finally threaten both sanity and selfhood. In "One Trip Abroad" we see him moving toward *Tender is the Night* through an analysis of expatriate corruption figured as symbolic geography. Meditating on the causes of Zelda's breakdown and his own dissipation, he came increasingly to associate expatriation with a compulsive yet random quest for absolute freedom and pleasure, for a life based on hedonistic impulse, facilitated by wealth, and conducted without regard for those local customs or cultural differences which might by comparison afford insight into one's own values and practices.

In a subsequent story, "Babylon Revisited," he offers closer analysis of this rootless existence, exposing both its inherent unreality and its potentially tragic toll. Set in Paris shortly after the stock market crash, the story depicts the dilemma of Charlie Wales, who wishes to escape the memory of past dissolution but who must return to the site of those escapades to reclaim his daughter Honoria, who has been raised since his wife's death by his sister-in-law, Marion, and her husband, Lincoln. Transparently the story thus portrays Charlie's effort to recover his honor; yet he cannot quite shake the dissolute past personified by his tipsy friends Duncan and Lorraine, who disrupt a crucial meeting with Marion and scuttle his negotiations. Noting that Charlie invites trouble by leaving Marion's address for Duncan at the Ritz, Roy R. Male points out the protagonist's ambivalence: "He *still* wants both worlds," the world of family and respectability and the world of irresponsible pleasure.[16] Fitzgerald compresses the fantastic quality of the "crazy years" in the story of Helen Wales' death, which—following a hysterical outburst at the Hotel Florida where she has just "kissed young Webb at the table"— results from her wandering about Paris in a snowstorm, "too confused to find a taxi." For his part, Charlie is one of those negligent revelers "who locked their wives out in the snow, because the snow of twenty-nine wasn't real snow."[17]

As a sketch for *Tender is the Night*, "Babylon Revisited" anticipates the fate of Dick Diver, who (like Charlie) loses his wife and family, "everything [he] wanted." Indeed Fitzgerald would repeat almost verbatim in the novel his summary of Charlie Wales's misfortune: "He wasn't young any more, with a lot of nice thoughts and dreams to have by himself" (633). Perhaps more importantly, the story sheds light on the disjointed Parisian section comprising the last half of book one in the novel. Returning to Paris, Charlie now sees the city as an alien place and laments, "I spoiled this city for myself" (618). He finds the Ritz "strange and portentous" and remarks that the bar is no longer American, having "gone back into France" (616). His taxi ride also betrays a basic topographical confusion; in a passage echoed in the novel Charlie travels from the Right Bank to the Left: "The Place de la Concorde moved by in pink majesty; they crossed the logical Seine, and Charlie felt the sudden provincial quality of the Left

Bank" (617). Yet in the next sentence he directs the driver back to the avenue de l'Opéra—to the Right Bank from which he has just come—before again rolling "on to the Left Bank." Whether intended or inadvertent, this zigzag route contributes to the sense of Charlie's ambivalence and disorientation. For him the bars and cabarets of Montmartre seem menacing: "Zelli's was closed, the bleak and sinister cheap hotels surrounding it were dark. . . . the Café of Heaven and the Café of Hell still yawned—even devoured, as he watched, the meager contents of a tourist bus" (620). Unlike the crazy years, when wealth insulated him from the foreign, Charlie now perceives himself as a stranger in a strange land. But the effect of strangeness conceals the irony that he now sees Paris more or less as it is, not as it appeared during the alcoholic binges of the twenties.[18]

By representing the city as a "Babylon," a scene of riotous living and emotional betrayal, Fitzgerald anticipates key elements of the Paris section in *Tender is the Night*. Charlie Wales looks back on a dizzying epoch just reaching its peak when Dick and Nicole Diver arrive in Paris in 1925. Projecting a more intricate sense of time and place, the novel effects a distorted but revealing image of the city. Indeed, insofar as this section depicts a pivotal phase in the career of Dick Diver, it also reflects the crisis of modernity itself and suggests that the city, in its fantastic unreality, embodies the terms and conditions of this immense upheaval. The improbable events which transpire in Paris typify the irrationality, violence, and uncertainty which in part define the climate of modernism. As Bruce L. Grenberg has argued, the city here represented by Fitzgerald constitutes "the image and substance of modern, postwar life-in-death."[19]

Although the novel contains only a few formal traits which might be associated with modernism—such as the cinematic foreshortening of time in book two—the story of the Divers and their relationship to Rosemary Hoyt incorporates many signs of modernist culture and its discontents which cohere in the image of Paris.[20] Among these, the most evident is the psychoanalytic matrix within which Fitzgerald frames the narrative. Via Yale, Oxford, and Johns Hopkins, Dick Diver has trained as a psychoanalyst in Vienna, presumably under "the great Freud" himself (115). At one point Doctor Dohmler gives Nicole "a little Freud to read," and though Dick does not cite specific Freudian texts, concepts associated with psychoanalysis (such as hysteria, schizophrenia, transference, and repression) traverse the novel and inform its crucial scenes. For example, the so-called "father complex" evoked by the title of Rosemary's film "Daddy's Girl" clarifies the incestuous coupling between Nicole and Devereux Warren and elucidates her subsequent attraction to Dick, an authority figure whom she addresses in letters as "captain." Similarly, when Collis Clay alludes to the "heavy stuff going on" (88) between Rosemary and a Yale man aboard a train, he constructs a primal scene which for Dick becomes a virtual fixation. Glimpses of clinical work call attention to the etiology of neuroses and suggest the curious ways in which childhood relationships with parents affect later emotional and sexual experience. The case of Señor Pardo y Ciudad Real and his intractably homosexual son (243–45) marks one such demonstration. But Fitzgerald's psychoanalytic perspective achieves a larger purpose than simply documenting the subculture of a Swiss psychiatric clinic; he suggests that the exploration of the unconscious in modernism has radically problematized identity and sexuality by calling into question the boundaries which had previously circumscribed both self and gender.

As a consequence, *Tender is the Night* presents personality as an unstable and indeterminate nexus of tendencies. The novel relentlessly questions the distinction between self and other, and even as Nicole receives treatment for a "split" personality, Fitzgerald implies that all personalities are multiple and that people tend to "become" the persons with whom they associate. In the stream-of-consciousness section which cinematically telescopes Nicole's transformation, she thinks: "When I talk I say to myself that I am probably Dick. Already I have even been my son, remembering how wise and slow he is. Sometimes I am Doctor Dohmler and one time I may even be an aspect of you, Tommy Barban" (162). Lest we construe this as evidence of her derangement, the narrator himself later tells us that "somehow Dick and Nicole had become one and equal, not opposite and complementary; she was Dick too, the drought in the marrow of his bones. He could not watch her disintegrations without participating in them" (190–91). As the preceding sentence implies, Nicole is not alone in her psychic assimilations; Dick too possesses a composite personality and feels "condemned to carry with him the egos of certain people, early met and early loved, and to be only as complete as they were complete themselves" (245). When Nicole's lover Tommy Barban calls her "a little complicated after all," her ironic reply sums up Fitzgerald's implicit theory of personality: "No, I'm not really—I'm just a—I'm just a whole lot of different simple people" (292). In a novel informed by an obsessive attention to psychoanalytic patterns of relationship—to conflicted ties between fathers and daughters, fathers and sons, or mothers and daughters—Fitzgerald suggests that unconscious incorporation makes it impossible to say precisely where one's own personality ends and others begin.

Through various strategies he also represents the distinction between male and female as relative rather than absolute, fluid rather than fixed; as in *The Garden of Eden* (a work surely influenced by Fitzgerald's novel) androgynous metamorphosis surfaces repeatedly, and scenes of gender ambivalence mirror the broader sexual confusion of the culture of modernism. Early in the novel, Rosemary witnesses an odd episode on the beach in which Dick goes into his dressing tent and emerges wearing only a pair of "transparent black lace drawers" which Nicole has handed him. Albert McKisco's quip—"Well if that isn't a pansy's trick!"—crudely associates Dick's stunt with homosexuality, perhaps to taunt the homophiles, Campion and Dunphry, who witness the display. Yet the joke (Nicole has lined the panties with flesh-colored cloth) literally invites closer examination. Dick's gratuitous exhibitionism, really a transvestite performance, signals not only his own tendency to assume conventionally female functions but also the pattern of gender reversal which runs through the novel. One notable transposition has occurred prior to the opening of the novel: Fitzgerald had initially conceived of the Rosemary Hoyt character, the young American with the overbearing mother, as a boy named Francis Melarky.[21] Traces of this sex change remain in Mrs. Spears' advice to Rosemary about pursuing a relationship with Dick: "Whatever happens it can't spoil you because economically you're a boy, not a girl" (40). Mrs. Spears' own name too obviously implies the phallic authority which she assumes in her daughter's life. Conversely Dick plays a maternal role with respect to Nicole, who continues "her dry suckling at his lean chest" (279). Later, in a symbolic metaphor, she severs the umbilical cord which links her to Dick, deciding to "cut the cord forever" (302). Her presenting the black lace panties to Dick in the opening scene may thus be seen as a prefiguration of the sexual transformation which she must effect in him to free herself from the dominating father.[22]

But sexual reversal may also be associated, as McKisco insinuates, with homosexuality. Thus Fitzgerald tells us that Luis Campion affects a "disinterested motherliness" (34) and that the son of Señor Pardo y Ciudad Real flaunts his inversion as "the Queen of Chili," whereas Mary North and Lady Caroline Sibly-Biers dress as French sailors to pick up two girls. These instances of deviance belong to a larger pattern of aberration which includes Mr. Warren's incest and Dick's late problem with nympholepsy in which "he was in love with every pretty woman he saw" (201). Fitzgerald tells us that in Rome, an angry crowd mistakes Dick for "a native of Frascati [who] had raped and slain a five-year old child" (234). Through such details he hints at the ubiquity of perversion in a novel marked by sexual turmoil, ambiguous erotic relations, and indefinite gender roles. In this sexual economy, desire itself seems inevitably displaced, deflected, or deformed.

Linked to his emphasis on psychoanalysis, Fitzgerald's treatment of the Great War also posits a modernist perspective in *Tender is the Night*. With the exception of a battlefield visit which colors the events of the Paris section, the war emerges almost entirely through oblique, fugitive references. Fitzgerald sums up the doctor's war experience in two meager sentences: "After he took his degree, he received his orders to join a neurological unit forming at Bar-sur-Aube. In France, to his disgust, the work was executive rather than practical" (117–18). Yet the conflict remains for Dick an obsession manifesting itself in dreams; on one occasion he awakens from "a long dream of war" which Fitzgerald summarizes: "His dream had begun in sombre majesty; navy blue uniforms crossed a dark plaza behind bands playing the second movement of Prokofieff's 'Love of Three Oranges.' Presently there were fire engines, symbols of disaster, and a ghastly uprising of the mutilated in a dressing station." Analyzing his own dream, Dick arrives at a "half-ironic" diagnosis: "Non-combattant's shell-shock" (180). This dream of uniformed men juxtaposed against the "ghastly" image of *mutilés de guerre* resonates with his later experience of waking to find passing beneath his window "a long column of men in uniform" who were "going to lay wreaths on the tombs of the dead" (200). Through such brief and seemingly incidental touches, Fitzgerald establishes the idea that although Dick did not see action at the front, he—like others of his generation— has been traumatized by the horrific carnage. The story of Dick and Nicole unfolds specifically within "the broken universe of the war's ending" (245), and Grenberg contends that the novel even implies a "precise" analogy between Nicole's illness and American involvement in the conflict.[23] Be that as it may, Fitzgerald's broad implication is that as a consequence of the Great War, the Divers move within a sphere of pervasive disillusionment and pent-up violence. Noting the postwar tendency among combat veterans toward escapist fantasy, historian Modris Eksteins makes a comment strikingly relevant to the world of *Tender is the Night:* "What was true of the soldiers was true with somewhat less immediacy and poignancy of civilians. The crowded nightclubs, the frenzied dancing, the striking upsurge of gambling, alcoholism, and suicide, the obsession with flight, with moving pictures, and with film stars evinced on a popular level these same tendencies, a drift toward irrationalism."[24]

The various eruptions of violence or insanity which mark the novel thus contribute to its modernist, postwar *vraisemblance.* Fitzgerald also represents the culture of modernism through his attention to new conceptions of time and space. For example, the Bergsonian notion of personal or subjective time forms the implicit basis of a comparison between Dick and Nicole: "For him time stood still and then every few years accelerated in a rush, like the quick rewind of a film, but for Nicole the years slipped away by clock and calendar and birthday" (180). The reference to the rewinding of a film as a metaphor for time implicitly recalls the tropes which Bergson used to describe the uncoiling or unwinding of time in "real duration."[25] In another passage, Fitzgerald alludes to a new, modern mode of keeping time when he describes Dick sitting "in the big room a long time listening to the buzz of the electric clock, listening to time" (171). Like Proust's *A la recherche du temps perdu,* Woolf's *To the Lighthouse,* and Faulk-

ner's *Sound and the Fury, Tender is the Night* reflects a peculiarly
modernist concern for the psychological experience of time; as
critics have often observed, the narrative structure calls attention
to the effects of time by bracketing the story between two beach
scenes, set five years apart, which dramatize basic changes in the
principal characters. According to Alan Trachtenberg, the disintegration of Dick Diver results in part from his "dislocated sense
of historical time."[26]

In a less obvious way, the novel also embodies certain modernist attitudes about space and place. Fitzgerald depicts the Gare
St. Lazare, for example, as a locus of metamorphosis for home-
bound Americans: "Standing in the station, with Paris in back of
them, it seemed as if they were vicariously leaning a little over the
ocean, already undergoing a sea-change, a shifting about of atoms
to form the essential molecule of a new people" (83). This comment resonates with his later observation that "on the long-
roofed steamship piers one is in a country that is no longer here
and not yet there" (205). That is, international postwar tourism
effects a displacement by problematizing the very concept of
place. To some extent, Dick suffers from that sense of "placelessness" expressed by Mrs. Miles in "One Trip Abroad." In Rome,
when Dick visits the house where Keats died, Fitzgerald notes
that "he cared only about people; he was scarcely conscious of
places except for their weather, until they had been invested with
color by tangible events" (220). Elsewhere the author implies that
an indifference to place may reflect a specifically American tourist mentality; he observes about Rosemary and her mother that
"after lunch they were both overwhelmed by the sudden flatness
that comes over American travellers in quiet foreign places. No
stimuli worked upon them, no voices called them from without,
no fragments of their own thoughts came suddenly from the
minds of others, and missing the clamor of Empire they felt that
life was not continuing here" (13). Their inability to respond to
"quiet foreign places" reveals not only a crass preference for excitement ("the clamor of Empire") but also an indifference—
endemic to the moneyed expatriate—to the physical realities of
daily life in ordinary European towns and cities.[27]

In the incessant movement of his major characters, Fitzgerald implies the superficiality of their grounding in the world.

When Dick flies to Munich, he gazes down on the landscape from an implicitly abstract, modernist perspective which yields delight: "It was simple looking at the earth from far off, simple as playing grim games with dolls and soldiers" (195). As this glancing allusion to soldiers implies, Fitzgerald sees the Great War itself as a product of the technology of power which has placed Dick far above the countryside he surveys with detachment. From a certain height, human beings shrink to nothingness, communities become indistinguishable, and geography assumes a fantastic unreality which bears no relationship to an earthbound sense of scale and distance. Dick's gaze from the airplane in fact epitomizes Fitzgerald's treatment of place in *Tender is the Night*, which is not so much realized as sur-realized by the experience of displacement.

Nowhere is this tendency more apparent than in the bewildering Paris section of the novel, which arguably marks a decisive turn in the Divers' marriage, in Dick's loss of professional discipline, and in Nicole's reliance upon Dick as a source of emotional protection. Yet these crucial developments unfold within the context of scenes that seem disconnected, hallucinatory, and even incoherent. When the action shifts to Paris, Fitzgerald discloses through a chaotic sequence of events the impulsive, irrational forces at large there. The two shootings which punctuate this section seem grotesque and initially reveal little except the presence of racial and sexual hostilities beneath the dreamlike surface of life in the capital of modernism. Ostensibly the Divers have come to Paris with Rosemary to see the alcoholic Abe North off to America. During five momentous days which blur together through a surfeit of movement and scene-shifting, we witness a developing romance between Dick and Rosemary, played out against an increasingly fantastic urban backdrop. In this treatment, the palpable unreality of place objectifies the confusion and ambivalence felt most keenly by Dick; the kaleidoscopic settings represent Paris as a locus of volatile change and cultural multiplicity.

In an opening scene in a Right Bank restaurant, Fitzgerald alludes to the touristic dislocation of his characters: "They had been two days in Paris but actually they were still under the beach umbrella" (52). For the Divers, the Norths, and Rosemary, actual surroundings scarcely matter; place is the immaterial context for social pleasure. At Voisin's (261, rue St.-Honoré), the group seems mainly concerned with distancing themselves from other Americans: Dick amuses them by pointing out American men lacking "repose," while Fitzgerald observes that "their own party was overwhelmingly American and sometimes scarcely American at all" (52), thus raising the problem of American identity which becomes associated with their various destinies. But the crux of this chapter lies in a conversation between the Divers, overheard by Rosemary from a telephone booth:

> "—So you love me?"
>
> "Oh, *do* I!"
>
> It was Nicole—Rosemary hesitated in the door of the booth then she heard Dick say:
>
> "I want you terribly—let's go to the hotel now." Nicole gave a little gasping sigh. For a moment the words conveyed nothing at all to Rosemary—but the tone did. The vast secretiveness of it vibrated to herself.
>
> "I want you."
>
> "I'll be at the hotel at four." (53–54)

While revealing the Divers' passion for each other, the dialogue enables Rosemary to imagine an "assignation" which she soon wishes to reenact with Dick, just as Collis Clay's story of Rosemary on the train later excites Dick's longing for her. Through these reciprocal moments of voyeuristic arousal, Fitzgerald advances the tacitly Freudian theory that desire originates in a primal scene which evokes rivalry and which persists through a mimetic doubling which, among other results, generates the symbolic repetition apparent throughout *Tender is the Night*. For Dick and Rosemary, the formation of their mutual sexual fantasies significantly begins in Paris, a city linked increasingly with the eruption of forbidden impulses.

After a brief shopping trip with Rosemary in which Nicole indulges in material excess, Fitzgerald transports his characters from Paris to a French battlefield near Amiens. Between the villages of Thiepval and Beaumont Hamel, where in 1914 the British had engaged the Germans in the bloody Battle of the Somme, Dick explains to Rosemary (though apparently not to Nicole) the

human cost of the campaign; "his throat straining with sadness,"
he expounds the notion that it was "a love battle" fought to
preserve nineteenth-century nationalistic values. Melodramat-
ically Dick announces: "All my beautiful lovely safe world blew
itself up here with a great gust of high explosive love" (57). Little
does he guess the personal, prophetic implications of his reference to the "explosive" potentialities of love. Partly confession,
partly romantic posturing, Dick's remark expresses a conventional sentiment about the loss of traditional certainties, but he
also portrays himself as a victim of the war's violence. His battlefield commentary reflects a sympathetic identification with
the "Wurtemburgers, Prussian Guards, Chasseurs Alpins, Man-
chester mill hands and old Etonians" who "pursue their eternal
dissolution under the warm rain"; yet it also betrays an awareness
of his effect on the tearful Rosemary, who tells him, "You know
everything" (57). If Dick's historical consciousness enables him to
grasp the significance of the battle, however, his sense of place
seems pretentious, markedly less genuine than that of Abe North,
who has at least seen combat. At the end of the chapter Fitzgerald
confides that to impress Rosemary, Dick has used a battlefield
guidebook to make "a quick study of the whole affair, simplifying
it always until it bore a faint resemblance to one of his own
parties" (59). The gentle derision implies that Dick has exploited
the sentimental possibilities of place to launch his own "love
battle" for Rosemary's affections.[28]

His tactic meets with quick success: following their return to
Paris, Nicole retires to the hotel while Dick, Rosemary, and the
Norths visit an exposition and then sip champagne at a houseboat
café, enjoying the picturesque view: "The river shimmered with
lights from the bridges and cradled many cold moons" (60). Shortly
after learning that Dick is a medical doctor—like her own de-
ceased father—Rosemary attempts to seduce him. Despite his
infatuation Dick resists, but the effort exposes his vulnerability:
"He was suddenly confused, . . . and for a moment his usual grace,
the tensile strength of his balance, was absent" (65). At the battlefield Dick had waxed eloquent about the "tremendous sureties"
destroyed by the war; now in his private life he confronts for the
first time a wavering sense of appropriate conduct. Rosemary's
charms have aroused in him an unconscious need to become the

lover of yet another eighteen-year-old girl with a father complex, to reenact with Rosemary his romance six years earlier with Nicole. On this night he fights the temptation, but after a few more days in the unreal city he will be ready to yield to desire.

Fitzgerald stretches out the next day over three chapters, depicting events which intensify the strangeness of the Parisian scene and expose the unconscious urges at work on the principal characters. When Rosemary and Nicole meet in the morning for "a series of fittings," the author implies a developing rivalry: in the taxi Rosemary "looked at Nicole, matching herself against her" (67). The twinning implied here finds a geographical correlative, as Rosemary and Nicole discover that as girls they have both lived on the rue des Saints-Pères, the street of the Holy Fathers, an address hinting at the father-fixation which they share. After a luncheon at the Norths' apartment on the rue Guynemer (where the Murphys lived in 1928), Dick, Nicole, Rosemary, Abe, and Mary meet young Collis Clay at Franco-American Films in Passy for a screening of *Daddy's Girl*. Here and elsewhere in *Tender is the Night*, Fitzgerald's representation of the film industry, the cult of stardom, and the phantasm of cinema itself bears witness to that "flight from reality" which Eksteins associates with the twenties. Dazzled by Rosemary's Hollywood aura, Dick begins to see her as a glamorous incarnation of modernity itself.[29] If his clinical training exposes the crude psychoanalytic meaning of her film role—which involves "a father complex so apparent that he winced for all psychologists at the vicious sentimentality" (69)— the screening also quickens a desire to be "united" with Rosemary like the father in the film.

After the Norths and Nicole leave to run errands, Dick and Rosemary attend a tea party on the Left Bank. This hallucinatory episode offers a glimpse of the lesbian community there and plunges Rosemary into the confusion of sexual ambiguity. Again the street name carries a suggestive connotation: the women's salon is located on the rue Monsieur. Through a bit of creative geography, Fitzgerald hints at the dissolving of sexual difference which occurs at this address.[30] At the moment of entering the house, Rosemary feels that she has entered a new age:

> Once inside the door there was nothing of the past, nor of any present that Rosemary knew. The outer shell, the masonry,

seemed rather to enclose the future so that it was an electric shock, a definite nervous experience, perverted as a breakfast of oatmeal and hashish, to cross that threshold, if it could be so called, into the long hall of blue steel, silver-gilt, and the myriad facets of many oddly bevelled mirrors. (71)

Perceiving the unreality of the place, Rosemary has the momentary sensation of being on a motion-picture set. The physical setting creates the impression of crossing a boundary or threshold into a realm of sensation in which "oddly bevelled mirrors" fragment reality into multiple, incongruous images—in effect, into the perspective of modernism. Fitzgerald depicts an interior room which conveys the idea of ambiguous change: "no one knew what this room meant because it was evolving into something else, becoming everything a room was not" (71–72). Rosemary faces a crowd composed mostly of women and notices a striking trio sitting on a bench: "They were all tall and slender with small heads groomed like manikins' heads, and as they talked the heads waved gracefully about above their dark tailored suits, rather like long-stemmed flowers and rather like cobras' hoods" (72). These stylish yet venomous lesbians are gossiping about the Divers, and as Rosemary masks her indignation she finds herself talking to "a neat, slick girl with a lovely boy's face" who begins to "play up" and beg for a date. Confused by the odd ambience and by sexual advances from a girl who looks like a boy, Rosemary quickly departs with Dick, "moving over the brief threshold of the future to the sudden past of the stone façade without" (74). In a scene which anticipates Djuna Barnes' *Nightwood*, Fitzgerald represents a lesbian subculture which in its appropriation of bourgeois conventions embodies the subversive force of modernism itself.[31]

Another kind of unreality typifies the moveable feast which Dick stages later that night, presumably for Rosemary's benefit. The party involves "a quick Odyssey over Paris" in a caravan featuring a jeweled car owned by the shah of Persia. The Norths, the Divers, and Rosemary attract an international group which includes "the heir to a Scandinavian throne." Fitzgerald reports that "people joined them as if by magic, accompanied them as specialists, almost guides, through a phase of the evening" (76). Dick's organization of events, his "technic of moving many varied types" into position, as if he were commanding "an infantry battalion," delights Rosemary, who compares the evening to a Hollywood party. At the Ritz bar, the Americans dupe the waiters into singing war songs for Abe North, who impersonates General Pershing. The revelers insist that the general "brooks no delay. Every man, every gun is at his service" (78). The reconnoitering of Paris, the use of "guides," Dick's marshaling of his "battalion," and the evocation of Pershing all suggest that the party in some obscure way unfolds as a parodic military exercise in which Dick and his friends turn their recent, melancholy visit to Thiepval and Beaumont Hamel into madcap escapism. Their hilarity obliquely implies the emotional and psychological burden which the war has imposed.

On another level the pace and extravagance of the party, together with the associations of royalty, underscore Fitzgerald's familiar claim that the rich are different because they lead unimaginably fabulous lives. For Dick and his cohorts, Paris provides an ideal space for the staging of fantasies: it offers a visual spectacle which for a certain amount of money can be requisitioned as image or illusion. The denouement of the party illustrates this point: after Dick and Nicole have returned to their hotel, Rosemary finds herself atop a market wagon filled with "thousands of carrots," rolling along with the Norths, Collis Clay, and two improbable nouveau riche types, "a manufacturer of dolls' voices from Newark and . . . a big splendidly dressed oil Indian named George T. Horseprotection" (79). Fitzgerald's giddy expatriates have commandeered a farm wagon en route to market, not to indulge in agricultural nostalgia but precisely to flaunt their privileged status as rich Americans and their class difference from the wagon's owner. The economic reality expressed by the fresh produce never impinges on Rosemary's fantasy: "The earth in the carrot beards was fragrant and sweet in the darkness, and Rosemary was so high up in the load that she could hardly see the others. . . . Their voices came from far off, as if they were having experiences different from hers, different and far away" (79). The external scene seems a mere extension of her desire, and when she notices at dawn's early light a truck transporting "a huge horse-chestnut tree in full bloom bound for the Champs-Elysées," she sees it as a "lovely person," identifies herself with it, and imagines that "everything all at once seemed gorgeous" (79). Paris has

Figure 17. The Gare St. Lazare, where Maria Wallis shoots a man in *Tender is the Night.*

on this evening become the narcissistic reflection of her all-American loveliness.

The following morning, though, a darker fantasy envelops Fitzgerald's characters. At the Gare St. Lazare (fig. 17), a dissipated Abe waits "under the fouled glass dome" for the boat train which will take him back to the United States. His sullen demeanor betrays his "will to die" (83), and as events later confirm, he will indeed disappear "into the dark maw of violence," beaten to death in an American speakeasy.[32] On this occasion, however, violence erupts in Paris; just as the train is pulling out, a young American woman, Maria Wallis, pulls a revolver from her purse and shoots a man on the platform. Signaling a theme of mounting importance, Fitzgerald notes that the victim, an Englishman, has been shot "through his identification card" (84). The attack seems unmotivated, and we never discover what "dark matter" precipitated it; yet we may infer that a relationship has gone horribly awry. The shooting has a temporary, estranging effect even upon the would-be lovers, Dick and Rosemary: "For a moment each seemed unreal to the other." Through rhetorical hints, Fitzgerald indicates that Dick experiences "a loss of control" and feels "panic" while Rosemary suffers from "a totality of shock." The scene at the station has "ended the time in Paris" and stunned Fitzgerald's characters:

The shots had entered into all their lives: echoes of violence followed them out onto the pavement where two porters held a post-mortem beside them as they waited for a taxi.

"Tu as vu le revolver? Il était très petit, vraie perle—un jouet."

"Mais, assez puissant!" said the other porter sagely. "Tu as vu sa chemise? Assez de sang pour se croire à la guerre." (85–86)

Once again the author invokes the memory of the war, here to suggest an implicit connection between the shooting at the Gare St. Lazare and the bloodshed of 1914–18. A contagion of violence has infected the world, and its eruption at the train station—at a precarious moment in the intimate relations between Dick, Nicole, and Rosemary—displays the deadly force of "high-explosive love."

At an alfresco luncheon "across from the Luxembourg Gardens," the three subsequently try to forget the morning's horrors. But Rosemary develops menstrual cramps, Dick feels "profoundly unhappy," and even Nicole exhibits testiness. They dine in an atmosphere of tension and mounting suspicion; Dick privately wonders, "What did Nicole think?" The afternoon takes a Freudian turn, however, after the departure of Rosemary and Nicole; Collis Clay happens along, shares some wine with Dick, and casually relates the story of Rosemary and a Yale man on the train to Chicago. "Seems they locked the door and pulled down the blinds," Clay says, "and I guess there was some heavy stuff going on when the conductor came for the tickets and knocked on the door." The story has an immediate, unnerving effect on Dick:

With every detail imagined, with even envy for the pair's community of misfortune in the vestibule, Dick felt a change taking place within him. Only the image of a third person, even a vanished one, entering into his relation with Rosemary was needed to throw him off his balance and send him through waves of pain, misery, desire, desperation. The vividly pictured hand on Rosemary's cheek, the quicker breath, the white excitement of the event viewed from outside, the inviolable secret warmth within.

—Do you mind if I pull down the curtain?
—Please do. It's too light in here. (88)

Through successive reiterations of the last lines, Fitzgerald implies the obsessive force of the story as a primal scene. When Dick later drops by his bank to cash a check, his manner implies agitation; he tries to calculate which clerk "would guess least of the unhappy predicament in which he found himself and, also, which one would be least likely to talk" (89). Even if he is withdrawing funds to finance an affair, it is hard to imagine how a bank clerk could surmise the specific nature of Dick's "predicament." As he sorts through his mail, finding a letter for Rosemary, a distressing question flashes through his consciousness: "Do you mind if I pull down the curtain?" In the wake of the shooting, the story of her presumed deflowering has shattered Dick's composure, triggering desire as well as prospective guilt.

At this juncture Fitzgerald uses Parisian topography to signal Dick's disorientation. Instinctively pursuing Rosemary, he hires a taxi to take him to her studio in Passy. "Go to the Muette," he tells the driver. "I'll direct you from there." Yet Dick does not give directions: "He was rendered so uncertain by the events of the last forty-eight hours that he was not even sure what he wanted to do" (91). He gets out at La Muette, a park near the Bois du Boulogne, and brandishing his briefcase and walking stick—signs of his precarious respectability—he walks along "swayed and driven as an animal." Soon he finds himself in the midst of a "melancholy neighborhood," surrounded by strangely portentous signs: " 'Vêtements Ecclésiastiques,' 'Déclaration de Décès' and 'Pompes Funèbres.' Life and Death" (91). Clerical clothing, death notices, funerals: Dick, the minister's son from Buffalo, perceives in these signs a reflection of his fateful errancy.[33] "He knew that what he was now doing marked a turning point in his life," Fitzgerald remarks. "It was out of line with everything that had preceded it— even out of line with what effect he might hope to produce upon Rosemary." His behavior represents, instead, the "projection of some submerged reality"; Dick, the psychologist, has surrendered to the irrational, to the unconscious urges which have been exposed and activated by the unreal city in which his dreamlike experience unfolds.

For three-quarters of an hour, Dick paces the rue des Saintes-Anges, an invented street which ironically evokes the image of Rosemary as one of Dick's "holy angels."[34] At this acknowledged "turning point," Fitzgerald stages a puzzling confrontation in

which an American war veteran with a "sinister smile" accosts
Dick on the sidewalk. Though his "menacing eyes" seem to be-
speak criminal intent, the stranger boasts that he has "made
plenty money" in Paris selling newspapers to American tourists;
he carries a cartoon depicting "Americans pouring from the gang-
plank of a liner freighted with gold" (93). The fellow obviously
typifies that swarm of American opportunists which inundated
Paris in the twenties; Fitzgerald here suggests a vast qualitative
difference between the two compatriots.[35] Yet late in the novel, he
undercuts this contrast: on the Riviera, at yet another turning
point, Dick again meets the same American "of sinister aspect,"
recognizing him by the clipping with "cartooned millions of
Americans pouring from liners with bags of gold" (309). While the
man is still hawking newspapers to rich tourists, Dick himself
has now become an antithetical caricature of the American mon-
eybags—a ruined and depleted expatriate about to return to the
United States.

As he languishes in Passy, Dick has already yielded to that
complex "submerged reality" which will effect his deterioration.
At a corner café, his telephone call to Rosemary (who is back at
the hotel) reveals his "extraordinary condition"; when he asks if
she is alone, the primal scene again flashes through his mind (94).
Under its spell, he has only one desire: to be alone with her, to pull
down the curtain himself as a prelude to lovemaking. As they
talk, Dick imagines her room and remembers the "dust of powder
over her tan," surrendering to the fantasy constructed by his own
longing. When he emerges from the café, still carrying the ac-
coutrements of class and profession, his disorientation seems
complete: "In a minute he was out in the street marching along
toward the Muette, *or away from it*, his small brief-case still in his
hand, his gold-headed stick held at a sword-like angle" (94, my
emphasis). With his stick poised for action, announcing his sexual readiness, Dick's topographical confusion betrays a concomitant loss of moral direction. Ironically, he makes his way back to
the hotel only to discover that Rosemary, feeling "not very well"
at the onset of her period, has elected to dine alone.

The last nightmarish day in Paris begins, appropriately, in
confusion, as Nicole awakens to find Dick's bed empty (a sign of
his unrest) and a police officer at the door looking for one "Mr.

Afghan North." Though Nicole declares that Abe has "gone to America," she learns that he is indeed still in Paris; the officer explains that North has been robbed by a Negro and must identify a suspect. "Mystified" by the account, Nicole sends the officer away; she brusquely slams down the receiver when the hotel office calls to ask whether she will speak to a Negro named "Crawshow," whose friend Mr. Freeman has been mistakenly put in prison. The situation becomes more muddled when Abe later explains to Dick that he has "launched a race riot" and that he intends to "get Freeman out of jail" (98). Abe's predicament offers further evidence of his dissolution, leading Nicole to wonder why "so many smart men go to pieces nowadays" and to ask Dick pointedly: "Why is it just Americans who dissipate?" Abe's disin- tegration of course prefigures Dick's decline; and both in effect herald the crash of the American stock market in 1929. But Ni- cole's question goes to the very heart of Fitzgerald's critique of American identity and implies the existence of a self-destructive contradiction at its very core.

At lunch downstairs, the three find themselves surrounded by "families of Americans staring around at families of Americans"; a waiter identifies them as "gold-star muzzers"—mothers of the American war dead. Again an incidental detail evokes a remem- brance of combat casualties; slipping into a reverie Dick recalls not only the Great War but also the Civil War: "Momentarily, he sat again on his father's knee, riding with Moseby while the old loyalties and devotions fought on around him" (101). The presence of the Gold Star mothers puts Dick in touch with "an older America" and briefly stirs his faith in the nineteenth-century ideals of his father. But Dick is caught between two sets of values, one belonging to an idealistic past and the other to a crass, acquisi- tive present; in Fitzgerald's mythography he embodies the contra- dictory essence of the American self. If the Gold Star mothers represent an old-fashioned gallantry, Nicole and Rosemary epito- mize "the whole new world in which he believed"—the world of pleasure, wealth, glamour, and power. Ironically as he dines in the company of "sobered women who had come to mourn for their dead," an overwhelming question stirs his brain: "Do you mind if I pull down the curtain?" (101). Here Fitzgerald again hints at the potent connection between death and desire, helping us to understand how the slaughter of 1914–18 might have triggered what he elsewhere called the "precocious intimacies" of the twenties.³⁶

After an uneventful chapter which depicts Abe North in the Ritz bar, drinking to forget the "nightmare" in which he has become involved, Fitzgerald resumes Dick's libidinal quest, noting the early stages of his psychic fragmentation: "Dick moved on through the rain, demoniac and frightened, the passions of many men inside him and nothing simple that he could see" (104). Troubled by the events of the previous twenty-four hours, Rosemary, too, has been "playing around with chaos," yet when Dick enters her room, the sexual consummation of their romance seems imminent. They are not exactly in love with each other; rather, they are in love with the illusions each has created about the other. Rosemary presses her lips "to the beautiful cold image she had created" and then in a moment of rare insight tells Dick, "Oh, we're such *actors*—you and I" (105), perhaps suspecting the psychoanalytic truth that each is acting out a rehearsed, fantasized scene with the other. But a knock at the door interrupts their tryst and plunges them both into the racial nightmare excited by Abe North.

Incongruities multiply when North introduces "a very frightened, concerned colored man," a "Mr. Peterson of Stockholm" (105), who has witnessed "the early morning dispute in Montparnasse" (106). This is the very man earlier identified as "a Negro from Copenhagen" in Abe's report of "a race riot in Montmartre" (98). Peterson has falsely accused one black man who was not even present at the time of the robbery; when those charges were dropped, the police then wrongly arrested "the prominent Negro restaurateur, Freeman." A third black man, the actual "culprit," has surfaced to explain that he had grabbed a "fifty-franc note to pay for drinks that Abe had ordered." The net effect of this wild account is that "Abe had succeeded in the space of an hour in entangling himself in the personal lives, consciences, and emotions of one Afro-European and three Afro-Americans inhabiting the French Latin quarter" (106). Fearing retribution from Freeman, the "Afro-European" Peterson begs Dick for help and then withdraws to the hall to let Abe plead his case. When Rosemary returns to her room moments later, looking for her wristwatch, she discovers "a dead Negro . . . stretched upon her bed" (109).

This unlikely sequence of events, which most critics have ascribed to Fitzgerald's thematic overreaching in *Tender is the Night*, raises a number of disconcerting issues.[37] The principal difficulty concerns the relation of Peterson's murder to the intrigue involving Dick, Nicole, and Rosemary. This problem seems linked, moreover, to the larger question of Fitzgerald's construction of racial and ethnic difference. In the elegant milieu of the Divers, Abe North has committed an expatriate social blunder by "entangling himself" with black people, by creating the situation of "unfamiliar Negro faces bobbing up in unexpected places and around unexpected corners, and insistent Negro voices on the phone" (106). These intrusions of the black into the privileged space of the (white) American expatriate are made to seem both offensive and threatening. Dick fails to "appreciate the mess that Peterson's in," because he regards the whole affair as "some nigger scrap" (110); a dispute between two blacks can have no claim to his attention. He tries to stereotype Peterson as "a small, respectable Negro, on the suave model that heels the Republican party in the border states" (106). Yet as a Scandinavian black, Peterson represents an ethnic anomaly, perhaps even an affront to some unspoken notion of Nordic purity. (One recalls Tom Buchanan in *The Great Gatsby* spouting racist theory.) For Dick, Peterson is a nuisance not simply because he has attached himself to Abe North but also because he represents the potential collapse of those social barriers which have long kept the darker races in their supposed "places."[38]

Thus when Rosemary finds Peterson's bloody corpse in her bed, Dick acts quickly to remove the body, to reinscribe the boundaries of racial difference, and thus to restore order. He knows that the discovery of a black man, even a dead one, in the bed of the white, putatively virginal "Daddy's girl" would generate a scandal disastrous to Rosemary's career. But the bizarre coincidence of Peterson's being found precisely in that place where Dick had hoped to be raises a more complicated issue, compelling us to ask what it means when a black man displaces a white at the site of erotic fantasy. Does it disclose a fear of sexual encroachment by the dark-skinned Other? Does it imply that Rosemary's status as a cultural goddess is assured by a system of patriarchal domination which requires the sacrifice of the black?

Fitzgerald offers no explanations, and it seems highly unlikely that he even considered such theoretical implications. But with an instinct for suggestive "grotesquerie," he places Peterson in Rosemary's bed so that the black man's blood saturates her coverlet and blanket, effecting another intriguing substitution—here, for the menstrual (if not hymenal) stain which might have resulted from her intercourse with Dick.

The stained coverlet and blanket of course produce another, more perplexing substitution. Dick disposes of the bedding by handing it to Nicole, who carries it to the bathroom where she suffers a mental relapse at the sight of the blood. Releasing a torrent of "verbal inhumanity," she accuses Dick of intruding on her privacy with his bloody bedspread, thereby alluding to yet another primal scene, that of her father's incestuous violation. Because the bedding which precipitates this breakdown actually comes from the bed of "Daddy's girl," Nicole's outburst obviously reinforces the symbolic parallel between her situation and Rosemary's. But what does Nicole's loss of virginity have to do with the bloody death of Jules Peterson, the Afro-European? Perhaps the clue lies in Peterson's role as a "small manufacturer of shoe polish," driven into exile because he refused to divulge his formula in Stockholm. If Devereux Warren is the prototype of the successful white capitalist, Peterson represents the emerging black entrepreneur bidding to compete for wealth and power. As the dark rival of the white capitalist, Peterson has been driven from Scandinavia; as the black counterpart of Devereux Warren, he also functions as a scapegoat, undergoing an absolute reversal of Warren's fate in what René Girard would call an act of "sacrificial substitution." Innocent of any impropriety with Rosemary, he sheds his *own* blood in the bed of Daddy's girl, suffering the death that Warren "didn't have the nerve" to inflict upon himself. Far from causing psychological damage to Rosemary, Peterson by his death frees her from Dick's paternal attachment; after the crime, she moves to another hotel and leaves Paris without saying good-bye to the Divers. Patently a sacrificial figure, Peterson also restores at least a semblance of devotion to the marriage of Dick and Nicole; by his blood they are redeemed, temporarily at least, from suspicion and enmity.

The histrionic scene which unfolds in the Divers' bathroom

caps a sequence of confrontations and discoveries which occur in Paris and which associate the city with a dreamlike or hallucinatory unreality. These uncanny scenes expose unconscious desires and anxieties, fantasies of power or sexual conquest, and nightmares of violence or powerlessness. Through such episodes as the lesbian party on the rue Monsieur, the "fabulous" mobile fête, the shooting at the Gare St. Lazare, Dick's disorientation in Passy, and the assassination of Jules Peterson, as well as through the evocation of three secret sexual scenes, Fitzgerald exposes the social and psychological chaos beneath the seemingly ordered surface of everyday life. The recurrent intrusion of the unconscious manifests those forces which are commonly repressed or denied: the irrational urges and volatile tensions masked by legal constraints and hierarchical social practices. Fitzgerald allows us to glimpse, in the Paris section, an impending explosion; Nicole's breakdown in the hotel bathroom seems emblematic insofar as it represents the return of the repressed, the eruption of chaos. Three times Dick tells her, "Control yourself." Yet what the bloody bedspread has summoned forth is precisely the irrepressible and uncontrollable. In the Freudian scheme of the novel, this scene acknowledges the power of the unconscious, and throughout the Paris section, a relaxed morality allows the unconscious to manifest itself repeatedly.

Within the novel's historical framework, this moment also discloses on the social level a ubiquitous violence. The bloody result of a "race riot," Peterson's death implies the presence of a rage which rarely obtrudes upon the comfortable world of the Divers. Yet Fitzgerald means by this and other details to uncover a seething, revolutionary fury loosed upon the dying Western world. His references to Russians displaced by the Bolsheviks or to ethnic types (like George T. Horseprotection) who appear in unlikely places all point toward a vast social upheaval, implicitly disconcerting to the Dick Divers whose sense of personal security is grounded in a notion of "the exact relation that existed between the classes." *Tender is the Night* calls attention to the breakdown of class differences and expresses alarm at the transgression of social boundaries. Jules Peterson personifies the social transformations associated with the modern age, with what Fitzgerald (following Spengler) assumes to be the decline of the West. The shoe polish manufacturer defies the stereotype of Nordic racial purity, threatens the hegemony of white capital, and at last violates the sanctum of the all-American white goddess. He embodies the principle of social chaos which figures to disrupt the caste system to which Dick Diver subscribes.

The Paris section occupies roughly one-fifth of *Tender is the Night;* yet it marks a pivotal phase, a point of crisis, for the Divers. If their respective destinies form a criss-crossed plot through the reciprocal stories of Nicole's recovery and Dick's collapse, the vectors of change intersect in Paris. Clearly, by pursuing Rosemary, Dick commits himself to a project as compulsive as it is destructive; his yearning for "Daddy's girl" soon becomes a generalized obsession for young women which undermines his professional discipline.[39] As we see in the bathroom scene, Nicole likewise suffers a crisis in Paris. Whereas her hysteria on the Riviera had not been so serious, "the collapse in Paris was another matter, adding significance to the first one. It prophesied possibly a new cycle, a new pousse of the malady" (168). In her bathroom ravings, Nicole seems to confuse Dick with her father, telling him, "I'll wear [the bloody spread] for you—I'm not ashamed, though it was such a pity" (112). This breakdown of the distinction between the wounding, biological father and the nurturing, symbolic father implies an erosion of Nicole's trust. The week in Paris changes her relationship to Dick and injects an element of doubt which paradoxically opens the way to her eventual self-reliance.

Judged by locodescriptive criteria, Fitzgerald's representation of Paris in *Tender is the Night* seems comparatively superficial. The author did not possess that attentiveness to the inner life of the city which excited Miller; he never shared Hemingway's fetish for geographical precision. Jean Méral characterizes the Paris of Fitzgerald's novel as "a vague limbo in which characters hang suspended." In only two incidents—the party on the rue Monsieur and the shooting at the Gare St. Lazare—do tangible places assume interpretive significance. The third-person Frances Melarky version of the novel included a wild scene with the Norths, George T. Horseprotection, and the manufacturer of dolls' voices carousing at a Montmartre night spot called the Georgia Cabin.[40] But in the published version, that episode becomes a mere allusion to Montmartre by Abe North. The novel offers glimpses of Voisin's restaurant, the Ritz bar, the Hotel Roi George (the Georges V), the Muette quarter of Passy, the Luxembourg Gardens, the rue de Rivoli, and the Champs-Elysées. Expressing a French perspective, Méral insists that these backgrounds possess "the unreality of a theater set."[41] But that is exactly Fitzgerald's point: the city is fundamentally a locus of the imaginary. For Dick and his expatriate cohorts, Paris is a theater of dreams, a scene of fantasy and excess which becomes a terrifying site of violent change.

Fear and loathing also pervade the Parisian setting of Djuna Barnes's *Nightwood* (1936), a novel which propels us into an even stranger and denser atmosphere of unreality. For all of its Gothic flourishes and Elizabethan sonorities, the narrative projects an unmistakably modernist vision of exile as it juxtaposes the problem of gender against the dilemma of American identity. In this formulation, nocturnal Paris objectifies the libidinal confusion of the novel's personae, who move in seemingly random fashion as if caught in a circular dream of longing and betrayal. Their various journeys home (or to places once conceived to be home) help to illuminate the experience of exile, yet *Nightwood* resists the operations which would reduce it to paraphrase. Its modernity resides in its representation of ambiguous, undecidable relations and in its insistence upon the enigmatic duality of the human animal. Barnes raises the latter issue repeatedly by collapsing the distinction between the human and the bestial. Andrew Field has commented on the clash in Barnes's writing between "contrary forces of bestiality and rectitude," a conflict which produces odd tensions and perplexing contrasts.[42] Yet despite its singularities, the novel nevertheless affords a suggestive comparison with *Tender is the Night* as a reconstruction of American disorientation in Paris in the late twenties.

After establishing herself in New York as a free-lance journalist linked to the bohemian community of Greenwich Village, Barnes began to find newspaper features a limited genre; she left for France in 1920 under an informal agreement with *McCall's* to act as a European correspondent.[43] In her 1922 essay "Vagaries Malicieux," she recounted her first trip abroad (at age twenty-eight) on a boat jammed with "disappointed teachers from the Middle West, who sat on deck eating gift fruit sarcastically."

Arriving at the Gare St. Lazare, Barnes confronted the foreignness of Paris and what sounded to her like the gabble of the French language. "It took me several days to get over the sensation of dangerous make-believe," she confessed, expressing the essential dislocation of the exile. From her hotel on the rue Jacob, Barnes visited the church of St. Germain des Prés, met James Joyce at Deux Magots, and admired "the chic of Paris, the beauty of its women, the magic of its very existence." Yet she refused to romanticize the city, informing a Frenchman that "the multiplication of Paris had been its destruction." She feared that "too many people had reported Paris,—it had the fame of a too beautiful woman." Dismissing such touristic sites as Napoleon's tomb, the Luxembourg Gardens, and the Folies-Bergère, she conceded a liking for men's walking styles and women's cosmetics, for cafés, for religious paintings ("dwindled Christs and Madonnas"), and for churches. She also liked the Cluny museum where amid its medieval treasures she sought an effigy of the mythical Thaïs. "I was told," she confesses, "that in one museum or other, there lay the body of the most beautiful woman,—brief of flesh and of legend immortal, and . . . I had come to Paris more on her account than she on mine, and herein lay my pleasure and my pain."[44] As this remark implies, Barnes had come to Paris in part to search for female beauty and to explore her lesbian inclinations, confronting the pleasure and pain of her attraction to women.

Apart from three relatively brief visits to America, Barnes lived in Paris continuously from 1920 until 1932. During those dozen years she published numerous magazine and newspaper articles; a score of short stories (collected in three different volumes); a parodic illustrated survey of lesbianism in Paris (*The Ladies' Almanack*); and a baroque, mock-epic novel (*Ryder*), which served roughly the same function in Barnes's career that *The Making of Americans* did in Stein's: to throw off the patriarchal influence of her American past through a disguised version of family history.[45] Paris provided the requisite distance from which Barnes could satirize the bucolic childhood world of Storm-King mountain near Cornwall-on-Hudson, a world dominated in the novel by the polygamist-patriarch, Wendell Ryder, a figure palpably inspired by Wald Barnes. Field suggests that in *Ryder* Barnes grappled with the dominance of her father, whose unorthodox notion of an extended family apparently induced him to offer his teenage daughter as a sexual "gift" to his brother-in-law, with the collusion of Djuna's grandmother, Zadel Barnes Gustafson.[46] Whether or not Barnes suffered precisely this fate, she detested her father, assumed thereafter a loosely feminist view of gender relations, and struggled throughout much of her adult life with a deeply conflicted sense of affectional preference. After a three-year heterosexual affair with a New York journalist named Courtenay Lemon, Barnes lived during the twenties in Paris (at 9, rue St.-Romain) with Thelma Wood, an American sculptor and silverpoint artist. In a famous remark Barnes later declared: "I'm not a lesbian. I just loved Thelma." Biographical evidence partly supports her claim: the liaison with Thelma Wood was Barnes's only significant love affair with a woman; by contrast, she had many briefer, intimate relationships with men.[47] Yet as she hints in "Vagaries Malicieux" and elsewhere in her writing, she felt irresistibly attracted to certain women and stirred by desires which she was reluctant to name or to acknowledge publicly.

Nowhere did Barnes articulate more brilliantly the contradictions of her own situation as an American exile of uncertain sexual affinity than in *Nightwood* (1936). Composed mostly in England in the aftermath of her break with Thelma, the novel rewrites that troubled romance as a "haunted" relationship between two radically dissimilar women, Nora Flood and Robin Vote, who are separated by a meddlesome intruder, the "squatter" Jenny Petherbridge. Yet Barnes's text goes far beyond a roman à clef: to this trio of American women the author links Felix Volkbein, an Austro-Italian Jew obsessed by the idea of aristocracy and consumed by the need to beget and protect the son who will carry on his spurious nobility. As a commentator on the dark universe inhabited by these characters, Barnes retrieves from *Ryder* Dr. Matthew O'Connor, the homosexual obstetrician, who emerges in *Nightwood* as a garrulous poseur, a transvestite whose raging, impossible desire is to be a mother.

As several critics have remarked, O'Connor's role resembles that of Eliot's Tiresias insofar as he witnesses the sexual rivalry provoked by Robin Vote and though male displays an empathetic understanding of female experience. The parallel seems deliberate; Barnes admired *The Waste Land*, later acceded to Eliot's

editorial ideas about cutting the novel, and welcomed his suggestion for its eventual title. As Donna Gerstenberger has noted,
Nightwood "stakes out the same territory as Eliot's poem, which
is that of a civilization (particularly Western European) in decay,
an aristocracy in disarray, a people estranged from a sense of
identity." But she goes further, arguing that Barnes's novel is "a
more radically experimental work than *The Waste Land*."[48] Initially this last claim seems extravagant: *Nightwood* followed Eliot's poem by fourteen years (as it did another influential text,
Joyce's *Ulysses*). More than a decade of subsequent literary expe-
rimentation—much of it conducted in the little magazines published in Paris and elsewhere—helped Barnes to achieve the modernist effects of her second novel.[49] In some respects her novel
seems, moreover, scarcely innovative: Barnes divides the narrative into separate chapters which form a chronological progression; the characters' lives connect intelligibly; an effaced, seemingly omniscient narrator tells much of the story; certain motifs
(such as animal imagery, or the gesture of "bowing down") give
the story a modicum of formal unity.

Yet there can be no question about the novel's status as an
innovative modernist text. Despite the role of Barnes's narrator,
Karen Kaivola rightly remarks that "many voices speak in *Nightwood*, undermining the authority of any one position and producing a contradictory and heterogeneous discourse composed of an
amalgam of styles." Judith Lee perceives the novel as "distinctively modern . . . in its consideration of what our concepts of
masculine and feminine imply," while Jane Marcus discusses
Nightwood as "the representative modernist text, a prose poem of
abstraction, tracing the political unconscious of the rise of fas-
cism."[50] While all of these claims have validity, Gerstenberger
locates the quintessential, modernist feature which distinguishes
Nightwood from *The Waste Land:* "It is a novel that rages against
the imprisoning structures of the language and narratives of the
'day,' which create a history built on the oppositions of night/day,
past/present, reason, madness, 'normal'/'abnormal,' truth/false-
hood, gender, and origins (both historical and textual). It is a book
that relentlessly undermines grounds for categorization. The ideal
and the real, the beautiful and the ugly, subject and object become
irrelevant distinctions."[51] Her observation resonates with a claim

by Jane Marcus, that *"Nightwood* is about merging, dissolution, and, above all, hybridization—mixed metaphors, mixed levels of discourse from the lofty to the low, mixed 'languages' from medical practice, circus argot, church dogma, and homosexual slang."[52] That is, Barnes's novel relentlessly subverts those "rational" distinctions and differences which, until the advent of modernism, held in place traditional notions of moral and social order and conventional ways of defining the self.

Precisely in the way that it challenges the concept of identity, *Nightwood* exposes a crisis symptomatic of modernism and justifies Barnes's attention to the experience of exile. In some sense all of her expatriate characters suffer from a profound uncertainty about who they are, where they "belong," and what they desire. Apart from portions of the first chapter set in Vienna and Berlin and some brief American scenes, the drama of their various anxieties takes place—significantly—in what Marcus calls "the night world of lesbian, homosexual, and transvestite Paris." In the chapter entitled "Watchman, What of the Night?" Barnes suggests that the nocturnal world over which O'Connor presides is figuratively the region of the irrational, the unconscious, and the bestial. The doctor himself explains that "the very constitution of twilight is a fabulous reconstruction of fear, fear bottom-out and wrong side up" (80). Fantastic metamorphoses occur in this shadow world where the self becomes another. Nora tells O'Connor, "Now I see that the night does something to a person's identity, even when asleep" (81). More radically the doctor describes an "unknown land" where the dreamer, in the company of anonymous "merrymakers," commits unspeakable acts "in a house without an address, in a street in no town, citizened with people with no names to deny them" (88). In the Freudian logic of the narrative, these phantom conspirators are always projections of the dreamer: "Their very lack of identity makes them ourselves." The night world thus dissolves the difference between subject and object, making the other a double of self even as that self remains anonymous and unknowable; it is the place where, as Karen Kaivola says, "one most directly encounters the instability and contradictions of identity."[53]

Nightwood thus projects the condition of uncertainty as the distinguishing sign of modernist experience. "There are only con-

fusions," O'Connor tells Nora, "confusions and defeated anxieties" (22). In her fictional analysis of the turmoil of modernism,
Barnes returns insistently to the question of identity, tying the
ontological perplexities of her characters to the enigma of self.
This question arises at a dinner party in Berlin when the Duchess
of Broadback asks Felix Volkbein, "Am I what I say? Are you? Is
the doctor?" (25). Later, Felix formulates what appears to be the
author's skeptical conclusion when he observes that "the more
we learn of a person, the less we know" (111). More pointedly
O'Connor frames the issue as an exclamation, a cry of exaspera-
tion, rather than a query: "Who is anybody!" (154). Yet this elemental uncertainty marks the speculative crux of *Nightwood;*
Barnes engages the problem at several levels and contemplates
not only the fate of identity under modernism but also the general
dilemma of the exiled self and the specific vicissitudes of the
American exile, male and female. Her exploration of the problematic aspects of modernist identity emphasizes three constituent
features, indicated by one's relation to gender, to memory, and to
place, respectively. By linking the stories of her principal characters, Barnes suggests ways in which these conditions of being
impinge upon the sense of self. Ultimately she examines three
kinds of dissociation which destabilize personal identity. Paris
provides the essential context for this study, insofar as its nocturnal unreality evokes those compulsions and fears which expose
the inherent confusions of modernism.

Within what James B. Scott calls "the inverted and introspec-
tive world of *Nightwood,*" gender and the ambiguities of desire
pose the most formidable problem for Barnes's characters.[54] Her
representation of "deviance" can scarcely be summarized, for
each figure incorporates an idiosyncratic notion of gender and
acts out a different search for love; indeed, her characters represent an array of alternative sexualities, implied by specific preferences, fetishes, and fantasies. Yet this novel so manifestly about
gender and sexuality has little to do with eroticism.[55] Barnes
glosses over the impregnation of Robin by Felix and depicts only
fleeting scenes of passion between women, such as the groping of
Jenny and Robin in the carriage, which prompts O'Connor to
voice what may have been the author's own cynical view of desire: "Love, that terrible thing!" (75). In some sense, all of her

characters are prisoners of the flesh, alienated from their own bodies and their own sexualities. The recurrent animal imagery connects the carnal with the bestial, suggesting Barnes's underlying perception of lust as horror.

But her characters suffer as well from other forms of alienation. Effectively cut off from the past and from history itself, they are exiled in the modernist moment; the marginality of these misfits excludes them from what Julie L. Abraham calls "the history of the official record."[56] Moreover, each has an ironic relation to memory which complicates the construction of identity and the articulation of a gendered role. As in *Tender* is the *Night*, a psychoanalytic matrix focuses attention in *Nightwood* upon repetition mechanisms which betray repressed material. But Barnes's characters are typically unable to reconstruct the past in ways which free them from its effects; they remain only obscurely aware of prior events which might explain present confusions. They seem likewise displaced geographically and circulate in the city of exile in ways which which suggest the ironies of their dislocation. That is, their patterns of movement and association within the Parisian milieu provide an index to their alienation from themselves.

Felix Volkbein, who clings to the title of Baron "to dazzle his own estrangement," suffers because he has no real past and no meaningful attachment to his native Vienna except as a locus of illusion. Orphaned from birth, his passion for history springs from an anxiety about his antecedents—a problem represented by the portraits said to be of his grandparents, which in fact depict two "ancient actors" whose likenesses his father Guido purchased to provide "an alibi for the blood" (7). Guido has in fact concealed his Jewish heritage with a fraudulent Austrian pedigree; this ambiguous fiction of nobility, passed on to Felix by his aunt, comprises all that the son understands of his origins. Tormented by insecurity, he launches a patriarchal project: "He wished a son who would feel as he felt about the 'great past' " (38). At age forty Felix plans to validate his dubious claim to aristocracy through descendants; he hopes to define the paternal line by extending it. His need for self-legitimation thus leads him to France, where he seeks the wife destined to bear "sons who would recognize and honour the past" (45).

Judging Paris to be the center of European social elegance, Felix thus arrives in 1920 "bowing, searching, with quick pendulous movements, for the correct thing to which to pay tribute: the right street, the right café, the right building, the right vista" (9). He delights in the "old and documented splendour" of the Musée Carnavalet and finds lodging in rooms hallowed because "a Bourbon had been carried from them to death" (9). But the location of this apartment remains unspecified, suggesting his attachment to a dream of history rather than to a tangible place. We see Felix only fleetingly in the sixth arrondissement: "fate and entanglement" lead him to the Hôtel Récamier, where (with O'Connor) he first gazes upon the literally unconscious American, Robin Vote. Carrying two volumes of "the life of the Bourbons," he next meets Robin on the rue Bonaparte (a wry historical irony) and walks with her in the "bare chilly" Luxembourg Gardens, describing his banking position with Crédit Lyonnais. They visit unnamed museums and "an antique shop facing the Seine"; their perfunctory courtship ends—in a subplot reminiscent of Henry James—in marriage between the European and the American.

Yet here Barnes dismantles the international romance: after an abortive wedding journey to Vienna which bores Robin and disillusions Felix (who finds how slight his connections to that city really are), they return to Paris to take up the chore of producing an heir.[57] The heterosexual contact is a trial for both: "He came and took her by the arm and lifted her toward him. She put her hand against his chest and pushed him, she looked frightened, she opened her mouth but no words came. He stepped back, he tried to speak, but they moved aside from each other saying nothing" (47). Felix must overcome his own "lack of desire" (8) and his "unaccountable apprehension" of sensuality (42) to sire an heir, while Robin responds to his advances by cursing. She expresses her aversion to marriage and maternity by leaving Paris after the birth of her sickly son.

What then does the sad case of Felix Volkbein reveal? Lacking any memory of a significant past, Felix suffers from a confusion of identity which impels his scheme to beget a son. This contradictory project, undertaken despite his own sexual reticence with a woman uncertain of her gender, produces the ultimate expression of his alienation, a boy "too estranged to be argued with" whose

existence entails the "demolition of [Felix's] own life" (108). Realizing that young Guido will never justify his own nobility, Felix
appeals to the church to accept his son into a sacred order. The
irony of this strategy lies in the recognition that Felix attempts to
relieve his alienation by delivering his son into Christendom. But
from the outset Barnes indicates that Felix, a veritable Wandering
Jew, will never solve the problem of his exile and displacement:
"No matter where and when you meet him you feel that he has
come from some place—no matter from what place he has come—
some country that he has devoured rather than resided in, some
secret land that he has been nourished on but cannot inherit, for
the Jew seems to be everywhere from nowhere" (7). Detached from
history, bereft of a homeland, and obscurely alienated from his
own sexuality, Felix suffers the classic ruptures of modernity.
Clinging pathetically to traces of the Bourbon monarchy in Paris,
he tries to assert the difference of his nobility in a period marked by
the dissolving of such archaic distinctions.[58]

Explaining his attraction to Robin Vote, Felix declares his
preference for an American wife because "with an American anything can be done" (39). In some way she epitomizes American
democracy, for her surname alludes to the Nineteenth Amend-
ment, which belatedly extended the ballot to American women.
Her ambiguous, indefinite personality makes her (in the eyes of
Felix) the mother of all possibilities. She indeed tries "to make
everyone happy" (155), yet she remains distracted and desperate,
the victim of ineradicable difficulties with gender, memory, and
place. Barnes characterizes her as a "born somnabule, who lives in
two worlds" (35), and of all the characters in *Nightwood*, Robin
seems caught most precariously between the human order and
the bestial, "a wild thing caught in a woman's skin" (146). As
implied by her androgynous first name, her sexuality partakes of
both genders; recurrently associated with white trousers, she is "a
tall girl with the body of a boy" (46). Profoundly conflicted, she
seems at once unsexed and promiscuous, devoid of desire yet
wanton in behavior. In Paris she seeks out bars and churches,
moving between the profane and the sacred; she shuttles between
France and America, between heterosexuality and lesbianism.
She moves from Felix to Nora, then to Jenny, then briefly to a girl
named Sylvia. To all she remains a riddle; even the possessive

Jenny admits: "I don't understand her at all, though I must say I understand her better than other people" (115).

Barnes displays this confusion most tellingly in Robin's peculiar fugue-like travel and compulsive cruising of the Parisian night world. When Felix begins to force his patriarchal, heterosexual will upon her, she reacts in singular fashion: "Robin prepared herself for her child with her only power: a stubborn cataleptic calm, conceiving herself pregnant before she was; and, strangely aware of some lost land in herself, she took to going out; wandering the countryside; to train travel, to other cities, alone and engrossed" (45). *Nightwood* projects her crisis of gender and identity in specifically geographical terms, as the search for a "lost land" within herself, perhaps some dreamed-of female utopia or simply the surrendered terrain of her privacy. When she returns to Paris, Robin takes "the Catholic vow" and attempts to find a literal sanctuary: "Many churches saw her: *St. Julien le Pauvre*, the church of *St. Germain des Prés, Ste. Clothilde*. . . . She strayed into the *rue Picpus*, into the gardens of the convent of *L'Adoration Perpetuelle*" (46). Her anxiety returns after the birth of Guido: "Robin took to wandering again, to intermittent travel from which she came back hours, days later, disinterested" (48). Then her search—a differently motivated, female version of Felix's quest for "the right street, the right café, the right building"—leads to her incessant prowling in bars and cafés among "people of every sort" (49). After visiting the United States, Robin returns to Paris with Nora and gradually resumes her roving ways; in the cafés she moves from "table to table, from drink to drink, from person to person," into the "night life" of the city. (59). Much later, she goes back to America with Jenny Petherbridge but again strays: "She began to haunt the terminals, taking trains into different parts of the country, wandering without design, going into many out-of-the-way churches, sitting in the darkest corner or standing against the wall" (167).

From the outset, Nora senses in Robin a profound disorientation and worries, after setting up housekeeping with her new companion, that "if she disarranged anything Robin might become confused—might lose the scent of home" (56). Barnes points out that even people on the street recognize Robin's displacement: "It was this characteristic that saved her from being asked too sharply 'where' she was going; pedestrians who had it on the point of their tongues, seeing her rapt and confused, turned instead to look at each other" (60). Through their intimacy Nora realizes that "Robin had come from a world to which she would return" (58); she sings songs of a secret unknown life, "snatches of harmony as tell-tale as the possessions of a traveller from a foreign land." Yet Robin's actual provenance remains unidentified; though she has (according to Felix) a certain " 'odour of memory,' like a person who has come from some place that we have forgotten and would give our life to recall" (118), she has no remembrance of that place of origin. Nowhere does she reflect explicitly upon her past; it seems not to exist. O'Connor observes that "she has difficulty in remembering herself" (121) and Nora suggests a connection between amnesia and errantry: "Robin can go anywhere, do anything . . . because she forgets" (152). This gap between present and past, so characteristic of modernism, estranges Robin Vote from any sense of American identity and leaves her exiled within a Parisian scene which fails to provide the refuge that she seeks. Hinting at this lack, Robin keeps "repeating in one way or another her wish for a home" (55). Her relentless, unconscious travels through the cities of Europe and America bring her no closer, however, to that "lost land" which stirs her nostalgia.

Her radical displacement and loss of memory seem linked ultimately to the gender confusion which complicates her emotional life. We know that Robin's indefinite sexuality and ambivalent desire make her a puzzle to others; Nora speculates that she "wants to be loved and left alone, all at the same time" (155). Robin indeed desires both "love and anonymity" (55), relationship and separateness, and the strange pattern of her compulsive wandering may be the acting out of this uncertainty. For we see that in each instance, her journeys coincide with new emotional encumbrances; they manifest her bid for the freedom of solitude. More poignantly, they perhaps reflect her effort to solve the dilemma of gender by avoiding the scene of desire.

Just as Robin's anguish arises from the undecidability of her sexual orientation, her repetition of symbolic infanticide expresses the very ambivalence which impels her wandering. Robin's first violent gesture occurs just after the birth of Guido: "One night, Felix, having come in unheard, found her standing in the centre of the floor holding the child high in her hand as if she were about to dash it down, but she brought it down gently" (48). Explaining her desperation to Felix, she exclaims furiously, "I didn't want him!" (49). She later repeats this gesture to different effect with Nora, who tells O'Connor: "Sometimes, if she got tight by evening, I would find her in the middle of the room in boy's clothes, rocking from foot to foot, holding the doll she had given us—"our child"—high above her head, as if she would cast it down, with a fury on her face" (147). To hurt Nora, Robin eventually smashes the doll, hurling it to the floor and "crushing her heel into it" until the china head has been reduced to dust. Marcus sees this violence as a reaction to Nora's love, said to be "possessive, patriarchal in its insistence on monogamy and control of the beloved."[59] But this reading conflates the original scene of threatened violence with its truly violent sequel, reducing Robin's act simply to a female resistance to male oppression. Through the "boy's clothes" that Robin wears, Barnes indicates, however, that the smashing of the doll has a different meaning than her threat to Guido. O'Connor speculates that "the last doll, given to age, is the girl who should have been a boy, and the boy who should have been a girl." He sees the doll as a sign of the gender trouble which causes its destruction. But his subsequent comment exposes the crux of Robin's problem: "The doll and the immature have something right about them, the doll because it resembles but does not contain life, and the third sex because it contains life but resembles the doll" (148). By suggesting a resemblance between the homosexual or lesbian and the doll, Barnes points to the paradox of the "third sex": that it both "contains life" and precludes procreation; that its members are alive but unable to reproduce. Nora later remarks that when a woman gives a doll to a woman, "it is the life they cannot have" (142). What Robin destroys is a figure of lesbian sterility, and the repetition of her gesture implies the despair of her bisexual androgyny: because she is both male and female, she can be neither homosexual nor heterosexual. Her tormenting ambivalence, projected in her wandering between intimacy and anonymity, makes Robin in some sense a victim of modernism and its erasure of difference.

The other androgyne of *Nightwood* presents quite a different version of the problem of modernist identity. Ironically Matthew

O'Connor idealizes the maternal role which Robin rejects. The fantastic doctor tells Nora: "No matter what I may be doing, in my heart is the wish for children and knitting. God, I never asked better than to boil some good man's potatoes and toss up a child for him every nine months by the calendar" (91). This "womb envy" perhaps explains his blatant transvestism; when Nora comes to learn about the night, she finds him surrounded by cosmetics and lingerie: "From the half-open drawers of this chiffonier hung laces, ribands, stockings, ladies' underclothing and an abdominal brace, which gave the impression that the feminine finery had suffered venery" (78–79). With his cheeks "heavily rouged" and his "lashes painted," the doctor lies in bed wearing "a woman's flannel nightgown." This spectacle of cross-dressing, a travesty of the "feminine," reinscribes sexual difference only to imply that conventional markers of gender (rouge, stockings, painted lashes) are superficial, arbitrary, and potentially ludicrous.[60]

The doctor's transvestism forms but part of his complicated, ambiguous sexuality. As his monologues indicate, he possesses an extensive knowledge of homosexual Paris; he haunts the pissoirs and boasts that he can tell a man's arrondissement and quarter by the "size and excellence" of his sexual equipment. In matters anatomical he insists upon a geographical determinism: "Sea level and atmospheric pressure and topography make all the difference in the world!" (92). For O'Connor the "best port" for such trade is the place de la Bastille, though he himself inhabits the quarter around the Eglise St. Sulpice, lives on the rue Servandoni, and patronizes the Café de la Mairie du VIe. When Robin awakens in the Hôtel Récamier, she cannot quite identify the doctor: "She had seen him somewhere. But, as one may trade ten years at a certain shop and be unable to place the shopkeeper if he is met in the street or in the *promenoir* of a theatre, the shop being a portion of his identity, she struggled to place him now that he had moved out of his frame" (36–37). The doctor's "frame," the place St. Sulpice, indeed forms "a portion of his identity"; he has been seen there "buying holy pictures and *petit Jésus* in the *boutique* displaying vestments and flowering candles" (29). Barnes's designation of this neighborhood with its ecclesiastical shops as "the doctor's 'city'" helps to account for the tension between O'Connor's homosexual lubricity and his tirades against modern love and its maculate forms. The full extent of O'Connor's conflict with his own sexuality becomes apparent in the chapter "Go Down, Matthew," which (as its title suggests) functions as a prophetic utterance, a jeremiad against this "bloody time" (165).

In the café a defrocked priest extracts from O'Connor a clue to his contradictory sexuality. Asked if he has ever been married, the doctor claims that he has but adds, "What if the girl *was* the wife of my brother and the children my brother's children?" He subsequently demands, "Who's to say that I'm not my brother's wife's husband and that his children were not fathered in my lap?" (159–60). These allusions to incest, which might otherwise be dismissed as characteristic prattle, echo his self-incriminating question to Jenny and Robin: "What manner of man is it that has to adopt his brother's children to make a mother of himself, and sleeps with his brother's wife to get him a future—it's enough to bring down the black curse of Kerry" (73). This implied sexual transgression may explain both O'Connor's self-loathing and his homosexual orientation: he associates heterosexuality with the violation of a taboo.

Such a view reduces his gender confusion to an intelligible psychosexual complaint. But clearly the problem is more complicated, as we see when O'Connor (commenting on Nora's preference for "a girl who resembles a boy") delivers his most challenging analysis of sexual difference and desire:

What is this love we have for the invert, boy or girl? It was they who were spoken of in every romance that we ever read. The girl lost, what is she but the Prince found? The Prince on the white horse that we have always been seeking. And the pretty lad who is a girl, what but the prince-princess in point lace—neither one and half the other, the painting on the fan! We love them for that reason. We were impaled in our childhood upon them as they rode through our primers, the sweetest lie of all, now come to be in boy or girl, for in the girl it is the prince, and in the boy it is the girl that makes the prince a prince—and not a man. They go far back in our lost distance where what we never had stands waiting; it was inevitable that we should come upon them for our miscalculated longing has created them. (136–37)

Barnes here reformulates the fairy-tale romance to show that its conventional grounding in heterosexual difference implies an equivalence between the "girl lost" and the "Prince found." In O'Connor's tortuous reading, the powerful fascination of the Prince lies precisely in his incorporation of the feminine. The doctor's critique effaces sexual difference to suggest that the androgynous Prince arouses "the prince" in the girl and "the girl" in the boy, producing by this transposition a longing for the same-sex figure in the romantic paradigm.[61]

This modernist version of the fairy-tale romance helps to explain the rampant sexual confusion of *Nightwood* and the particular difficulty of O'Connor, who persistently refers to himself as a "girl" and fancies that long ago he has been female: "In the old days I was possibly a girl in Marseilles thumping the dock with a sailor, and perhaps it's that memory that haunts me" (90–91). The doctor's alienation from his own sexuality becomes obvious in the darkness of the Eglise St. Merri when, weeping in anguish, he holds his penis (Tiny O'Toole) and asks, "What is this thing, Lord?" (132). For all of his theorizing with Felix and Nora, O'Connor is unable to fathom the mystery of himself and can only sigh: "C'est le plaisir qui me bouleverse" (it is pleasure which undoes me).[62] Like Robin, he vacillates between the night world of homosexual Paris and the churches within which he seeks to reconcile his male anatomy with his female longings. However, unlike Robin, who expresses gender ambivalence through evasions of sexuality, the doctor flaunts both his homosexuality and his transvestism. Though he inhabits the St. Sulpice quarter, his true domain is the "Town of Darkness" and the "unknown land" of night (81, 87); within this unreal, nocturnal world he acts out his estrangement from the world of everyday reality. The doctor articulates his fundamental displacement by insisting that "he's been everywhere at the wrong time and has now become anonymous" (82). Alienated from his American roots (the Barbary Coast of Pacific Street, San Francisco), from a past made unthinkable by incest, and from the sexual mistake of his male body, he lives out his exile in the shadow of St. Sulpice, apocalyptically warning fellow patrons of the Café de la Mairie du VI[i]: "It's all over, everything's over, and nobody knows it but me. . . . Now, . . . the end—mark my words—now *nothing, but wrath and weeping*" (165–66).

In contrast to the grotesque afflictions of the doctor, the confusions of Nora Flood seem more plausible, perhaps because insofar as *Nightwood* carries autobiographical resonances, Nora most closely resembles Barnes herself.[63] Nora's significant connections with an American past and a native landscape appear in the chapter "Night Watch," where we learn of her estate near New York—a house "couched in the centre of a mass of tangled grass and weeds," a burial ground, and a "decaying chapel." In her home Nora hosts a strange salon "for poets, radicals, beggars, artists, and people in love; for Catholics, Protestants, Brahmins, dabblers in black magic and medicine" (50). At these "incredible meetings" of "paupers" and misfits, the mood is retrospective: "one felt that early American history was being re-enacted." In this singular ambience,

> the Drummer Boy, Fort Sumter, Lincoln, Booth, all somehow came to mind; Whigs and Tories were in the air; bunting and its stripes and stars, the swarm increasing slowly and accurately on the hive of blue; Boston tea tragedies, carbines, and the sound of a boy's wild calling; Puritan feet, long upright in the grave, striking the earth again, walking up and out of their custom; the calk of prayers thrust in the heart. And in the midst of this, Nora. (51)

Whereas Robin Vote recalls American democracy and women's suffrage, Nora becomes more broadly identified with the land and its settlers. She somehow personifies the idea of the "Westerner," conjures up images of "covered wagons," and has "the face of all people who love the people" (50–51). Thus rooted in a specific place and involved in American history, Nora seems an unlikely exile.

But when she meets Robin at the Denckman circus in New York in 1923, her orientation begins to change. Significantly, Robin's first words to Nora at the circus initiate escape: "Let's get out of here." Outside, Robin's destination seems uncertain: "She looked about her distractedly. 'I don't want to be here.' But it was all she said; she did not explain where she wished to be" (55). Although this remark indeed signals the dislocation from which Robin can never escape, Nora with characteristic generosity assumes the impossible task of providing shelter, first in her home and then abroad. Their European travels take them "from Munich, Vienna and Budapest into Paris," where Nora buys an apartment—chosen by Robin—in the rue du Cherche-Midi.[64] The courtyard contains a symbolic figure, "a tall granite woman bending forward with lifted head," her hand "held over the pelvic round as if to warn a child who goes incautiously." The apartment amounts to a physical emblem of their relationship: "Every object in the garden, every item in the house, every word they spoke, attested to their mutual love, the combining of their humours" (55). After the onset of Robin's straying, however, this "museum of their encounter" becomes a source of suffering and "punishment" for Nora. While Robin wanders the cafés at night, Nora either stays home or stalks the streets "looking for what she's afraid to find," searching for "traces of Robin" yet "avoiding the quarter where she knew her to be, where by her own movements the waiters, the people on the terraces, might know that she had a part in Robin's life" (61).

Nora's relationship to Robin thus determines her movements and evasions in Paris. But the meaning of Nora's exile from America emerges only through the cryptic dream which recurs one night while she waits for Robin to return from her nocturnal adventures. This intricate dream re-presents Nora's American past, the house of her childhood, and a confusing encounter with her grandmother. Nora sees herself upstairs in her grandmother's room, which though full of furnishings seems empty, as "bereft as the nest of a bird which will not return." On the wall are "portraits of her uncle Llewellyn, who died in the Civil War," linking the place both to family history and to nineteenth-century America. From this room Nora looks down into an interior space, sees Robin, and calls out: "From round about her in anguish Nora heard her own voice saying, 'Come up, this is Grandmother's room,' yet knowing it was impossible because the room was taboo" (62). As Nora cries out, Robin seems to recede from her, and the room becomes suddenly strange and haunted: "This chamber that had never been her grandmother's, which was, on the contrary, the absolute opposite of any known room her grandmother had ever moved or lived in, was nevertheless saturated with the lost presence of her grandmother, who seemed in the continual process of leaving it." This bent, spectral figure recalls to the dreaming Nora an earlier incarnation of her grandmother, whom she had run into "at the corner of the house—the grandmother who, for some unknown reason, was dressed as a man, wearing a billycock and a corked mustache, ridiculous and plump in tight trousers and a red waistcoat, her arms spread saying with a leer of love, 'My little sweetheart.'" Nora subconsciously links the image of her grandmother disguised as a man with "something being done to Robin, Robin disfigured and eternalized by the hieroglyphics of sleep and pain" (63).

As improbable as any sequence in Kafka, this dream bears witness to a complex estrangement. It stages the conditions of Nora's exile from her own past and from the proprieties of her American childhood through the bizarre transformation by which her crossdressed grandmother seems to express some form of sexual danger. While she is in the upstairs room, in the place of the grandmother, Nora makes an overture to the woman whom she loves; but she instantly recalls the "taboo" which places the room off limits and proscribes lesbian lovemaking.[65] Though she feels an attraction to Robin as the symbolic counterpart of her grandmother, whom she "loved more than anyone" (148), such a relationship literally has no place within the American setting: Robin, in the floor below, seems increasingly remote. In her apparition as a male, the grandmother subsequently acts out the confusion of gender and the deformation of desire, producing an image which may express the grandmother's experience of denial within marriage or (alternatively) the threat posed by Robin's androgyny or by her vulnerability to a disfiguring desire.

Ironically, as Nora awakens from this dream, she sees Robin outside her window in the embrace of Jenny Petherbridge. This moment marks a decisive turn, for as Barnes reports, "It was not long after this that Nora and Robin separated; a little later Jenny and Robin sailed for America" (77). Nora thus finds herself alone in Paris, an exile for love yet deserted by her lover. Devastated by loss, she expresses her alienation through travel which seems aimless: "I sought Robin in Marseilles, in Tangier, in Naples, to understand her, to do away with my terror" (156). She also consults O'Connor, hoping to learn from him something about the unconscious urges which have led Robin away from her into the night world. Noting that "the day and the night are two travels," the doctor explains that while the French accept creatureliness and "filthiness," thinking of the day and night "as one continually," the American, obsessed by cleanliness, "separates the two for fear of indignities" (85). By this line of reflection, O'Connor means to suggest that Nora's own puritanical tendencies have alienated Robin. Later, Nora herself recalls a night in Montparnasse when Robin has reproached her: " 'You are a devil! You make everything dirty!' (I had tried to take someone's hands off her. They always put hands on her when she was drunk.) 'You make me feel dirty and tired and old!' " (143). Ironically, though Nora has left America (presumably) to find the cultural freedom in which to pursue her unconventional relationship with Robin, the moral instincts of her American past obtrude to complicate her life in exile.

But Nora's problem goes beyond the puritanical inhibitions which she has carried to France. In a subsequent conversation with O'Connor, she tries to comprehend her continuing fixation upon Robin—her compulsive fascination with "a girl who resembles a boy" (136). Increasingly she understands the narcissistic aspect of this attraction: "A man is another person—a woman is yourself, caught as you turn in panic; on her mouth you kiss your own" (143). She later asks O'Connor: "Have you ever loved someone and it became yourself?" (152). Nora's discovery of her own narcissism exposes a paradox, however, for while she recognizes that her desire for Robin lies in the fact that she is not male and that in kissing this woman Nora kisses herself, still Robin "resembles a boy" and thus on some level represents to Nora the possibility of kissing and loving a male or, more radically, of becoming a male so that she can love a woman without encountering in her own guilt the resistance of patriarchal law. In Robin's androgyny, that is, Nora confronts the unresolved problem of her own unconscious sexual ambivalence. Through O'Connor's revelations of the bestial night world, she also glimpses the fearful aspect of her American rectitude: "There's something evil in me that loves evil and degradation—purity's black backside!" (135). These insights reveal Nora's estrangement from her prior American identity and suggest the emergence of an exilic self more attentive to the ambiguities which mark her relation to gender, memory, and place.

Out of these stories of obsession and displacement, Barnes constructs her haunting, dissonant novel. While Felix Volkbein embodies, almost prophetically, the fate of the Jew as the outcast of European modernism, O'Connor, Robin, Nora, and even the contemptible Jenny Petherbridge—about whom it is said that "the places [she] moults in are her only distinction" (97)—reflect the peculiar confusions of the American who is both exiled from homeland and marginalized in Paris as a denizen of the homosexual/lesbian night world. Although *Nightwood* closes with an American homecoming which reunites Robin and Nora in the deserted chapel, Barnes avoids romanticizing the exile's return, projecting it instead as a revolting event: into the night the distraught Nora runs "cursing and crying," only to find Robin "in her boy's trousers" in the throes of bestial frenzy, apparently attempting to mate with Nora's dog. In this scene, the "confusions and defeated anxieties" of *Nightwood* reach a grotesque climax; long alienated from her body, emptied of memory, and dislocated geographically, the anonymous Robin has at last become estranged from her own humanity, abandoning herself to animal instinct. In an age profoundly influenced by Freud's privileging of the id and his foregrounding of sexuality as the crucial determinant of psychic adjustment, Robin's "obscene" barking perhaps serves as Barnes's sardonic reminder that the unconscious, that locus of unspeakable urges, is not a pretty site.

During the early 1930s, Fitzgerald and Barnes both worked under heavy emotional burdens to complete novels which indirectly summarized their responses to the experience of exile and to the culture of modernism. Away from France, both portrayed characters caught up in and to some extent corrupted by the decadence of Paris (and Europe generally) in the late twenties and early thirties. Neither writer presumed to analyze the crisis of values which ensued in the decade after the Great War; rather, both took for granted an undercurrent of cynicism and despair, a revolution in sexual attitudes and practices, a pervasive sense of drift, and a widespread rootlessness, born of the recognition that one could not go home again because there was no place of retreat from the violent, alluring transformations of modernism itself. Their respective novels portray a period of experiential perplexity, marked by the breakdown of those conceptual oppositions which seemed to give structure and certainty to everyday life.

Within this cultural matrix, Fitzgerald and Barnes saw Paris as a physical emblem of unreality; both portrayed the city through incongruous images reminiscent of dreams and nightmares, thereby reinforcing the psychological—and at times patently Freudian—implications of the stories they told. Though neither writer had much interest in geography for the sake of verisimilitude, both found the context of Paris in the twenties, particularly the city at night, conducive to the representation of *les années folles*, the crazy years. In the titles of their respective novels, these authors alluded to a nocturnal world at times seductive but more often chaotic or irrational. *Tender is the Night* and *Nightwood* project an oneiric unreality through seemingly random movement, bizarre encounters, and disconcerting settings. For Fitzgerald, the house on the rue Monsieur which generates an "electric-like shock" with its unusual decor and "oddly bevelled mirrors" typifies his dreamlike distortion of Parisian places. Barnes likewise depicts an unreal scene when Nora looks out on the garden "in the faint light of dawn" to see "a double shadow falling from the statue, as if it were multiplying" (64). In *Nightwood*, as in *Tender is the Night*, the strangeness of Paris conveys the alienation and confusion of characters who are themselves displaced and thus psychically detached from the city of exile.

The sense of place in these novels may be contrasted with the hallucinatory versions of Paris by French surrealist authors of the twenties and thirties. In narratives by Aragon, Breton, Soupault, Desnos, and Péret, the effect of strangeness emerges not from the perceived unreality of the material environment but conversely from an intimate knowledge of its particularity. For example, Aragon's *Paysan de Paris* transforms the Parc des Buttes-Chaumont into a fantastic site partly through a summary of inscriptions on an obelisk containing a directory of the nineteenth arrondissement.[66] This meticulous scrutiny of banal municipal "facts," in the context of a nighttime quest for mystical illumination, has the effect of defamiliarizing the obelisk and exposing its oddities—including the disclosure that the project was concocted by a traveling salesman. Similarly in *Nadja*, Breton exhibits his knowledge of Parisian places while recalling encounters with the visionary title character; in the place Dauphine, which Breton calls "one of the most profoundly secluded places I know of, one of the worst wastelands in Paris," a distracted Nadja seems to see a crowd of dead people massing in the darkness.[67] The dull, "wasteland" aspect of the place Dauphine contributes to the sinister impression which the narrative thus evokes. In Soupault's *Dernières Nuits de Paris* the narrator remarks that "places and environment have a profound influence on memory and imagination," and for several years the peculiarities of Paris obsessed the surrealists. Despite their disdain for certain aspects of French society and politics, they consistently manifested what Relph would call the perspective of "insideness" in their projections of a city rife with esoteric metaphors and signs.[68]

Their method of defamiliarizing a place understood in intimate detail helps to clarify the exilic perspective of "outsideness" in Fitzgerald and Barnes. By projecting a strangeness upon an obscure and sometimes incomprehensible cityscape, both writers suggest the anxieties of central characters afflicted by problems of American identity. Unfamiliar or threatening aspects of the Parisian scene objectify their intensely personal dilemmas. The surrealists represent the city mindful of its complex cultural meanings (which their works often subvert or challenge), whereas Barnes, Fitzgerald, and their American contemporaries inevitably write from the outside, even when they affect—as Hemingway does—what Relph aptly calls "vicarious insideness."[69] Allowing for obvious differences of style and content, we can see that both *Tender is the Night* and *Nightwood* portray the experience of exile as a crisis in which the expatriate, opened to new desires in a seemingly unreal place, discovers internal contradictions and tensions. Paris thus figures as a fantastic scene of conflict and possibility, presenting those dilemmas of choice through which the self constructs and defines itself.

This is perhaps only an exaggerated version of the situation recreated in the narratives of Stein, Hemingway, and Miller. For them, Paris was the indispensable "world elsewhere" (to appropriate Richard Poirier's phrase), a city foreign enough in architecture, customs, and language to seem on some level exotic and thus to grant them a freedom from the constraints and inhibitions of American life as well as from the failures, real or imagined, of an

American past. (It is worth noting that all of the writers discussed here had reached vocational impasses in America.) Paris granted the American a certain anonymity, a release from old routines and responsibilities, even an exemption from the duty to be one's old self. It presented the expatriate with the opportunity for metamorphosis, for the reformulation of ambitions, habits, and inclinations; the city thus nurtured an exilic identity, a different way of conceiving one's connections to place and populace. Paris also provided the conditions for writing, its very indifference to the foreigner ensuring the privacy essential to creative work. Finally, the strangeness of the French-speaking milieu produced a heightened consciousness of language itself and the tenuous relation between words and things which can be altered by crossing a linguistic border.

For these American writers, the city of exile thus remained to some extent alien and illegible. Amid the novelties of the modernist era, they gazed upon the same physical surroundings and social transformations observed by their French contemporaries. But they did so from a position of exteriority, tending to regard the city on some level as an illusory spectacle. Displaced from a native setting which though forsaken continued to determine their perception of difference, these writers developed attachments to Paris reflecting various levels of geographical understanding, cultural awareness, and linguistic competence. None, however, became entirely assimilated; none lost altogether that residual habit of mind which, for want of a more precise term, might be called "American." Repeatedly encountering those differences which set Paris and France apart from remembered American scenes, Stein, Hemingway, Miller, Fitzgerald, and Barnes all composed works which directly or indirectly contemplated the relationship between place and identity. These writers faced a common predicament: far from the homeland which once formed the ground of being, they found themselves in a great foreign city which remained ultimately elusive or inscrutable despite the local knowledge each had acquired. In texts as diverse as their own experiences, they portrayed the dilemma of the expatriate self, projecting imaginary versions of Paris which in their differing particulars suggest each writer's accommodation to the possibilities and risks of modernist displacement. Insistently, these narratives of exile also evoked the nagging question of American identity, because the encounter with cultural difference typically exposed—as it did for James's Lambert Strether—the presence of an obstinate American self. Reflecting upon his return from Europe in "American Letter," Archibald MacLeish examined his simultaneous longing for "a land far off, alien" and his bone-deep ties to a country that is "neither a place nor a blood name." Summing up these contradictions he observed: "It is a strange thing to be an American." Nowhere was that strangeness more keenly felt or more brilliantly translated into modernist texts than in the Paris of writing.

Notes

Preface

1. Joshua Meyrowitz, *No Sense of Place: The Impact of Electronic Media on Social Behavior* (New York: Oxford University Press, 1985), 125.

2. Archibald MacLeish, *Collected Poems, 1917–1952* (Boston: Houghton Mifflin, 1952), 63–64. The original version appears in *Letters from the Lost Generation,* ed. Linda Patterson Miller (New Brunswick, N.J.: Rutgers University Press, 1991), 35–38.

Chapter One. Place, Self, and Writing

1. E. E. Cummings, *The Enormous Room,* ed. George James Firmage (1922; reprint, New York: Liveright, 1978), 50. Subsequent parenthetical page references to the novel correspond to this edition.

2. Cummings, *The Enormous Room,* xiv.

3. E. E. Cummings, *Complete Poems, 1913–1962* (San Diego: Harcourt Brace Jovanovich), 93.

4. E. E. Cummings, *I: Six Nonlectures* (Cambridge: Harvard University Press, 1953), 53.

5. Leonard Lutwack, *The Role of Place in Literature* (Syracuse: Syracuse University Press, 1984), 12, 31. Subsequent page references to this work will be noted parenthetically.

6. Yi-Fu Tuan, *Space and Place: The Perspective of Experience* (Minneapolis: University of Minnesota Press, 1977), 6, 12; Edward Relph, *Place and Placelessness* (London: Plon, 1976), 43.

7. Relph, *Place and Placelessness,* 50–56, 61.

8. Tuan, *Space and Place,* 54. The expression "knowing one's place" appeals to just this sense of being where one belongs, though

it also figures in the discourse of repression to exclude individuals or groups from a guarded, symbolically important place.

9. Pierre Sansot, *Poétique de la ville* (Paris: Editions Klinksieck, 1969), 23; Gaston Bachelard, *The Poetics of Space,* trans. Maria Jolas (Boston: Beacon Press, 1969), 14, 17.

10. Relph, *Place and Placelessness,* 43.

11. Roger M. Downs and David Stea, *Maps in Minds: Reflections on Cognitive Mapping* (New York: Harper and Row, 1977), 27.

12. Marcel Proust, *Swann's Way,* trans. C. K. Scott Moncrieff (New York: Modern Library, 1956), 59. Subsequent references to this edition will be noted parenthetically.

13. Ernest Hemingway, *The Short Stories of Ernest Hemingway* (New York: Scribner's, 1939), 54. Subsequent parenthetical page references to the story correspond to this edition.

14. Ernest Hemingway, *Across the River and into the Trees* (New York: Scribner's, 1950), 123.

15. Downs and Stea, "Cognitive Maps and Spatial Behavior: Process and Products," in Roger M. Downs and David Stea, eds., *Image and Environment: Cognitive Mapping and Spatial Behavior* (Chicago: Aldine, 1973), 9.

16. Kevin Lynch describes victims of brain injury who "cannot find their own rooms again after leaving them, and must wander helplessly until conducted home, or until by chance they stumble upon some familiar detail." See Lynch, "Some References to Orientation," in Downs and Stea, eds., *Image and Environment,* 301.

17. *The Early Diary of Anaïs Nin,* vol. 3 (San Diego: Harcourt Brace Jovanovich, 1983), 40. Subsequent citations from the *Early Diary* refer to this edition. The question of Nin's national identity is complicated by the fact that her father was of Spanish and her mother of French-Danish descent; both parents were born in Cuba. Nin moved to New York with her mother in 1914 at the outbreak of the Great War.

18. *The Early Diary of Anaïs Nin,* vol. 4 (San Diego: Harcourt Brace Jovanovich, 1985), 42.

19. Downs and Stea, *Maps in Minds,* 78. Kevin Lynch also develops a theory of "imageability"—the "quality in a physical object which gives it a high probability of evoking a strong image in any given observer." See his *Image of the City* (Cambridge: M.I.T. Press, 1960), 9.

20. Those volumes of the diary (from 1934 on) which Nin herself prepared for publication reflect careful revision and purging of indiscreet entries. So, for instance, the published diary deletes references to her sexual liaisons with Henry Miller and others. The recent appearance of *Henry and June* (1987), edited by Rupert Pole, makes available some of this previously suppressed material.

21. Lutwack, *The Role of Place in Literature,* 21.

22. A fine recent study of British and French fiction reinforces the importance of place as a repository of meaning and demon-

strates new interest in this aspect of narrative. See Gillian Tindall, *Countries of the Mind: The Meaning of Place to Writers* (London: Hogarth, 1991).

23. E. V. Walter, *Placeways: A Theory of the Human Environment* (Chapel Hill: University of North Carolina Press, 1988), 121, 205.

24. See, e.g., the bibliography appended to *Autobiography: Essays Theoretical and Critical*, ed. James Olney (Princeton: Princeton University Press, 1980), 343–52. Six of the fifteen contributors to this important collection address the problem of time in autobiographical narrative; none, however, deal substantively with the problem of place.

25. Eudora Welty, *Place in Fiction* (New York: House of Books, 1957), 11.

26. See Harry Levin, "Literature and Exile," *The Listener* (15 October 1959): 613–17. My thanks to Lewis P. Simpson for bringing this essay to my attention and for sharing his work-in-progress on Robert Penn Warren as a figure of internal exile.

27. Gertrude Stein, *Paris, France* (New York: Scribner's, 1940), 2.

28. Henry Miller, *Tropic of Cancer* (1934; reprint New York: Grove Press, 1961), 153.

29. Lloyd S. Kramer, *Threshold of a New World: Intellectuals and the Exile Experience in Paris, 1830–1848* (Ithaca: Cornell University Press, 1988), 9.

30. William Boelhower, "Avant-Garde Autobiography: Deconstructing the Modernist Habitat," in *Literary Anthropology*, ed. Fernando Poyatos (Amsterdam: John Benjamins: 1988), 274, 276. Thanks to Paul Smith for bringing this essay to my attention.

31. Walter, *Placeways*, 98, 99.

32. Italo Calvino, *Invisible Cities*, trans. William Weaver (San Diego: Harcourt Brace Jovanovich, 1974), 28–29.

33. Martin Heidegger, *Poetry, Language, Thought*, trans. Albert Hofstadter (New York: Harper and Row, 1971), 161.

34. Kramer, *Threshold of a New World*, 10.

35. Andrew Gurr, *Writers in Exile* (Sussex: Harvester, 1981), 14.

36. See Malcolm Bradbury's suggestive essay "The Cities of Modernism," in *Modernism 1890–1930*, ed. Malcolm Bradbury and James McFarlane (London: Penguin, 1976), 96–104.

37. Kramer, *Threshold of a New World*, 18, 20–21.

38. Jerrold Siegel, *Bohemian Paris: Culture, Politics, and the Boundaries of Bourgeois Life, 1830–1930* (New York: Viking, 1986), 7–13. The Bohemians were, as Siegel suggests (51), often products of middle-class culture who harbored contradictory attitudes toward wealth and comfort.

39. Walter Benjamin, *Charles Baudelaire: A Lyric Poet in the Era of High Capitalism*, trans. Harry Zohn (London: Verso, 1983), 166, 176.

40. Benjamin, *Charles Baudelaire*, 171.

41. Leonard Shapiro remarks that it is "quite certain that the future Emperor Alexander II was influenced by the *Sketches* in his final decision to put through the emancipation of the serfs, and Turgenev regarded this as his main achievement in life." See Shapiro, *Turgenev: His Life and Times* (New York: Random House, 1978), 66.

42. *Parisian Sketches: Letters to the New York Tribune 1875–76*, ed. Leon Edel and Ilse Dusoir Lind (London: Rupert Hart-Davis, 1958), 3.

43. See Edwin Sill Fussell, *The French Side of Henry James* (New York: Columbia University Press, 1990).

44. Roger Shattuck, *The Banquet Years: The Origins of the Avant-Garde in France, 1885 to World War I* (New York: Vintage, 1968).

45. August Strindberg, *Inferno and From an Occult Diary*, trans. Mary Sandbach (New York: Penguin, 1979), 111.

46. Naomi Segal, "Rilke's Paris—'cité pleine de rêves,'" in *Unreal City: Urban Experience in Modern European Literature and Art*, eds. Edward Timms and David Kelley (New York: St. Martin's, 1985), 103.

47. Rainer Maria Rilke, *The Notebooks of Malte Laurids Brigge*, trans. M. D. Herder Norton (New York: Norton, 1964), 67.

48. Kramer, *Threshold of a New World*, 230.

49. J. Nicholas Entrikin, *The Betweenness of Place: Towards a Geography of Modernity* (Baltimore: Johns Hopkins, 1991).

50. Henri Bergson, *Time and Free Will: An Essay on the Immediate Data of Consciousness*, trans. F. L. Pogson (1910; reprint, New York: Harper and Row, 1960), 129.

51. Entrikin, *The Betweenness of Place*, 13.

52. See especially Fussell's *French Side of Henry James*, 177–214, and Michael Seidel, *Exile and the Narrative Imagination* (New Haven: Yale University Press, 1986), 131–63, for discussions which foreground the problem of place and the displacement of exile.

Chapter Two. The Outside and the Inside of Stein's Paris

1. Details of the 1900 visit can be inferred from Leo's letter to Gertrude, 9 October 1900, in Leo Stein, *Journey into the Self*, ed. Edmund Fuller (New York: Crown, 1950), 3. She mentions the visit to the exposition in *Wars I Have Seen* (New York: Random House, 1945), 34. For details of Stein's disappointments in Baltimore, see James Mellow, *Charmed Circle: Gertrude Stein & Company* (New York: Avon, 1975), 62–64; 78–83. Stein's affair was complicated by the fact that her friend Mabel Haynes was also in love with May, traveled with her, and treated her as a protégée.

2. Leon Katz, Introduction to Gertrude Stein, *Fernhurst, Q.E.D., and Other Early Writings* (New York: Liveright, 1971), xxix.

3. Gertrude Stein, "An American and France," typescript of 1936 lecture, in the American Literature Collection, Beinecke Rare Book and Manuscript Library, Yale University.

4. Shari Benstock, *Women of the Left Bank: Paris, 1900–1940* (Austin: University of Texas Press, 1986), 14.

5. Gertrude Stein, *Paris, France* (New York: Scribner's, 1940), 1. Subsequent parenthetical page references to this work correspond to this edition. Judith P. Saunders, "Gertrude Stein's *Paris, France* and American Literary Tradition," in *Modern Critical Views: Gertrude Stein,* ed. Harold Bloom (New York: Chelsea House, 1986), 122.

6. Joanna Richardson, *The Bohemians: La vie de Bohème in Paris, 1830–1914* (London: Macmillan, 1969); and Jerrold Siegel, *Bohemian Paris: Culture, Politics, and the Boundaries of Bourgeois Life, 1830–1930* (New York: Viking, 1986).

7. Having moved in early 1938 to a new apartment at 5, Rue Christine, Stein here rationalizes her abandonment of the famous atelier at 27, rue de Fleurus—which the landlord had reclaimed for his newly married son—as a response to changing needs ("now we need the picturesque the splendid we need the air and space you only get in old quarters"). Picasso was also working in this neighborhood in the late thirties.

8. Saunders, "Gertrude Stein's *Paris, France,*" 127.

9. George Wickes, *Americans in Paris* (1969; reprint, New York: Da Capo Press, 1980), 2.

10. Gertrude Stein, unpublished letter to W. G. Rogers, 1936 [n.d.], American Literature Collection, Beinecke Rare Book and Manuscript Library, Yale University.

11. Gertrude Stein, *The Making of Americans* (New York: Harcourt, Brace: 1934), 39. Lisa Ruddick considers this novel a crucial phase in Stein's "self-creation" in *Reading Gertrude Stein* (Ithaca: Cornell University Press, 1990), 55–136.

12. Gertrude Stein, *Portraits and Prayers* (New York: Random House, 1934), 169–72.

13. Richard Bridgman, *Gertrude Stein in Pieces* (New York: Oxford University Press, 1970), 92n.

14. Gertrude Stein, *Two: Gertrude Stein and Her Brother and other Early Portraits* (New Haven: Yale University Press, 1951), 351–52. Subsequent parenthetical page references to this composition, as well as to "Flirting at the Bon Marché" and "Rue de Rennes," correspond to this edition.

15. Bridgman, *Gertrude Stein in Pieces,* 94.

16. Marianne DeKoven, *A Different Language: Gertrude Stein's Experimental Writing* (Madison: University of Wisconsin Press, 1983), 58.

17. Gérard Genette, "Structure and Functions of the Title in Literature," trans. Bernard Crampé, *Critical Inquiry* 14 (1988): 713.

18. Marianne DeKoven, "Gertrude Stein's Landscape Writing," *Women's Studies* 9 (1982): 221.

19. Gertrude Stein, *Geography and Plays* (Boston: Four Seas, 1922), 416.

20. Gertrude Stein, *Painted Lace and Other Pieces* (New Haven: Yale University Press, 1955), 156.

21. Stein, *Geography and Plays*, 32–33.

22. Stein, *Painted Lace*, 243.

23. Stein, *Painted Lace*, 243, 247.

24. Gertrude Stein, *Lucy Church Amiably* (Paris: Plain Editions, 1930), 47. Subsequent page references to this work correspond to this edition.

25. DeKoven, in "Gertrude Stein's Landscape Writing," argues that the landscape compositions mark an "affirmation" of a "female vision": "the happy, easy union of the human and the physical, the spirit and the flesh, over the patriarchal mode of tragic separation and yearning" (234).

26. Ulla Dydo, "Landscape is not Grammar: Gertrude Stein in 1928," *Raritan* 7 (1987):102.

27. Stein, *Painted Lace*, 241.

28. Stein acknowledges the influence of Bertie Abdy in *Everybody's Autobiography* (New York: Random House, 1937), 300; she also described the writing process in "The Story of a Book," in *How Writing is Written*, ed. Robert Bartlett Haas (Santa Barbara: Black Sparrow Press, 1974), 61–62. Mellow discusses the backdrop of Stein's relations with other artists and writers in *Charmed Circle*, 421–22.

29. S. C. Neuman, *Gertrude Stein: Autobiography and the Problem of Narration* (Victoria, B.C.: English Literary Studies, 1979), 17, 29.

30. Stein, *The Autobiography of Alice B. Toklas* (New York: Vintage, 1961), 79, 132, 90, 211. Subsequent parenthetical page references correspond to this edition.

31. Roger Shattuck, *The Banquet Years: The Origins of the Avant-Garde in France, 1885 to World War I* (New York: Vintage, 1968), 66–70, 360. Stein disdainfully described how André Salmon "went off his head" with drink. She was the only woman there not cast as the wife or lover of an artist, though it should be noted that Marie Laurencin attended both as artist and mistress of Apollinaire.

32. Benstock, *Women of the Left Bank*, 12, 143–93. This pattern is of course bound up with the sibling rivalry between the Steins, which is one reason why Gertrude (prior to 1914) had to get away from the rue de Fleurus to establish her acceptance by male modernist painters.

33. Benstock, *Women of the Left Bank*, 190.

34. It is worth noting—as Benstock does—that although Stein created a feminized domain on the Rue de Fleurus and wrote with increasing openness about her lesbianism, she remained generally aloof from the community of lesbian women in Paris, assumed "masculine authority in her private life," and continued to gauge

her career by male recognition and approval. See Benstock, *Women of the Left Bank*, 184, 189.

35. Leon Lutwack has argued, for example, that Stein "hardly needed the stimulus of place, and her writing depends not at all upon localization." See Lutwack, *The Role of Place in Literature*, 114.

36. Stein, *Everybody's Autobiography*, 311.

37. "A Transatlantic Interview 1946," in *A Primer for the Gradual Understanding of Gertrude Stein*, ed. Robert Bartlett Haas (Santa Barbara: Black Sparrow Press, 1976), 18. The relationship between Stein's experimental methods and modern painting receives lucid treatment in Randa Dubnick, *The Structure of Obscurity: Gertrude Stein, Language, and Cubism* (Urbana: University of Illinois Press, 1984).

38. Stein, *Paris, France*, 5.

39. Stein, *Everybody's Autobiography*, 289.

40. DeKoven, *A Different Language*, xiii.

41. See Mellow, *Charmed Circle*, 518.

42. Sherwood Anderson, letter to Gertrude Stein, April 1939 [?], Newberry Library, Northwestern University.

43. One of Stein's rare publications in French, "Le Retour à Paris" appeared in the monthly magazine *Fontaine* 41 (April 1945), 135–36. The cited passage is my translation.

Chapter Three. City of Danger

1. Ernest Hemingway, unpublished letter to Clarence and Grace Hall Hemingway, [June 1918], Hemingway Manuscripts III, Lilly Library, Indiana University.

2. Michael Reynolds, *The Young Hemingway* (New York: Basil Blackwell, 1986), 4, 143.

3. For example, Hemingway once illegally shot a heron and hid from the game warden; at the lake he also developed a sexual interest in Katy Smith. See Reynolds, *The Young Hemingway*, 71–72, 75, 121. For a correlation of the landscape Hemingway knew with the geography of the stories, see Joseph Flora, *Hemingway's Nick Adams* (Baton Rouge: Louisiana State University Press, 1982), 7, 9. The Michigan country also figures in Hemingway's 1926 parody, *The Torrents of Spring*.

4. Ernest Hemingway, "On Writing," *The Nick Adams Stories*, ed. Philip Young (New York: Scribner's, 1972), 238. Subsequent parenthetical page references will correspond to the Young edition.

5. Reynolds, *The Young Hemingway*, 252–53.

6. Michael Fanning, *France and Sherwood Anderson: Paris Notebook, 1921* (Baton Rouge: Louisiana State University Press, 1976), 46–47.

7. Fanning, *France and Sherwood Anderson*, 49.

8. Ernest Hemingway, *A Moveable Feast* (New York:

Scribner's, 1964), 21. Subsequent parenthetical page references to the memoir correspond to this edition.

9. Impressions of Paris and the apartment appear in an unpublished letter to Katy Smith, 27 January 1922, Dos Passos Collection, Manuscript Department, University of Virginia. The article on *bals musettes* was reprinted in Ernest Hemingway, *Dateline: Toronto*, ed. William White (New York: Scribner's, 1985), 117.

10. For a discussion of the suppression of sexual matters in Oak Park, see Reynolds, *The Young Hemingway*, 122–23. The apaches, who emerged from the bohemian counterculture, wore improbable costumes (sometimes inspired by the American Indian) to manifest scorn for bourgeois convention and attire. Reynolds comments on Hemingway's conflicted response to sexual ambiguity in Paris in *Hemingway: The Paris Years* (Oxford: Blackwell, 1989), 34. On the first page of *A Moveable Feast*, the author calls the Café des Amateurs "the cesspool of the rue Mouffetard."

11. Hemingway, *By-Line*, 23.

12. Hemingway, *Dateline: Toronto*, 114–15.

13. Reynolds, *Hemingway: The Paris Years*, 24–25.

14. Hemingway's *Toronto Star* dispatches in early 1922 include, in addition to the aforementioned description of the Café Rotonde, articles on bargains in Paris, on Russian immigrants, on "wild night music," on Parisian rudeness, and on foreign impostors. See Hemingway, *Dateline: Toronto*, 88–89, 98, 114–20.

15. Item 647a, Ernest Hemingway Collection, John F. Kennedy Library, Boston. Permission to quote from Item 647a of the Hemingway Collection has been granted by the Ernest Hemingway Foundation, which retains publishing rights. This version differs from the one included by Carlos Baker in *Ernest Hemingway: A Life Story* (New York: Scribner's, 1969), 90–91. Baker (who apparently transcribed the piece from a 1962 letter by Bill Smith) reorders the last four sentences, omitting or altering certain details in the present version.

16. My thanks to Paul Smith for bringing to my attention the connection between the prostitute and the Eglise Madeleine, noted in his address "Hemingway Learning to Write Like Hemingway," at the John F. Kennedy Library, Boston, 13 June 1991.

17. Hemingway apparently completed one draft of this composition by the early summer of 1922, well after the May Day riots in Paris. Reynolds speculates that Hemingway reconstructed the lost text from memory about the time of his letter to Pound on 23 January 1923, which mentions the loss of his "juvenilia." See Reynolds, *Hemingway: The Paris Years*, 95.

18. Hemingway had been covering the peace conference in Lausanne in November 1922, and Hadley decided to make a surprise visit, bringing with her all of his working manuscripts. Reynolds gives the date of "My Old Man" as the late summer of 1922 and discusses its composition in *Hemingway: The Paris Years*, 58–61.

19. Ernest Hemingway, "My Old Man," in *The Complete Short Stories of Ernest Hemingway* (New York: Scribner's, 1987), 153–54.

20. Convinced that Anderson had lost his discipline and self-respect, Hemingway in November 1925 concocted his parody *The Torrents of Spring* as a reproof to his former mentor. For a summary of critical positions on Anderson and "My Old Man," see Paul Smith, *A Reader's Guide to the Short Stories of Ernest Hemingway* (Boston: G. K. Hall, 1989), 11–14.

21. In an unpublished sketch, apparently drafted for *A Moveable Feast*, Hemingway advances a system of café classification: the private café where writers never invited anyone; the secret café where they met their mistresses; the neutral café where they might invite others to meet their mistresses; and the famous cafés of Montparnasse, where (by implication) writers blatantly invited public attention. See Item 185a, Ernest Hemingway Collection, John F. Kennedy Library, Boston.

22. Letter to Bill Horne, 17–18 July 1923, *Ernest Hemingway: Selected Letters*, ed. Carlos Baker (New York: Scribner's, 1981), 85. Hemingway knew Horne from the ambulance corps in Italy, had lived with him briefly in Chicago, and had fished with him in Michigan in 1920. Reynolds mentions the map of Michigan in Hemingway's Paris apartment in *The Young Hemingway*, 40–41.

23. Hemingway, *Selected Letters*, 153.

24. Recent discussions of *In Our Time* as metafiction include Debra A. Moddelmog, "The Unifying Consciousness of a Divided Conscience: Nick Adams as Author of *In Our Time*," *American Literature* 60 (December 1988): 591–610, and Louis A. Renza, "The Importance of Being Ernest," *South Atlantic Quarterly* 88 (Summer 1989): 661–89. Both readings must be balanced against Hemingway's reference to "all that mental conversation" in the deleted conclusion as "the shit" in a letter to Robert McAlmon, c. 15 November 1924, in *Selected Letters*, 133.

25. Hemingway, *Nick Adams Stories*, 237–39.

26. Hemingway, *Nick Adams Stories*, 234–35.

27. An early, discarded fragment depicts Nick getting off the train at Seney with two companions. The elimination of these characters in subsequent drafts underscores my point. See Item 279, Ernest Hemingway Collection, John F. Kennedy Library, Boston. Thanks to Michael Reynolds for pointing out this detail.

28. Hemingway, *A Moveable Feast*, 5.

29. Item 194, Notebook 1, 9, Ernest Hemingway Collection, John F. Kennedy Library, Boston. Permission to quote from Item 194 of the Hemingway Collection has been granted by the Ernest Hemingway Foundation, which retains publishing rights. For a study of the novel's composition and early drafts, see Frederic Joseph Svoboda, *Hemingway and "The Sun Also Rises": The Crafting of a Style* (Lawrence: University Press of Kansas, 1983).

30. Ernest Hemingway, *The Sun Also Rises* (New York:

Scribner's, 1926), 11–12. Subsequent parenthetical page references to the novel correspond to this edition.

31. David Morgan Zehr, "Paris and the Expatriate Mystique: Hemingway's *The Sun Also Rises," Arizona Quarterly* 33 (1977): 157–58, 162–63.

32. The deleted introductory material cited here appears in Svoboda, *Hemingway and "The Sun Also Rises,"* 134–35.

33. Item 194, Notebook I, Chap. III, Ernest Hemingway Collection, John F. Kennedy Library, Boston.

34. See, e.g., the ingenious discussion of homosexuality and *The Sun Also Rises* in Kenneth Lynn's *Hemingway* (New York: Simon and Schuster, 1987), 318–25. For a broader discussion of Hemingway and homosexuality, see Scott Donaldson, *By Force of Will: The Life and Art of Ernest Hemingway* (New York: Viking, 1977), 182–88.

35. Ernest Hemingway, *Three Stories & Ten Poems* (Paris: Contact Publishing, 1923), 56.

36. Brassaï, *The Secret Paris of the 30s,* trans. Richard Miller (1933; reprint, New York: Pantheon Books, 1976), n.p. Although Brassaï describes the dance hall as it appeared six years after the action of *The Sun Also Rises,* its homosexual character had been well established for years.

37. Hemingway, letter to Howell E. Jenkins, 9 November 1924, *Selected Letters,* 132.

38. Lynn contends that "while the full extent of his injury is unspecified, Jake remains capable of achieving a degree of satisfaction through oral sex." See Lynn, *Hemingway,* 324.

39. H. R. Stoneback reads the reference to the Rue St.-Jacques as a clue to Jake's spiritual destination, Santiago (St. Jacques) de Campostela in Spain. See Stoneback, "From the rue Saint-Jacques to the Pass of Roland to the 'Unfinished Church on the Edge of the Cliff,'" *Hemingway Review* 6 (1986): 17.

40. Carlos Baker, *Hemingway: The Writer as Artist* (Princeton: Princeton University Press, 1952), 85.

41. Reynolds, *Hemingway: The Paris Years,* 230.

42. Hemingway, unpublished letter to Jane Heap, [c. 25 August 1925], Jane Heap Papers, University of Wisconsin-Milwaukee.

43. For an account of the book's composition, see Reynolds, *Hemingway: The Paris Years,* 334–38.

44. Ernest Hemingway, *The Torrents of Spring* (1926; reprint, New York: Scribner's, 1972), 74–75.

45. Lynn, *Hemingway,* 305.

46. *The Complete Short Stories of Ernest Hemingway,* 261. For a discussion of the composition history of this story, see Scott Donaldson, "Preparing for the End: Hemingway's Revisions of 'A Canary for One,'" in *New Critical Approaches to the Short Stories of Ernest Hemingway,* ed. Jackson J. Benson (Durham, Duke University Press, 1990), 229–37.

47. The remark about having been "long enough in Europe" appeared in Hemingway's letter to Perkins, 24 July 1926, *Selected Letters*, 212. In a letter to Scott Fitzgerald, about 15 September 1927, Hemingway speaks of having spent only one night in the Quarter during the past year. See *Selected Letters*, 262.

48. *The Complete Short Stories of Ernest Hemingway*, 302–05.

49. J. F. Kobler, "Hemingway's 'The Sea Change': A Sympathetic View of Homosexuality," *Arizona Quarterly* 26 (1970): 322. Smith notes Hemingway's equivocal comments about the source of the story and suggests the influence of "intrigues gossiped about in the Parisian cafés in 1929" in *A Reader's Guide*, 224.

50. The story "How We Came to Paris" appeared originally in *Collier's* (7 October 1944) and was reprinted in *By Line: Ernest Hemingway*, ed. William White (New York: Scribner's, 1967), 383.

51. Ernest Hemingway, *Islands in the Stream* (New York: Scribner's, 1970), 60. Subsequent parenthetical page references to this novel correspond to this edition.

52. See, e.g., the last three paragraphs of Hemingway's letter to Hadley, 23 July 1942, in *Selected Letters*, 537.

53. Scott Donaldson identifies the motif of "paradise lost" in *By Force of Will*, 149.

54. Hemingway, *Garden* manuscript, Item 422a, Folder 37, 24–25, Ernest Hemingway Collection, John F. Kennedy Library, Boston. Permission to quote from Item 422a of the Ernest Hemingway Collection has been granted by the Ernest Hemingway Foundation, which retains publishing rights. See also my essay-review, "Life as Fiction: The Lure of Hemingway's *Garden*," *Southern Review* 24 (1988): 451–61.

55. While casting some doubt on the existence of the trunks supposedly recovered from the Ritz, Jacqueline Tavernier-Courbin has provided a helpful inventory of the early notebooks in her article "The Paris Notebooks," *Hemingway Review* 1 (1981): 23–26. This discussion has since been incorporated in her recent informative book, *Ernest Hemingway's "A Moveable Feast": The Making of a Myth* (Boston: Northeastern University Press, 1991).

56. Among Hemingway's papers is a miscellaneous page where he remarks: "I do not know what I thought Paris would be like but it was not that way. It rained nearly every day." Item 186, Ernest Hemingway Collection, John F. Kennedy Library, Boston. Permission to quote from Item 186 of the Ernest Hemingway Collection has been granted by the Ernest Hemingway Foundation, which retains publishing rights.

57. A miscellaneous page related to *A Moveable Feast* refers to *The Garden of Eden*. A note about "poverty in Paris" and "the rich who collect people" and "the pilot fish," accompanies an outline for a book entitled "The Two Catherines" (Barbara Sheldon was initially named Catherine) and a cancelled title, "The Garden of the

Very Poor and Free." See Item 123, Ernest Hemingway Collection,
John F. Kennedy Library, Boston.

58. Ernest Hemingway, *The Garden of Eden* (New York:
Scribner's, 1986), 17. Subsequent references to the novel, unless
otherwise indicated, correspond to this abridged, published edition.

59. Hemingway, *A Moveable Feast*, 57.

60. That is, after the 1957 trip to Paris which uncovered Hemingway's lost notebooks and before the composition of the sketch
"Hunger Was Good Discipline," which gives a more polished account of the lost manuscripts. For a more complete examination of
the fragment and the connection between the two books, see my
essay "Hemingway's Gender Trouble," *American Literature* 63
(June 1991): 187–207.

61. Item 256, Ernest Hemingway Collection, John F. Kennedy
Library, Boston (1). Permission to quote from Item 256 of the Hemingway Collection has been granted by the Ernest Hemingway
Foundation, which retains publishing rights. Subsequent references
to this manuscript correspond to the page numbers or insert letters
assigned by Hemingway. My citations do not indicate Hemingway's
numerous interpolations or cancellations; instead, I have generally
ignored cancelled material and incorporated all legible insertions.

62. Lynn emphasizes the role of Grace Hall Hemingway in her
son's crisis of gender; Spilka tends to distribute the responsibility
between Grace and her passive husband but stresses the androgynous influence of late-Victorian literature. See Lynn, *Hemingway*, 38–48; Mark Spilka, *Hemingway's Quarrel with Androgyny*
(Lincoln: University of Nebraska Press, 1990).

Chapter Four. The Secret Paris of Henry Miller

1. Henry Miller, *Black Spring* (New York: Grove Press, 1963), 3.

2. Jay Martin, *Always Merry and Bright: The Life of Henry
Miller* (New York: Penguin, 1978), 37.

3. Miller's second wife, June, appears to have possessed few
maternal qualities, but Robert Ferguson notes that in her relationship to Miller "she thought of him increasingly as her charge, her
child." See *Henry Miller: A Life* (New York: Norton, 1991), 121.

4. Martin, *Always Merry and Bright*, 165–66. Mary Dearborn
writes of June's motives for sending Miller abroad that she had
"high hopes for Henry's future. But she was also desperate. He
seemed unable to function in the world, and he was not happy living on the fringes as she was. Perhaps in Paris, where prices were
low and the climate encouraging for artists, Henry might find so-
lace. Failing that, he would at least be less of a drag on her own attempts to make a livelihood." See Mary Dearborn, *The Happiest
Man Alive: A Biography of Henry Miller* (New York: Simon and
Schuster, 1991), 119.

5. Martin, *Always Merry and Bright*, 215, 181–82.

6. Malcolm Cowley, *Exile's Return* (1934; reprint, New York: Penguin, 1976), 284.

7. Henry Miller, *Letters to Emil*, ed. George Wickes (New York: New Directions, 1989). Subsequent parenthetical page references to the published letters correspond to this edition. Wickes made important use of the Schnellock letters in his discussion of Miller in *Americans in Paris* (Garden City, N.Y.: Doubleday, 1969), 239–61.

8. Wickes rightly observes that "Miller penetrated far deeper into Paris than any other American writer." See Wickes, *Americans in Paris*, 261.

9. Unpublished portion of Miller's [April 1930] letter to Schnellock (see *Letters to Emil*, 44–48), from the Henry Miller Collection, UCLA Research Library.

10. Unpublished portion of Miller's [March 1930] letter to Schnellock (see *Letters to Emil*, 29–34) in the Henry Miller Collection, UCLA Research Library.

11. Unpublished portion of 10 March 1930 letter to Schnellock (see *Letters to Emil*, 27–29), Henry Miller Collection, UCLA Research Library.

12. See Brassaï, *The Secret Paris of the 30s*. Miller apparently met Brassaï in early 1932, posed for him, and accompanied him on photographic outings. His admiration for Brassaï prompted an essay entitled "The Eye of Paris," published in *The Wisdom of the Heart* (New York: New Directions, 1941), 173–86.

13. Henry Miller, *Remember to Remember* (New York: New Directions, 1941), 309.

14. See Marie-Claire Bancquart, *Paris des Surréalistes* (Paris: Seghers, 1972), 79–98; 101–21.

15. In 1952, though, Miller listed *Nadja* among the hundred books which had most influenced him. See Henry Miller, *The Books in My Life* (New York: New Directions, 1952), 317.

16. Wickes, *Americans in Paris*, 245.

17. Ferguson, *Henry Miller: A Life*, 257.

18. *Henry Miller: The Major Writings* (New York: Schocken, 1986), 81.

19. Henry Miller, *Tropic of Cancer* (1934; reprint, New York: Grove Press, 1961), 11. Subsequent parenthetical page references to this work correspond to this edition.

20. Dearborn comments helpfully on the influence of Fraenkel and Lowenfels in *The Happiest Man Alive*, 133–35. Lowenfels later wrote: "We felt we had the real key to the horrors of civilized life in the 30s, when Hitler was on the way up, and we were half way between World Wars I and II." See Henry Miller, "Unpublished Preface to *Tropic of Cancer*," *Massachusetts Review* 5 (1964): 485.

21. Ihab Hassan, *The Literature of Silence: Henry Miller and Samuel Beckett* (New York: Knopf, 1967), 35.

22. Martin, *Always Merry and Bright*, 261.

23. References to Dante recur in the narrative and culminate in the section recounting the narrator's teaching stint in Dijon. Here Miller unmistakably evokes the bleak imagery of Cocytus, the frozen ninth circle of Dante's hell.

24. See, e.g., Joseph Campbell, *The Hero with a Thousand Faces* (New York: World Publishing, 1956), 90–94.

25. While revising *Tropic of Cancer*, Miller had (through Anaïs Nin) become interested in the ideas of Otto Rank, meeting the psychoanalyst in Paris in 1933; he knew Rank's *The Trauma of Birth*, citing a passage on uterine "strangulation" in an unpublished letter to Schnellock (25 August 1934) now in the Henry Miller Collection, UCLA Research Library. See also Miller's letter to Nin, 7 March 1933, in *Letters to Anaïs Nin*, ed. Gunther Stuhlmann (New York: Paragon House, 1965), 80–86. Whatever the etiology of Miller's sexual attitudes, he has become for feminist critics like Kate Millett the personification of a violent sexism which reduces the female to a commodity for purposes of subjugation and humiliation. Millett sees in Miller's obscenity an ironic hostility "toward sexuality itself." See Kate Millett, *Sexual Politics* (Garden City, N.Y.: Doubleday, 1970), 297, 307.

26. Wallace Fowlie, "Shadow of Doom: An Essay on Henry Miller," in *Henry Miller: Three Decades of Criticism*, ed. Edward Mitchell (New York: New York University Press, 1871), 36, 39.

27. Miller, *Letters to Emil*, 113.

28. Wickes, *Americans in Paris*, 240.

29. Miller, *Letters to Emil*, 152.

30. Miller, *Letters to Emil*, 120.

31. Miller, *Black Spring*, 9.

32. Kramer, *Threshold of a New World*, 9–10.

33. As Martin notes, Miller was actually born at 450 East Eighty-Fifth Street in Manhattan. Before he was a year old, however, his family moved to the Driggs Avenue address in Brooklyn which Miller associated with his earliest memories. See Martin, *Always Merry and Bright*, 3, 5.

34. Bachelard, *The Poetics of Space*, 15–16.

35. Miller went to New York in 1935 to be with Anaïs Nin, who was then working as an associate of Otto Rank. See Ferguson, *Henry Miller: A Life*, 237.

36. Martin, *Always Merry and Bright*, 338. Martin later remarks that by 1939 Miller "had really tired of Paris—he called it a 'city of sewers'" (356).

37. Though first composed in June 1940, *Quiet Days in Clichy* did not appear in print until 1956, when it was issued by Olympia Press in Paris.

38. Wasserman, cited in Henry Miller, *Remember to Remember* (New York: New Directions, 1941), 332–33. Miller quotes from *Deutscher und Juden*, in which Wassermann (as a Jew in the early thirties) accounts for his increasingly complicated relation to his German homeland.

39. Henry Miller, *My Life and Times* (New York: Playboy Press, 1971), n. p. Miller lived in Big Sur until 1959, when he moved to Pacific Palisades in Los Angeles.

40. Millett, *Sexual Politics,* 294. Granting Miller's "considerable achievement as an essayist, autobiographer, and surrealist," Millett delivers a provocative but reductive denunciation.

41. Henry Miller, "The Eye of Paris," in *Max and the White Phagocytes* (Paris: Obelisk Press, 1938), 246.

Chapter Five. Modernism as Exile

1. Stephen Kern, *The Culture of Time and Space: 1880–1918* (Cambridge: Harvard University Press, 1983). Subsequent references to Kern's study will be given parenthetically.

2. The standard accounts of these movements appear in Malcolm Cowley, *Exile's Return,* and Paul Fussell, *Abroad: British Literary Traveling Between the Wars* (New York: Oxford University Press, 1980), in which the comment on placelessness appears (70).

3. Alan Bullock, "The Double Image," in *Modernism, 1890–1930,* ed. Malcolm Bradbury and James McFarlane (New York: Viking Penguin, 1976), 66.

4. James McFarlane, "The Mind of Modernism," in *Modernism, 1890–1930,* 80–81.

5. See Roger Shattuck, *The Banquet Years: The Origins of the Avant-Garde in France, 1885 to World War I* (New York: Vintage, 1958), 340–45.

6. McFarlane, "The Mind of Modernism," 81.

7. Malcolm Bradbury, "The Cities of Modernism," in *Modernism 1890–1930,* 98–99.

8. Raymond Williams, "The Metropolis and the Emergence of Modernism," in *Unreal City: Urban Experience in Modern European Literature and Art,* ed. Edward Timms and David Kelley (New York: St. Martin's, 1985), 21.

9. See Matthew J. Bruccoli, *The Composition of "Tender is the Night"* (Pittsburgh: University of Pittsburgh Press, 1963). Bruccoli provides an indispensable reconstruction and analysis of the various manuscript and typescript versions.

10. James Mellow, *Invented Lives: F. Scott and Zelda Fitzgerald* (Boston: Houghton Mifflin, 1984), 168.

11. André LeVot, "Fitzgerald in Paris," *Fitzgerald/Hemingway Annual 1973,* ed. Matthew J. Bruccoli and C. E. Frazer Clark, Jr. (Washington: Microcard Editions, 1974), 49–50.

12. Edmund Wilson, letter to F. Scott Fitzgerald, 5 July 1921, *Letters on Literature and Politics, 1912–1972,* ed. Elena Wilson (New York: Farrar, Straus & Giroux, 1977), 63.

13. See André LeVot, *F. Scott Fitzgerald: A Biography,* trans. William Byron (Garden City, N.Y.: Doubleday, 1983), 235–37.

14. Scottie, a Parisian schoolgirl, was left in the custody of a nursemaid. In addition to his trips to Paris, Fitzgerald also made a

hasty journey to the United States in early 1931 to attend his father's funeral in Maryland.

15. *The Short Stories of F. Scott Fitzgerald,* ed. Matthew J. Bruccoli (New York: Scribner's, 1989), 580, 594.

16. Roy R. Male, " 'Babylon Revisited': A Story of the Exile's Return," in *Modern Critical Views: F. Scott Fitzgerald,* ed. Harold Bloom (New York: Chelsea House, 1985), 94.

17. *The Short Stories of F. Scott Fitzgerald,* 633. Subsequent parenthetical page references to "Babylon Revisited" correspond to this edition.

18. For an analysis of parallels between "Babylon Revisited" and *Tender is the Night,* as well as a discussion of two other Fitzgerald stories thematically related to the novel ("Two Wrongs" and "The Rough Crossing"), see Richard D. Lehan, *"Tender is the Night,"* in *"Tender is the Night:* Essays in Criticism," ed. Marvin J. LaHood (Bloomington: Indiana University Press, 1969), 61–85.

19. Bruce L. Grenberg, "Fitzgerald's 'Figured Curtain': Personality and History in *Tender is the Night,*" in *Critical Essays on F. Scott Fitzgerald's "Tender is the Night,"* ed. Milton R. Stern (Boston: G. K. Hall, 1986), 221.

20. See F. Scott Fitzgerald, *Tender is the Night* (New York: Scribner's, 1934), 159–62, for his emulation of cinematic montage. Subsequent parenthetical page references to the novel correspond to this edition.

21. From 1925–30, Fitzgerald worked on the Melarky version, which hinged on a young Hollywood technician's hatred of his mother and on his attraction to a glamorous expatriate couple, Seth and Dinah Roreback (or Piper). Bruccoli insists that "nothing of Francis' personality clings to Rosemary," who is a "completely feminine creature." See Bruccoli, *The Composition of "Tender is the Night,"* 95–96.

22. Commenting on Dick Diver's own ambivalent sexual impulses, James E. Miller, Jr. notes the "strange element in Nicole's relationship to him," presaged by a passage in one of her early letters to him: "I have only gotten to like boys who are rather sissies. Are you a sissy?" See Miller, *"Tender is the Night,"* in *"Tender is the Night": Essays in Criticism,* 98.

23. Grenberg, "Fitzgerald's 'Figured Curtain,' " 213–15.

24. Modris Eksteins, *Rites of Spring: The Great War and the Birth of the Modern Age* (Boston: Houghton Mifflin, 1989), 293.

25. See Kern, *The Culture of Time and Space,* 25.

26. Alan Trachtenberg, "The Journey Back: Myth and History in *Tender is the Night,*" in *Critical Essays on "Tender is the Night,"* 172. The problem of time also created nagging doubts for Fitzgerald about the proper arrangement of the novel—whether (as in the original version) to use a long flashback in book two to recount Dick's career and his romance with Nicole, or whether to tell the story chronologically, as in Malcolm Cowley's 1951 revised version.

27. Fitzgerald referred to a similar American deracination in

his notebooks: "In England, property begot a strong sense of place, but Americans, restless and with shallow roots, needed fins and wings." See *The Notebooks of F. Scott Fitzgerald,* ed. Matthew J. Bruccoli (New York: Harcourt Brace Jovanovich, 1978), 35.

28. Fitzgerald indulges here in subtle sentimentality; as Grenberg points out, the "red-haired girl from Tennessee" looking for the grave of her brother marks an anachronism: the American army did not fight at the Somme; the U.S. did not enter the war until 1917.

29. See Eksteins, *Rites of Spring,* 257–58. Grenberg sees Dick's "infatuation with Rosemary" as a symptom of his brief "love affair with modernity." See Grenberg, "Fitzgerald's 'Figured Curtain,' " 225.

30. Noting that the same setting was used in Fitzgerald's 1929 short story "The Swimmers," André LeVot points out Fitzgerald's topographical "mistake": although the house is said to be "hewn from the frame of Cardinal de Retz's palace," the seventeenth-century prelate never lived on the rue Monsieur, a street created in the eighteenth century. See LeVot, "Fitzgerald in Paris," 65.

31. In an early version of the novel, Francis takes a romantic interest in a young woman named Wanda Brested, who is associated with a lesbian coterie. In one scene, Francis finds Wanda in the company of three other girls with mannequins' heads. See the facsimile edition of the Melarky-narrator version, Matthew J. Bruccoli, ed., *F. Scott Fitzgerald Manuscripts, Tender is the Night,* vol. 2 (New York: Garland, 1990), 164.

32. Fitzgerald speaks of this wave of American violence in "Echoes of the Jazz Age," in *The Crack Up,* ed. Edmund Wilson (New York: New Directions, 1945), 20.

33. The same signs and shop windows appear in the opening paragraphs of the 1929 short story "The Swimmers."

34. There was no such street in the fashionable sixteenth arrondissement near Passy, but there was a passage St.-Ange (masculine) near the Porte de St. Ouen in a working-class neighborhood in the seventeenth arrondissement. By placing the Films Par Excellence studio at 341, rue des Saintes-Anges, Fitzgerald makes the angels feminine and plural, again implying the doubling of Dick's relationship to Nicole in his attachment to Rosemary.

35. In 1931 Fitzgerald superciliously noted the influx of American ethnic types in Paris about 1928: "There was something sinister about the crazy boatloads." See "Echoes of the Jazz Age," 20.

36. See Fitzgerald, "Echoes of the Jazz Age," 15–17.

37. Typical of extant criticism is Mary E. Burton's remark that "the inclusion of the Negro murder remains mysterious." She speculates that since earlier versions of the novel included a homicide, Fitzgerald "felt impelled to include a murder somehow—perhaps quickly to bring the reader up against the unreality and 'enchanted' quality of the Divers' lives by a shocking intrusion of reality from the passions and problems of another class and race." See Mary E.

Burton, "The Counter-Transference of Doctor Diver," *Journal of English Literary History* 38 (1971): 469.

38. This same anxiety recurs later when Dick worries about the bathwater his children have shared with the Indian stepchildren of Mary North Minghetti. Mary's Asian husband is said to be "not quite light enough to travel in a Pullman south of Mason-Dixon" (258). My own understanding of the race problem in this novel has been enriched by the work of Felipe Smith, who argues persuasively that the author's symbolic treatment of race in *Tender is the Night* "amounts to an elaboration of the racial holocaust he had hinted at in *The Beautiful and the Damned* and *The Great Gatsby.*" See Felipe Smith, "The Dark Side of Paradise: Race and Ethnicity in the Novels of F. Scott Fitzgerald," Ph.D. diss., Louisiana State University, 1988, 207.

39. At a Swiss ski resort about five months after the Parisian episode, Dick becomes briefly fixated upon a "special girl" at the table behind him (174); subsequently Fitzgerald reports: "He was in love with every pretty woman he saw now, their forms at a distance, their shadows on a wall" (201).

40. See *F. Scott Fitzgerald Manuscripts, Tender is the Night,* vol. 4, part 2, 251–55.

41. Jean Méral, *Paris in American Literature,* trans. Laurette Long (Chapel Hill: University of North Carolina Press, 1989), 162, 176.

42. Andrew Field, *Djuna: The Life and Times of Djuna Barnes* (New York: G. P. Putnam, 1983), 29.

43. As Field points out, Barnes's earliest contribution to *McCall's* did not appear until 1925; she may also have had an arrangement with *Vanity Fair,* where her articles, poems, plays, and satires began to appear in 1922. See *Djuna,* 104, 129. Throughout his eccentric book, Field rarely provides specific documentation for such biographical details; yet his is the only full-length study of Barnes' life currently available.

44. Djuna Barnes, "Vagaries Malicieux," *The Double Dealer* 3 (1922): 249, 251, 256, 258.

45. Barnes's short stories from this period appeared in *A Book* (1923), *A Night Among the Horses* (1929), and *Spillway* (1962).

46. See Field, *Djuna,* 43. Some of the evidence for the impromptu marriage rests on literary inference. In the original version of *Nightwood* (titled *Bow Down*) and in *The Antiphon* (1958), Barnes's late verse drama, there are scenes suggesting that the author experienced the "wedding" as a rape. See also Mary Lynn Broe, "My Art Belongs to Daddy," in *Women's Writing in Exile,* ed. Mary Lynn Broe and Angela Ingram (Chapel Hill: University of North Carolina Press, 1989), 42–43, 69–73.

47. For the remark about Thelma Wood, see Field, *Djuna,* 101. Barnes had friendships with a number of lesbian women, including Mary Pyne in New York and Natalie Clifford Barney in Paris. But

there was apparently no cohabitation or sustained intimacy. Such matters are, of course, crudely speculative; they arise here only because Barnes's sexual ambivalence figures crucially in *Nightwood*.

48. Donna Gerstenberger, "The Radical Narrative of Djuna Barnes's *Nightwood*," in *Breaking the Sequence: Women's Experimental Fiction*, ed. Ellen G. Friedman and Miriam Fuchs (Princeton: Princeton University Press, 1989), 130.

49. Carolyn Burke points out that "*Ulysses* and *Finnegan's Wake*, which she followed closely as *Work in Progress*, confirmed Barnes in her own idiosyncratic modernism." See Carolyn Burke, " 'Accidental Aloofness': Barnes, Loy, and Modernism," in *Silence and Power: A Reevaluation of Djuna Barnes*, ed. Mary Lynn Broe (Carbondale: Southern Illinois University Press, 1991), 73. To date, the most authoritative study of the little magazines is Hugh Ford's *Published in Paris: American and British Writers, Printers, and Publishers in Paris, 1920–1930* (New York: Macmillan, 1975).

50. See Karen Kaivola, *All Contraries Confounded: The Lyrical Fiction of Virginia Woolf, Djuna Barnes, and Marguerite Duras* (Iowa City: University of Iowa Press, 1991), 63; Judith Lee, "*Nightwood:* 'The Sweetest Lie,' " in *Silence and Power*, 207; Jane Marcus, "Laughing at Leviticus: *Nightwood* as Woman's Circus Epic," in *Silence and Power*, 231.

51. Gerstenberger, "The Radical Narrative of Djuna Barnes's *Nightwood*," 130.

52. Marcus, "Laughing at Leviticus," 223.

53. Kaivola, *All Contraries Confounded*, 94.

54. James B. Scott, "Reminiscences," in *Silence and Power*, 344.

55. Studies of the original, uncut manuscript suggest that Eliot may have excised some provocative material. But on the basis of the published text alone, we can infer that Barnes was not much inclined toward erotic relations; what matters, at least for the women in *Nightwood*, is the difference between solitude and companionship.

56. Julie L. Abraham, " 'Woman, Remember You': Djuna Barnes and History," in *Silence and Power*, 257. Attributing a prescience to Barnes, Jane Marcus goes further, seeing the "lesbians, blacks, circus people, Jews, [and] transvestites" of *Nightwood* as a prophetic grouping of "soon-to-be-exterminated human types," in "Laughing at Leviticus," 231.

57. Felix betrays the limits of his own memory when he shows Robin historical sites: "He tried to explain to her what Vienna had been before the war; what it must have been before he was born; yet his memory was confused and hazy, and he found himself repeating what he had read" (43).

58. Our last glimpse of Felix finds him back in Vienna, bowing madly and pathetically to a man he assumes to be the Grand Duke Alexander of Russia (123).

59. Marcus, "Laughing at Leviticus," 234.

60. Benstock points out that this transvestism "calls attention to woman's role as *ornament* in society." See *Women of the Left Bank*, 258.

61. Insisting that the "prince-princess" personifies not androgyny but narcissism, Judith Lee construes "the myth of romantic love" as "the sweetest lie" to support a circular argument that "male and female are inherently and inevitably incompatible." See *"Nightwood:* 'The Sweetest Lie,'" 209, 212.

62. Marcus speculates plausibly that O'Connor is a parodic version of Dr. Freud and that his "womb envy is so strong that it parodies Freudian penis envy mercilessly." See "Laughing at Leviticus," 233.

63. In a reminiscence, Hank O'Neal reports that Barnes identified the model for Nora as Henrietta Metcalf. See *Silence and Power*, 351.

64. Barnes doubtless chose the rue du Cherche-Midi because it was around the corner from the apartment she shared with Thelma Wood at 9, rue St.-Romain.

65. Mary Lynn Broe underscores the patently lesbian intimacy between Barnes and her grandmother, Zadel Gustafson Barnes, in "My Art Belongs to Daddy," in *Women's Writing in Exile*, 42. We may expect further elaboration of this issue in the forthcoming volume of Barnes' letters, *Cold Comfort*, being edited by Mary Lynn Broe and Frances McCullough.

66. Louis Aragon, *Nightwalker (Le Paysan de Paris)*, trans. Frederick Brown (1926; Englewood Cliffs, N.J.: Prentice-Hall, 1970), 133.

67. André Breton, *Nadja*, trans. Richard Howard (1928; New York: Grove Press, 1960), 80, 83.

68. Philippe Soupault, *Last Nights of Paris*, trans. William Carlos Williams (1928; New York: Macaulay, 1929), 53, 73, 129. Marie-Claire Bancquart speaks of the veritable "cult of Paris" developed by surrealists for whom the city was a site of quest and initiation as well as a source of metaphors and signs. See Bancquart, *Paris des Surréalistes*, 186, 189, 199.

69. Relph, *Place and Placelessness*, 52–53.

Index